Anger
Management

6 Critical Steps to a *Calmer* Life

By Peter Favaro, Ph.D.

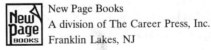

New Page Books
A division of The Career Press, Inc.
Franklin Lakes, NJ

ANGER MANAGEMENT: 6 CRITICAL STEPS TO A CALMER LIFE
EDITED BY GINA TALUCCI
TYPESET BY CHRISTOPHER CAROLEI
Cover design by Lu Rossman/Digi Dog Design
Printed in the U.S.A. by Book-mart Press

To order this title, please call toll-free 1-800-CAREER-1 (NJ and Canada: 201-848-0310) to order using VISA or MasterCard, or for further information on books from Career Press.

The Career Press, Inc., 3 Tice Road, PO Box 687,
Franklin Lakes, NJ 07417
www.careerpress.com
www.newpagebooks.com

Library of Congress Cataloging-in-Publication Data

Favaro, Peter
  Anger management: 6 critical steps to a calmer life / by Peter Favaro, Ph.D.
    p. cm.
  Includes index.
    ISBN 1-56414-834-3 (pbk.)
    1. Anger. I. Title.

BF575.A5F385 2006
152.4′7--dc22

2005049145

Dedication

For the love and patience she showed to all people, and for the adoration she showed for her children, this book is dedicated to my mother, Jeannie Favaro, who sends me her love every day from heaven.

Acknowledgments

I have never written a book alone, although sometimes it can seem that way at 5 a.m. when the only light in the room is the glow of my computer screen. The fact is, however, that I couldn not have made it through the difficult times in this process without the help of my family, my friends, my colleagues, and the good humor and kind support of my friends in Texas.

Contents

Preface

An Anger Epidemic

The other day I crossed the street with two teens who were push-ing one another and play fighting without regard for the fact that they were in the middle of a busy intersection. A driver coming down the street approached them, came to a full stop to avoid running them over, and beeped, at which point the boys gave him the finger, cursed at him, and strolled across the street. I am a forensic psychologist who evaluates criminal behavior and parents who are fighting over custody of their kids. Anyone who has experienced this kind of fight knows first hand what it is to live your life day after day, engaged in angry conflict.

I have worked as a forensic expert within family conflicts for the last 10 years and, in the course of my work, I have investigated cases of murder and attempted murder of one parent against the other. I have been involved in hundreds of cases where children, living in their anger-filled homes, become so enraged at one of their parents that they refuse to have contact with that parent after the divorce. I have also been appointed to many cases where children are the victims of violent crimes, ritualistic torture and abuse, as well as child abuse where parents have lost their tempers and beaten them with belts, burned them with cigarettes, or shaken them until the children could no longer breathe. The agencies where these crimes are reported have become powerless to deal with these incidents because they are over-whelmed with complaints of this nature and are too short-staffed to save all of the children from the uncontrolled anger of their caregivers. There is a tremendous amount of dangerously angry interactions within families these days: parents angry at parents, children angry at par-ents, parents angry at children, and children angry at the world. As this book goes to press, a 4-year-old in Texas went to his mother's handbag, took out her gun, and shot his 2-year-old sibling because he was touching his toys.

For a time I thought that I had a distorted view of the world, seeing more anger and hatred than the average person. After all, my line of work has placed me into personal contact with tens of thou-sands of very frustrated and angry people. That was until September 11, when I learned that there were quite a few angry and frustrated people whom I have never met, and who had taken it upon themselves to kill innocent people, seemingly for the sake of doling out a sort of idiosyncratic justice that still has not been adequately explained or justified. Taking the lives of 3,000 innocent people to show how angry you are at somebody else has left me, and other clear-minded people, numb as to the state of this seemingly angry world.

As I write this book, the country is on a "heightened state of alert," which as far as I or anyone else can tell, means that we should not be surprised if during the course of any given day, we are a target for attack or harm by other people we don't know, never had any contact with, and wouldn't expect to hurt us. We must live with the thought that the person sitting next to us on the train might have a bomb or explosive device hidden in their shoes or under their clothes. This heightened state of alert makes a lot of people frustrated, anxious, and angry. It makes them so angry that they talk about wiping out entire countries or sections of the Earth, where people who are our enemies and who have made us their victims are killed before they kill us. We might have to kill a few hundred thousand innocent men, women, and children to get to them, but that is the cost of doing business in an angry world.

Sometimes there is no political point to acts of anger and rage. Consider the rash of murders that have happened in schools such as Columbine High School over the past decade. Children killing children and adults, mostly out of boredom, frustration, and family problems—angry children imitating angry grown ups.

What relevance does all of this have to the person who does not abuse their child or spouse, is not a terrorist or mail bomber, and is generally a nonviolent person? It has a lot to do with all of us, if we believe that the big problems in the world affect us on a small scale. I believe the big problems trickle down to influence the smaller worlds of interaction that we operate in. If anger and aggression drive world politics, the smaller social environments we operate in cannot help but function in similar ways. Civilized problem-solving requires patience and tolerance. Moreover, it requires taking the perspective of our adversaries and antagonists in order to show an understanding of what causes them to be at odds with us. Living in a scary world puts these commodities in almost immediate short supply, and that reduces problem-solving to little more than a pattern of actions and reactions, the most powerful and aggressive of which usually wins. After all, who wants to listen patiently to someone who has openly stated his or her hatred of us, or at least acts that way without directly stating it?

From the world at large, to the interactions of smaller groups, poor or ineffective social models for coping with disagreements quickly begin to influence the smallest, but most meaningful, one-to-one or one-to-few relationships we have. These would include the relationships we have with our spouses, families, friends, and coworkers.

I wrote this book to address those issues and in the hopes that we can make our lives just a little more peaceful.

Introduction

What's Eating You?

What's eating you? Phrases like this humble me to the fact that most of psychology is and always will be the "science of common sense." This term of everyday slang acknowledges that when people become irritated or enraged over something, they are simultaneously consumed by it. Anger is a toxic emotion. Poor anger management destroys relationships, makes us lose our jobs and our families, keeps people we might want to get to know better at arms length, and in the very worst of all cases, results in behavior that injures or kills other human beings.

Most anger management programs teach anger control as a series of techniques that address the way you *think about your thoughts*. A "thinking about thinking" approach is part of this program, too, but there are other important ideas to follow and practice, and these ideas concentrate on how we perceive the world, how easy it is to develop angry habits, and how anger is not just your problem, it's almost everyone else's problem, too.

The organization of the concepts presented in this book is different that in most anger management education programs. The program uses the notion of "critical paths" to help you gain a deeper and more complex understanding of how anger operates. There are common elements and techniques in each path that focus on communication and thinking skills. There's no rush to get from the first step to the last step because once you dedicate yourself to the process, and master the very first step, you will already have achieved success. From that point, you can get a little better every day for the rest of your life, if you choose to get a grip on your angry habits.

> **✓ Check Point**
>
> *The Mastering Calm program teaches anger management in six stages or "critical paths." Each critical path is broken down into specific ways to help you cope, communicate, and implement the content into your daily life.*

This book places a good deal of emphasis on learning how to deal with the angry behaviors of others. Even if you may not have a problem with anger, you almost certainly know a couple of people who do. Anger is contagious. Dealing with angry people on their terms will almost always make you angry; but bringing angry people into a calmer, less hostile world (when possible) ultimately makes your life easier.

The first chapters of the book provide the basic framework for understanding why people use anger as their main way of interacting with the world. The chapters that follow go on to describe the many faces and styles of anger that we come across on a day-to-day basis. Whenever possible, I will provide you with "composite personalities": descriptions of fictional people that I have cut and pasted together from real life circumstances and clinical cases. My way of teaching is to help people relate to concepts through stories. It is up to you to read about the characters in the stories and say, "Hey, I do that," or "Hey my boss, (or husband, wife, third-grade teacher, and so on) is like that." After learning about different styles of anger, I will introduce you to my program on how to become a less-angry person. Be forewarned, though, that when you come into the program you sign up for a lifetime. What I will introduce is the "stages of mastery," each requiring that you succeed at integrating a new skill or lesson completely before you go on to the next path or goal.

Mastering the first stage will bring you some immediate success, and it should not take you long to get there. The more stages you master, the more success you will have. Mastering the stages is not a footrace. You don't get any extra points for doing it fast. You learn at whatever pace you are capable of because that is how all of the most important things in life are learned. People mature into their potential, and that takes time. This may sound very Zen-like to some of you, and to others it may be reminiscent of 12-step approaches. I can see the commonalities in both processes, but I have not set up my program quite that way. You do not start off as a

Check Point

This program combines principles of learning how to control your anger with principles and techniques for controlling the anger of others.

"grasshopper," and you do not have to bare your soul at weekly meetings. I am a big fan of finding others with common goals who will support your efforts, and if you can form a group or discuss your progress with other like-minded people who will cheer you on to new levels of success, I think that would be great for you, but this program is something you can do by yourself as well as with others.

The next chapter is where you begin your journey. Good luck. If you take this project seriously, your life should improve dramatically.

Chapter I

What Makes People so Angry?

Frustration-Driven Anger

In creating this program I struggled with the idea of how deeply I should go into the psychology of anger. There has been so much written on it and so many different points of view that I did not want to run the risk of getting you bogged down in theory. I want to keep this program practical and focused. What I will present in theory I will try to present as much in everyday terms as possible.

The Angry Lifestyle

Anger isn't always a toxic and sick human emotion. Anger is a perfectly normal human emotion and it is a normal reaction to events that are unpleasant to us. As a matter of fact, if you have ever observed a newborn baby, you might easily conclude that anger is the first reaction we seem to have as we are introduced to the world! This book is about how to manage what I refer to as "the angry lifestyle." A person has an angry lifestyle when the normal, natural way they look at life is pessimistic, aggressive, critical, nasty, and confrontational. All of us get grumpy from time to time, but the person who has problems with anger is angry almost *all* of the time. I will sometimes refer to the type of angry person who will benefit most from this program as the "chronically angry" person. The chronically angry person has forgotten that there is a more gentle, reasonable, and calm way of approaching the world and the conflicts we all face on a day-to-day basis. They simply lose track of the fact that there is more than one way to approach a difficult situation. Chronically angry people are angry when they wake up, drive, interact with others at work, and when they come home. They are angry at people they know and people they don't know. They are angry for things that people have done to them, and angry at people who didn't do anything to them. They are angry because anger is the most comfortable emotion for them to express almost constantly.

Check Point

The chronically angry person is angry almost all the time. It appears as though this is the emotion they feel most comfortable expressing.

The grandpappy of all shrinks, Sigmund Freud, spent a lot of time and effort trying to understand human aggression, and pinpointing its place as a natural instinct that man must work hard at trying to suppress. The suppression of aggression, Freud thought, was essential because without suppressing our natural tendencies to fight, kill, and compete, we could not live in a civilized society. Civilization does have its advantages. After all, killing our own food before putting on a three-piece suit and going to the office can interfere with one's productivity at work.

Unfortunately there is a downside to suppressing our anger. Freud reasoned that suppressing what is naturally aggressive places us in a state of conflict and turmoil, and screws us up in so many countless other ways that maybe we would be better off hunting a boar first thing after the clock radio goes off. The suppression of aggression, according to Freud, doesn't make the aggression go away, it just redirects it enough so that we don't destroy ourselves. Understand that I have taken great liberties in this interpretation of Freud's work. I pared it down substantially so that you would not fall asleep reading the first pages of the first chapter of my book. The main idea is that human beings are naturally aggressive animals, and learning how to control aggression is an important part of life. It requires hard work and keeping a lid on our naturally hostile and competitive tendencies.

Discussing Freud, even briefly, points at the problems with psychology from a technical point of view—lot's of good ideas, but so many building blocks of theoretical ideas, funky terms, and leaps of faith that it is hard to extract anything practical out of it. I had the same problem going through my professional education in psychology. I didn't want to memorize all of the terms and theories, I just wanted to know what made people tick. The next few sections will try to provide you with the two most meaty parts of what it takes to understand anger, which are:

1. What role does anger have in our emotional makeup?
2. Why does it become a problem for people?

Anger Is a Function of Two Main Emotional Systems

How many emotions do people have anyway? The number and type of emotions humans have, like every notion about human behavior, is subject to tremendous debate. For the sake of this book, and for my anger management program, there are only two main emotional responses: pleasure and displeasure. What we commonly describe as shades of many emotions such as fear, ambivalence, annoyance, rage, jealousy, elation, and joy, are really not different emotions. Instead, these emotional words and the thousands that I did not list, are functions of how human beings communicate pleasure or displeasure in response to their surroundings. An even simpler way of stating this is that life makes us feel "good" or "bad." The things that make us feel bad reflect a state of displeasure, and angry responses are a way of communicating that we are in a state of displeasure. The things that make us feel good, we do not have to concern ourselves with.

When someone cuts you off on the highway and you spill lava-hot coffee all over your private parts, that produces a state of displeasure. (All that wasted coffee!) Your immediate response might be to speed up to the offending driver and scream out something about one of his or her close family members, while pumping your middle finger wildly in the air. I choose this as an example because this is how we communicate displeasure while motoring in the greater five boroughs of New York as well as some of the surrounding geographic areas.

We do not *always* do things like this. Even the grumpiest of us will sometimes let an indiscretion like this slide. In other words, sometimes we are very motivated to let others know when they are displeasing us, and sometimes we are not so interested. We express anger when we are bothered enough to let someone "have it." Those who have problems with anger want to let people "have it," too often for their own good. What, then, determines how bothered we are and exactly when the "anger switch" is turned on? When do we let people "have it," and when do we show tolerance for the ignorance or bad behavior of others?

Fill–Hold–Release

"I've had it up to here! I'm going to blow my top!" These very familiar statements imply that there is only so much room a person has in the imaginary container that holds their displeasure, before that container is too full to hold any more unpleasant feelings, and those feelings spill out. I'm trying very hard to keep the number of psychobabble concepts down to a bare minimum, but I have to throw in one more at this point. I have already said that there are two main emotional systems: pleasure and displeasure. Pleasure is usually something we strive to attain, and displeasure is something we strive to avoid. Another way of talking about displeasure is to say that displeasure occurs not only when something bad happens, but when our attempts to attain pleasure are blocked or *frustrated*.

> ✓ **Check Point**
>
> *Anything unpleasant can fill up the imaginary container that manages and holds frustration. Too much displeasure can cause the mental equivalent of what happens when your car radiator overheats. That container can also fill up when our attempts to seek pleasure are blocked or frustrated.*

Frustration is an interesting emotional commodity. It does not dissipate as quickly as it grows. It is also not always compensated for by success in other areas. In other words, finally getting a break after many frustrating experiences is often not enough to remove all of the aggravation the original frustrating event caused. After 60 attempts at trying to set the time on the VCR, success at finally doing so may not remove all of the irritability that you have just previously experienced. If you burn that soufflé, all of the compliments you have received about the roast may not resolve your frustration and disappointment at wanting everything to be just perfect.

The fact that frustration does not go away as quickly as it comes on, and the additional fact that it is not necessarily relieved by a corresponding amount of pleasure or satisfaction, makes it *cumulative*. As frustrating events build, the imaginary container fills up until it can no longer hold any more. When it reaches a point of absolute fullness, people start to voice their displeasure in a way that human beings typically describe as "angry." Hold on, my explanation isn't over yet. We know that anger is a way of communicating displeasure. We also know that people communicate displeasure as anger when they experience an accumulation of displeasure that they can no longer contain. So far I have not exactly split the atom in terms of human psychology. We need just a little more background.

Some Containers Are Already Half Filled

We need to understand why some people's containers seem to overflow so quickly and so violently while some people's containers never seem to fill at all. Some people are always ready to blow, while some are perpetually calm and easygoing. The answer to that has to do with what types of things are in that container aside from the events that are happening around a person at the present time. Let's take a look at a *vignette* (a fancy French word for "anecdote," which is a fancy English word for "story") that describes two people with two totally different containers.

Bill, Bob, and the Electric Company

Bill and Bob are two honest, hardworking guys who, for the sake of this example, live in parallel universes; meaning whatever happens to Bob happens to Bill and vice versa. Everything is the same about them except for one thing—their view of the world. Bill looks at the world as a very disappointing place. He is mostly upset because he has not gotten what he feels he is "owed." You don't want to be around Bill when the newspaper prints a story about the latest big-money lottery winner. "Why do idiots always win the lottery? It's rigged I tell you. The people who really need the money, like me, never win." To Bill, waiters in restaurants are always incompetent. When you go shopping at the mall with Bill you can set your watch by the number of minutes that will transpire before Bill will look around and say, "Gee, there's no shortage of ugly people here today!"

Bob, on the other hand, is not as wound up as his otherworldly counterpart. He is more likely to say "good morning" to strangers, not give anyone an undo amount of grief, and is not likely to criticize or even notice the little tufts of hair that come out of his boss's nostrils.

On a day last week in both Bill and Bob's universes, they woke up to find their apartments engulfed in total darkness. None of their neighbor's apartments were blacked out. A call to the electric company was most certainly in order. The phones in the apartment did not work because they were powered by electricity. Being thoroughly modern individuals, cell phones were the next line of communication. Whoops, the cell phone batteries went dead because the electricity to the battery chargers went out during the night. Lugging a pocketfull of change to the corner pay phone, the Electric Company was finally contacted. After listening to a half hour of electronic prompts by the "automated customer service system," a representative told both Bill and Bob that the electricity was turned off because the bill had not been paid. "Is that so? I distinctly recall having paid that bill," said Bob. "No way, you guys must be morons. I paid that bill," said Bill.

"Billing errors are handled by another department," said the customer service representative, who transferred the call, which was then immediately disconnected. More change and a half hour later, Bill and Bob were both informed that due to a computer software upgrade their accounts were both mistakenly listed as unpaid. Unfortunately, the fact that the accounts were shut down for any reason automatically took up to 12 hours to be restored. Both Bill and Bob were annoyed. Check that. Bob was annoyed. Bill was screaming as loud as one would scream after accidentally stapling their thumb to the desk.

Upon returning home from the pay phones, Bill and Bob noticed that their collections of exotic tropical fish were having difficulties breathing. No electricity, no pump. No pump, no air. No air, a thousand dollars' worth of upside down navigating fish. More grief for Bob, and more agony and excruciating yelping from Bill.

At the end of the day, Bill was arrested for carrying a bazooka into the lobby of the Electric Company customer service area. Bob was home making funeral arrangements for his lost fish.

Why did Bill dust off that trusty bazooka? Why was his container full enough to overflow? The answer is that Bill's container was almost already full with all of the displeasure he receives just from living in the world and carrying along with him a suitcase full of angry attitudes. Bill has convinced himself that the world is a hostile, unfair, unlucky, uncomfortable, and unpleasant place. Bill's overall view of the world and the people in it create enough frustration to keep him at the point of exploding, *almost all the time*. Bob, on the other hand is more easygoing, looks at the world as difficult and unsettling from time to time, but doesn't "hate life." As a result, Bob's container can store more day-to-day discomfort. Temperament and genetics might describe the difference between Bill and Bob, but it is my position that angry attitudes about the world are practiced and become habits.

Threat Sensitivity, Perceptions About the World, and Anger Thresholds

The expression of anger is part of the lesson we all learned in Psychology 101 about human beings having a "fight or flight" system for coping with threats from the environment. Choosing to fight or flee is a very important part of being human. As a matter of fact, it is so much a part of being human that anger is processed by a very ancient part of the brain, which means that angry behavior has been around for a very long time in human evolutionary terms. You can bet that one of the standard options carved into the mentality of primitive man was a nasty temper, or at least the potential for one. We appear to have evolved that way.

When humans feel threatened they become naturally aggressive. Going back to the analogy of the "frustration container," one of the ways people know when that container is full, is they begin to feel so much displeasure that they feel threatened, and when people feel threatened, they communicate it as a matter of survival. They are communicating that they want the displeasure to stop. That is called "expressing frustration." When we express frustration before that container is bursting and overflowing we might appear angry but not necessarily threatened to the point of violence. We are likely to be in better control of our anger when we behave like this. When people start expressing their frustration and their displeasure after they have already contained all they can, they are usually feeling threatened to the point of exploding in anger or worse, rage.

This explains the difference between sitting down at the dinner table after a mildly difficult day at work and being served asparagus, a vegetable you really do not enjoy, versus being served asparagus after a horrible day at the office. After merely a rough day at the office you may proclaim, "I think I am going to pass on the asparagus tonight, Dear." After being chewed out by your boss, fired, and black-listed in your industry, you might be more likely to say, "How many times do I have to tell you how much I can't stand asparagus!" as you fling the innocent but nevertheless offending spears toward the trash.

> ✓ **Check Point**
>
> *People's ability to control their anger is, in part, a function of the way they view the world in general. For some the world is a hostile, ugly place. For others, it is as tolerable as we can make it.*

People who have chronic problems with their expression of anger are often always at or right below the point of feeling threatened, regardless of if they are having a good day or a bad day. That is because they have practiced a perception of the world that keeps them in a constant state of threat *all the time*. In other words, they talk to themselves all day long about what a horrible place the world is. They don't even realize they are talking to themselves, but they are.

When we say that people are "touchy," it means that their reactions are defensively out of proportion to whatever stimulus has caused them to react.

Jane: *"Did you do something new to your hair?"*

June: *"Why? Do you hate my hair?"*

June responding to what was probably a very innocent question by Jane. June operates under the presumption that a simple observation has an insulting or negative spin. You might say that a person who is overly touchy might simply have a poor self-esteem. Okay, I'll buy that; however, it is not at odds with what I have been saying. People with poor self-esteem operate under the burden of threats they place upon *themselves* with their own negative self-perceptions. Some might even say they don't like and are angry at themselves. They generate anger and threat to their own selves. For instance, the person with poor esteem might have a negative view of the world that can be translated into "the world will always be a horrible place to live because I am too incompetent to make it any better for myself." Not surprisingly, people with poor self-esteem often have lots of problems controlling their tempers. The hatred that they have for themselves and the world they live in often spills out onto the people they interact with. That is why shrinks such as me will often say, "You cannot like other people when you hate yourself."

Check Point

People who are chronically angry are always just at the point of feeling threatened enough to have to do something about it. They are always looking for a fight with themselves (creating poor self-esteem) or others.

To sum up, people who harbor negative perceptions about the world overburden themselves because the mere act of living in the world as they see it is unpleasant. Using the container analogy, this keeps them at a place that is very close to the maximum amount of frustration they can hold. They "go over the top" of their container more quickly than people who do not hold such a negative view of the world. As we get closer to filling that container, we activate the mechanisms that are associated with feeling threatened. A common response to feeling threatened is aggression, and anger is a component of aggression.

Finally, people who practice having a negative and unpleasant view of the world maintain and stoke their own anger. The more negative we are, the more we reinforce the notion that this is the reality of how the world operates. The more convinced we are that we live in a terrible, hostile world, the more "full" we keep that container. This includes people who do not feel positively about themselves, which can be an added burden that intensifies angry feelings.

Keeping our containers mostly full from negative perceptions we carry about the world reduces our ability to cope with the normal course of everyday lousy events. Releasing frustration in the form of anger often creates additional difficulties for us. This is very significant because it shows how self-replenishing an angry style of behavior is. It is the answer to the question of why grumpy, angry people can maintain themselves in such a seemingly negative state for such a long time, and in so many different situations. Their grumpy attitude towards life feels so bad that it merely proves how horrible life is.

How Did a Genius Such As Me Get Born Into a World of Morons?: The Power of AMPs

Forgive me, but I am going to throw out another term. I haven't thrown too many at you so far, and I promise there won't be that many more. I have been talking about how perceptions of the world take up a lot of room in the imaginary frustration-holding container that we blow the lid off of when we get angry. I am going to give those perceptions a name: *anger-maintaining presumptions,* or AMPs.

In the world of electronics, an amp is short for *ampere,* a unit of electrical power. I like the analogy between real amps and my own AMPs because

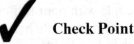
Check Point

We all have "pet perceptions" about how the world operates. This book uses the term AMPs (short for anger-maintaining presumptions) to describe negative beliefs about the world that seem to serve no other purpose but to maintain an angry mode of living.

both are types of energy that maintain a system in a certain state. The AMPs that I talk about in this book represent the energy that maintains a person's negative perceptions of the world, increases their sense of frustration (and therefore threat), and keeps them in a state of readiness to act in angry and aggressive ways. It is the force that keeps those containers we talked about always hovering close to the top.

There are countless anger-maintaining presumptions. When you live with or interact with a chronically angry person you will hear how often they speak directly and indirectly. Here are just a few to wind up the chapter. If you are the type who likes homework, keep track of how many AMPs such as these you hear every day. Don't be shy about owning up to those that are filling up *your* container.

AMPs are a very important part of this program. It is my goal to make you very aware of the AMPs that contribute to your perception of the world and how the people in it operate. We will be identifying many more AMPs in the following chapters. Let's move ahead.

Popular Anger-Maintaining Presumptions or AMPs:

- All people are assholes.
- All people who are not like me are assholes.
- The world is full of morons.
- I am the only intelligent person at my job.
- Most people I meet are out to screw me over.
- Almost everyone on the road is a lousy driver.
- I have stopped expecting anything pleasant from people a long time ago.
- The people who work in retail stores don't care about their jobs.
- Most people would rather see someone rot than to go out of their way to assist them.

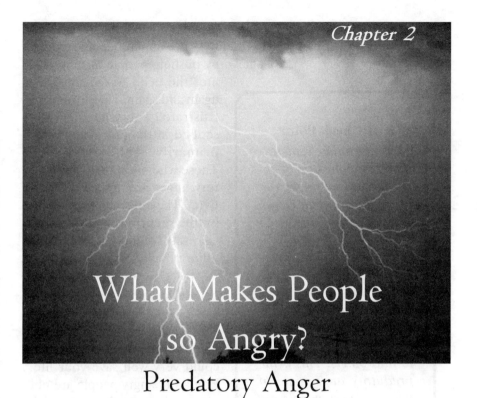

Chapter 2

What Makes People so Angry?

Predatory Anger

In the last chapter, we learned about the type of chronically angry person whose anger response is motivated by frustration. This frustration is maintained or reinforced by negative and unpleasant perceptions of the world. (We gave these unpleasant perceptions a term: called *AMPs*.) Life would be tough enough if the only type of anger we had to deal with was the anger that people store up as a result of living in a frustrated world. Unfortunately, this isn't the only type of angry person we might encounter. The frustrated angry person shows anger in response to displeasure and disappointment. There are people who use anger and aggression to create feelings of *satisfaction* as well. These are the most dangerous of all angry people. People who operate with *predatory anger* use anger as a technique. It becomes part of an arsenal used to compete, persuade, manipulate, control, and intimidate others. Ultimately, the feelings of competence and power that predatory angry people achieve by pushing people around creates the need to feel this way again and again. The chronically frustrated angry people I described in the last chapter are primarily self-destructive. Those who operate with predatory anger are "other destructive." They elevate themselves by persecuting others. They gain satisfaction out of hurting other people.

> ✔ **Check Point**
> *Unfortunately, there is more than one type of angry person we might run into out there in the world. First, there is the frustrated angry person, who is angry because he or she is perpetually disappointed in life. Then, there is the person who actually derives pleasure and enjoyment from using anger to hurt others. This is the predatory angry type of person. These people are very, very dangerous.*

It is important to help people identify anger in others as well of themselves. Taking yourself out of the target sights of the predatory angry person could very well save your life. Predatory angry people are not always big, burly guys with chips on their shoulders. We find them in all walks and roles in life. One of the easiest places to find people who have problems with predatory anger is in our courts. The criminals are the easiest ones to spot—they are usually walking around with handcuffs on. Some lawyers are also high on the list. Here is a vignette about one:

The Story of Bartholomew A. Dabra, Esq.

Divorce attorneys can be the most vicious predatory individuals who practice within their profession. Notice I said "can be," which means I do not think all lawyers are this way. As a matter of fact, professional and ethical lawyers who practice matrimonial law often act as peace ambassadors to settle matrimonial disputes, helping unhappily married people part as friends and saving the children of broken marriages a lot of grief and stress in the process.

Lawyers' styles range from plain to flamboyant. Watching law-yers settle matrimonial disputes is a truly fascinating process. Some lawyers literally become married to their clients' causes, fighting with an adversary lawyer with fully vested egos. Winning is important to all lawyers, but seemingly more so with matrimonial lawyers. The winningest lawyers draw the highest fees, as well as the angriest clients—those that are less interested in separating from a marriage, and more interested in making a cheating spouse suffer embarrass-ment and humiliation in front of as many people as possible. Dividing money and property sparks some very heated disputes as well. In big-money cases, the difference between a mediocre lawyer and a good lawyer can mean dissolving a marriage with thousands to millions more in your pocket.

B.A.D, as he likes to be called, is a lawyer who is one of the "heavy hitters" in his profession. He usually does more than a good job for his clients, but his real passion is the mind games that follow cases and clients, as well as the outside-of-courtroom power plays that are the true forces that drive cases to victory. Observing B.A.D. in action is to observe an example of what I would consider the classic angry predator.

Attorneys do not always get the "good guy," and these are the cases where B.A.D.'s penchant for exercising his talent at manipula-tion and bullying are showcased. Winning a case where you are fight-ing for the client clearly in the right is easy. B.A.D. became bored by these cases long ago. However, winning a case, when all the odds are against you, is truly a feather in your cap. As B.A.D. often brags, "I can turn shit into gold in front of any judge in the state."

In one particular nasty divorce, B.A.D. represented a client who brutally assaulted his wife. The client, an extraordinarily angry preda-tory type himself, showed no remorse over his actions, and suggested that he should be complemented for exercising enough self-control for not hitting her sooner. The victim was a thin wisp of a woman, not even 100 pounds. She was the victim of a nasty divorce in her own childhood.

First, B.A.D. went to work on her psychology, insinuating that she was "damaged goods" because of her own parent's divorce. Next, he suggested that it was she who was abusive because her older daugh-ter who claimed she was too strict with her. This daughter wanted to live with the father, even though the father had assaulted the mother. My belief is that the child was terrified that she would be next. The woman, who had been abused for most of the marriage, became defensive because she felt like she was under attack, both by her husband and his lawyer. She did not feel that, after being beaten up by her husband, she should be humiliated by the type of insults B.A.D. was hurling at her.

Just prior to her being placed on the witness stand to testify, B.A.D. confronted her in the hallway and told her that her own mother was flying in from Nebraska to testify against her and tell the court she was an unfit mother. She did not think it was possible that her mother would ever do this, but things had been going so terribly lately that she began to have some doubts. She did not have the best relationship with her mother, but it was at least cordial. Could her own mother turn against her at a time like this? The woman was crushed. She took the witness stand frightened and demoralized. Her responses were defensive and she made a horrible impression on the judge. When B.A.D. finished examining her, he puffed out his chest, turned to the audience in the back of the courtroom and exclaimed, "That's why they call me Bartholomew A. Dabra."

B.A.D. was clearly pleased that he had once again "turned shit into gold." He successfully misdirected the case from the real issues of spousal abuse. And by the way, he had never had a moment's conversation with the abused woman's mother. It was all a con, carefully engineered to bully, manipulate, and intimidate.

What Maintains the Predatory Angry Personality?

All animals compete for superiority in their immediate environments. Some compete harder than others. In human social groups, successful competition brings a host of social rewards: money and status are two of the most obvious ones. People who have strong motivation to succeed can become extremely consumed with the prospect of attaining more and more, thus competing more and more, and using predatory aggression and anger to get what they want.

Many people avoid competitive environments because they do not enjoy how it feels to compromise someone else's position to advance their own. Others take great joy in proving their superiority. There are ways to survive and succeed in business and social environments without damaging others, but competing in a positively social way usually takes longer and is harder work. Some people choose a more direct way, and that way relies on anger and aggression. Angry predators are too impatient to succeed in socially positive ways such as using "win-win" strategies as the basis for advancing whenever possible. Instead "win-destroy" is the preferred protocol or tactic. For the angry predator, *every* human interaction is a game, and the prizes are domination, control, and the opportunity to eliminate all potential of threat.

The Angry Predator and Perceptions of Threat

In the last chapter I explained how angry frustrated people become threat-sensitive when they reach a certain point of saturation with displeasure. Feelings of discomfort ultimately lead to an angry mode of responding in the hopes of reducing feelings of helplessness and displeasure. Angry predatory people often eliminate any potential threat *before* it becomes a source of displeasure. The act of eliminating the threat becomes a source of relief ("that's one less enemy to have to worry about"), which in turn produces pleasure and satisfaction. Another way of describing the difference between people whose anger is supported by frustration versus those whose anger is supported by predation is that frustrated angry people *react* to feeling threatened. Predatory angry people are proactive—they eliminate even the *potential* of threat.

Other Calling Cards of the Predatory Angry Personality

There are differences between the angry, frustrated personality and the angry, predatory personality. The angry, frustrated person is likely to be self-isolating. Life is a painful experience for the angry, frustrated person. Like a wounded lion, the angry, frustrated person usually will not lash out unless you place additional demands on him or her. Angry responses are more of a lashing out to keep you away than a purposeful set of behaviors designed to hurt or attack.

Angry, predatory personalities operate very comfortably in social environments. They may not appear grumpy, irritable, or angry at all. While they are in the process of sizing up your "threat potential," they will be cordial, often helpful. Even after they have determined that you might be a potential threat, you may not see any outward signs of them wanting to do anything emotionally hurtful or destructive. Angry predators are smart and cunning. They are more likely to operate against you when they believe they have lost the ability to control you, or when the opportunity arises for them to benefit from hurting you. Angry predators are not always "rough and tough people." They can be sophisticated, cool, and calculating. They often use indirect or passive-aggressive acts to undermine your position in certain situations, as you will see in the next vignette:

Meet Missy Gabor

Missy Gabor is the picture of civic responsibility. She runs bake sales, heads up the PTA, and is the chairwoman for a committee that raises money for medical research. She is a volunteer. She knows how busy most of her friends are and cannot imagine how they would have the time to print calendars and hang fliers the way she does. So many volunteers come and go into her group, but she is lucky enough to have a few good friends who "coordinate" the details of events she plans and fundraisers that she is so often praised for. The local newspaper just recently ran a story about her being "a volunteer for all seasons." She was very proud of that.

Jane Tupilow had just moved in across the street from the elementary school. At first, Missy thought Jane was a "curious type." Missy observed Jane, and Jane seemed busy and interested, and was overheard asking the local librarian how she could get involved in the National Juvenile Diabetes Foundation. Apparently, Jane had a diabetic child and wanted to volunteer in the organization. "How nice," Missy related to a friend over coffee, "but if she was so interested in the foundation, all she had to do was look at the telephone poles on Main Street," which clearly listed Missy as the contact person for that organization. "Why didn't she just call?" Missy wondered.

Eventually, Jane did call. According to how Missy described Jane to another friend, she seemed like a "real go-getter." About a week later Missy contacted Jane about helping out with a fundraiser for the National Juvenile Diabetes Foundation. Missy had some ideas for what sort of fundraiser it should be. She thought a book drive would be fun. Later, when Missy was talking to one of her other friends, Mrs. Atkins, she mentioned that when she and Jane were talking about the fundraiser, Jane "chirped in" that she thought a book drive was more of a winter activity and because it was the summertime, maybe a car wash would be fun. "We've been doing book drives for *centuries* and they have all been successful," Missy mused. Mrs. Atkins just happened to mention that maybe a car wash would be fun as well.

After coffee, Missy passed by the school to see Jane unpacking a carload of groceries at the curb, and wouldn't you know it, Mr. Atkins was helping Jane unload groceries. Missy did not miss the opportunity to mention to Mrs. Atkins that she thought Jane seemed like "an extremely friendly" new community member. Embellishing just slightly on what she saw, she mentioned to Mrs. Atkins that if she was looking around for her husband, she had seen him walking out of Jane's front door just a few minutes ago.

Missy knew that Mrs. Atkins and her husband had been having some marital difficulties. The local gossip was that he had an affair with his secretary that nearly broke up the marriage. After Missy reported on the fact that her husband was over Jane's house, she made sure to end the conversation by saying to Mrs. Atkins, "...and remember, Sweetie, if you ever just want to unload and get things off your chest, I'm always here to listen."

"What a good friend Missy is," thought Mrs. Atkins. "A good friend always watches your back." The nerve of Jane, horning in on her husband after being in the neighborhood for less than a month. At the next National Juvenile Diabetes Foundation committee meeting, the suggestion to have a car wash as a fundraiser was unanimously opposed. Book drives had been successful for *centuries*, at least according to Mrs. Atkins.

Lack of Empathy: A Key to How the Angry, Predatory Person Operates

Angry predatory people succeed because they can "disconnect" a very important human trait—empathy. Empathy is the ability to look at life from someone else's perspective. Empathy is an important short-circuit for impulses that are angry, mean, or selfish because once we try to imagine how another person might respond to our angry actions, we tend to censor it. Many people find the thought of hurting people very unacceptable. This is a function of imagining how they would feel if treated the same way.

Take, for example the man who has asked his wife 100 times to keep the bathroom door closed while he is taking a shower because the new puppy likes to sneak in and poop on the throw rug in front of the shower stall. When he steps out and finds puppy poop squished under his foot, he can either scream and curse at his wife, beat the dog, or say, "Life is too short, I'm already in the shower. I'll just wash it off." Empathy permits the man to imagine his wife feeling upset for him berating her, and also allows him to forgive the puppy for being a puppy.

The predatory person does not have empathy. Their own feelings and desires take precedence over everything else. They don't care about the hurt feelings they cause by screaming at someone else, and the release that they achieve from throwing a fit is important to them. The damage they cause with their anger is justifiable because "it serves people right for being so stupid." Some predatory people enjoy the feeling of making other people suffer, merely for the sense of power and control it gives them.

Desensitization

I love to fish. When I first started fishing as a kid I was very squeamish about touching live bait. I was sensitive, so I did not enjoy the idea of putting a hook through a little fish's mouth to catch bigger fish. Over time, though, I would like to think that I remained sensitive as a human being. I have learned to bait a hook with live bait, although I am not exactly crazy about it as a task, nor am I crazy about filleting a fish I have caught so I can eat it. I do it, however, and I no longer feel nauseated by it. The fact that I have become less sensitive to the issue over time shows that I have become *desensitized* to it.

Angry predators become desensitized to their own empathic feelings and the feelings of others. When an angry boss stands over an employee and whittles that person down to a nub with insults about the employee's intelligence and work style, that boss has become completely desensitized to what it was like to work for someone else. Desensitization allows angry people to cause high degrees of pain and anxiety in others. This desensitization is rarely limited to one person in an angry person's life, so if you are spending time with a person who perpetually cuts down others, either with aggression, sarcasm, or insults, understand that eventually your time will come.

The next vignette is about "blame externalization." This is another characteristic of the angry, predatory person. It is a fancy way of saying that the angry, predatory person never feels responsible for any damage he or she causes. It is always someone else's fault. The angry predatory person believes that when he hurts people it is because he "had to" or because the person "asked for it."

The Story of Mark Barker, Double Parker: An Example of Blame Externalization

Mark Barker, always in a hurry, wanted to pick up his clothes at the dry cleaners on a busy urban boulevard. As usual, there were no parking spaces in front of the store. According to Mark, that was because the idiots that designed the town were too stupid to realize that people would actually want to park in front of the stores that were there. After circling the block once, Mark double-parked his vehicle, effectively tying up the right lane of a two-lane eastbound avenue. Mark reached around to the backseat to pick

 Check Point

Angry predatory people "disconnect" their ability to feel empathy for the people whose lives they affect negatively. In addition, they "desensitize" themselves to feelings of disgust or discomfort at the idea of hurting others.

up his pile of clothes and flipped open the handle on the driver's side door of his late-model car. He let the door fall open. The next sound Mark heard was the squeal of tires, a large bang, and the sight of his car door bouncing and skitching across the road. A driver, who did not realize Mark was parked and was not expecting to see the door open into his lane, could not avoid hitting the door.

After the initial shock of the incident subsided, Mark started walking toward the man in the other car. He could see from the rearview mirror that the driver of the vehicle was an older gentleman.

"Stupid old man," Mark muttered. "Why don't they make these blind, old bastards take driving tests once they hit 65." In the 10 feet between Mark's car and the older gentleman's car, Mark worked himself up into a rage, convincing himself that the entire event occurred because the man was too old to be driving. Mark walked up to the car and started banging on the window. The old man was saying, "Calm, down. We can take care of this. Let's make sure neither one of us is injured." Mark shot back angrily, "None of us is injured yet, you stupid, old bastard. If you don't haul your ass out of that car and tell me how you are going to replace that door, you will be plenty injured." "Please, please," said the old man, "there is no need for that." "Get out here, dammit," said Mark as he slammed his fist down on the hood of the car, leaving a large dent. The old man was dialing the phone. Mark presumed he was calling someone from his family. What a relief, Mark thought. Maybe this guy had a son who wasn't senile and who could get his father to pay for the damage.

Actually, the older man *was* calling his son, a lieutenant in the city police department, right in the jurisdiction where they were in right now. The old man was a retired police officer himself.

When the police arrived a few minutes later, two cops jumped out and wanted to know if Mark made a threatening remark to the older gentleman. "What do you mean, did I make a threatening remark? This stupid old fool nearly killed me. He took the door right off my car." The cop asked politely, "Were you double-parked? Were your hazard lights on? Did you look to see if there was any oncoming traffic?" The police officer continued, "More importantly, because you did not answer the last time I asked, Sir, did you tell this gentleman you were going to injure him if he did not get out of his vehicle, and then pound your fists on the hood?" Mark replied, "Well, yeah, I said that and did that, but he wasn't listening to me."

Click! The cuffs went on. Mark spent $800 fixing his car door and $2,800 in legal fees. When Mark saw the gentleman in court the old man said, "You know, if you hadn't acted like such a jerk, I would have never had you arrested. We could have settled the whole thing by swapping insurance cards." Mark replied, "I don't know what the hell you are talking about. You wrecked my car, and just because you have an 'in' with the police department, I got locked up. When I get through with this, I'll sue you."

Mark had a difficult time understanding that he was capable of doing *something* wrong. His mind was very quick at coming up with a lot of different reasons for why negative things that happen to him are always someone else's fault. This is called *blame externalization*. People who have problems controlling their anger have difficulty accepting responsibility for their behavior. They are very good at assigning blame to everyone and everything other than themselves. This is especially true in people who have predatory anger. They justify their angry behavior and the aggressive things they do by convincing themselves that everyone else is "wrong" and they are right. Ironically, one of the things that people who are like this will perpetually repeat is, "I am the first one to admit when I am wrong, *but*..." Then they will go on to tell you how, on this particular occasion, they are most certainly *not* wrong.

Check Point

Many angry predatory people have a difficult time accepting responsibility for the consequences of what they do. Nothing is ever their fault. This is called blame externalization.

A behavior that goes hand-in-hand with never admitting that one is wrong is also never being able to apologize for any harm that they have caused. Apologies are considered a sign of accepting blame or fault. They are also, to the predatory person, a sign of weakness. The predatory angry person reasons that, if someone decides to mess with them, that person might get hurt. They might get hurt really badly, as a matter of fact. Perhaps that will teach them to find out a little more about who they are starting in with the next time.

Revenge Motivation

The angry, frustrated person is not particularly interested in revenge. The angry, predatory person is often consumed by it. Replaying fantasies of revenge and imagining a "movie" of what the angry, predatory person will do reduces the normal process of censoring what should short circuit aggressive behavior. Playing it out in one's mind can make it more real and more likely to happen. Road rage is, in part, a function of revenge motivation. "That driver did something bad to me, so now I am going to do something bad to him to even the score."

Strong Sense of Entitlement

The world owes me. If reading this phrase immediately causes someone's name to pop into your head, I would be willing to bet that you also believe this person is excessively angry. The technical term for this attitude is "sense of entitlement," and it is another attitude or perception that drives the predatory personality.

Once someone feels as if they are "owed" something, it makes it easier for them to accept that the world should punish those who do not "pay up." It is very easy to identify people who have strong feelings of entitlement by the way they speak to or about other people. Their comments are rude, disrespectful, insensitive, impatient, and overly critical. For people with this trait, it is not something someone would notice once in awhile. It is a type of behavior that is active continuously, and expressed toward almost everyone they come in contact with.

✔ **Check Point**

Two more important features of angry predatory behavior are a high need for revenge and a sense that the world owes them something just because they are living in it. These two characteristics compliment each other in a very negative way. When the angry predatory person does not get what they feel is owed to them, they will seek revenge against those who do not give it to them.

AMPS of the Angry Predator

In the last chapter, I introduced you to the concept that chronically frustrated angry people keep themselves close to the point of overload or saturation by maintaining a negative view of the world in general. They do this by maintaining certain presumptions or conclusions about how the world operates (these presumptions were what I termed anger-maintaining presumptions, or *AMPs*). As a result, chronically frustrated angry people are hurt. Their anger is a mechanism of communicating that pain.

Angry, predatory people subscribe to some of the same AMPs as do angry, frustrated types of people, but their AMPs tend to take on a substantially darker and more vicious tone. Take, for example, the following very common AMP of people who have had difficult times in relationships:

"All men are scum."

"All women are vicious, high-maintenance tramps."

The frustration of experiencing bad feelings and resentment that unsuccessful relationships cause produces these perceptions, which help keep the person away from additional frustrating relationships. Again, for the frustrated person, the message is "I'm in pain, keep away."

When you start adding a component that implies that if you are hurt in a relationship, you will make it your business to hurt back. Or when you imply that using the opposite sex for money or for sexual gratification is a goal or aim of yours, then you are endorsing a set of presumptions that justifies a more predatory way of interacting with the opposite sex. If your beliefs about relationships take a turn toward using other people for sex or for other gain, your orientation is clearly not in the best interests of the other person, but in the best interests of yourself. Predatory angry people who engage in romantic relationships, friendships, or business relationships often become abusive and bullying.

As in the last chapter, items like those in the following list are a "starter set" of AMPs that maintain and encourage predatory behavior. Once you begin to notice them in yourself or in others, you will tune into many, many more. Also, understand that behavior can speak just as clearly as words, so you do not have to *hear* a person utter these ideas to know these AMPs are operating.

AMPS That Reinforce Predatory Behavior

+ "Life is tough, the strongest survive. If weak people get in my way and they get hurt, it is not my fault; it's merely an unfortunate fact of life."

+ "I do not mind hurting people who stand in the way of what I want."

(AMPS list continued on next page.)

- "If you come onto my playing field and you lose more than you bargained for, maybe you should think twice about it the next time. I might hurt you more than I have to in order to prevent you from doing it a second time."
- "You have no right to disappoint me. I don't care if you are having a bad day, if you do something bad to me and it makes me upset, you are going to get very little slack."
- "I might be right, and I might be wrong, but if you piss me off in the middle of an argument and get hurt, it doesn't matter. You just shouldn't have pissed me off."
- "All of life is a game. You play to win. If I break a rule and it doesn't hurt me, that's good for me. If I break a rule and it hurts you, that's tough for you. In the end the only thing that matters is winning."
- "Control of people and things is a necessary part of life. Without control there is chaos. People like me are given the opportunity to control because I am innately smarter and more powerful than most others. I may have to control something you do by intimidating you. If you allow yourself to be intimidated, you are meant to be controlled."

In the next chapter I will continue to show you how becoming more aware of and disputing the anger-maintaining presumptions that you endorse is an important part of learning how to live a happier, less stressful, and calmer life.

Chapter 3

People Perception: Increasing Anger Awareness, Your First Critical Path

(Part I)

The first thing people often want to know when they learn I am a psychologist is whether or not I am "analyzing" them. Sure I am, but not just because I am a psychologist. Most human beings analyze one another all the time. When you walk down the street at night and you see a person screaming, howling, spitting, and swearing, you most likely either turn back and walk to where you came from, or cross the street and walk on the other side. You have "analyzed" the person's behavior. We analyze people all the time when we speak to them, mostly because it is a *polite* thing to do. After all, listening to a person, and wondering why they said or did something is a sign we are paying attention.

Oddly, most people go through the trouble to observe and pay attention to behavior in people whom we associate closely with, only to *ignore* the things that ultimately produce problems later, when the things we have observed (and ignored) impact us negatively.

Being a keen observer of others is important for more than one reason. Knowing how someone treats others is a good indicator of how they will treat you. Also, if you are the type of person who can relate what you see in others to yourself, you will be able to change your own behavior more easily. Don't forget, this book is as much about dealing with the angry behavior of others as it is about dealing with anger in yourself. The best way to deal with excessively angry behavior in other people is to avoid them, but often people do not avoid what looks like trouble. It might be that people, in general, would rather think everything is always going to turn out fine, regardless of what red flags are raised or what their observations suggest. Social psychologists point out that this is a fundamental error in judgment that most people make.

> ✓ **Check Point**
>
> *Most people will agree that it is important to be a keen observer of others. Unfortunately, while people will take the time to observe others, they frequently fail to act on what they see. This is often because most people want to believe that "things will work out" despite early warning signs of problems. Angry people are often very good at identifying problems in other people, but cannot see those same difficulties when they are within themselves.*

The next vignette shows how closely we can observe others, while ignoring the impact or significance it may have to us.

I Thought I Was Different

A year after the start of a very stressful divorce for Jim, he met Diana, who was convinced Jim was the man of her dreams. What she did not realize, however, is that there are two types of dreams, and he wasn't the good kind. Diana was drawn to Jim because she felt sorry for how he was always being victimized by his vicious ex-wife, Jody.

Before they separated, Jody called the police on him frequently. Her agenda, according to Jim, was to get him out of the house and have him put in jail.

Jim was never particularly angry or rough with Diana, but she knew he could be put in a very bad mood with one five-minute telephone call to his ex. "Why don't you and your crooked bastard lawyer just put a gun to my head while you are at it?" he would scream into the phone. "If it were up to you, I would be out on the street. You deserve nothing from this marriage after all the aggravation you have caused." After he would hang up the phone he would look at Diana and apologize for his temper. "That woman pushes all of my buttons," Jim would say. Diana would advise him, "No one is worth getting yourself *that* angry over, Jim." Jim would agree. Diana was a good cheerleader. As a matter of fact, Jim's angry divorce and Diana's willingness to support him were the cornerstones of their relationship.

Diana was very tuned in to Jim. If Jim was having a "bad day," he would drive very aggressively and lose patience with people. Diana would give him a shoulder rub at home to calm him down. This always seemed to help.

Eventually Jim's problems with Jody were over. The divorce was finalized and he did not have to speak to her anymore. Jim and Diana moved in with one another. Two weeks after the divorce decree was signed Jim lost his temper with his boss at work and was fired. It seems they had an argument that escalated into a shoving match. Instead of just letting it "blow over," the boss had Jim escorted out of the building by security. "I guess you can afford to have any kind of argument you want with your employees when you've got three ex-marines as security guards to back you up," Jim told Diana. Diana could not believe Jim's bad luck. As soon as he was out of his marriage, his boss goes ape on him. She was beginning to wonder whether her man would ever catch a break.

About a month later, Diana asked Jim if he would accompany her to a family wedding. Jim wasn't exactly crazy about socializing with people he didn't know, but, reluctantly, he agreed. As they were getting dressed to go to the affair, Diana asked Jim if he would change his tie. Maybe he didn't realize that there was a pretty noticeable spot on it. "For crying out loud, Diana, do I have to worry that the geeks in your family are going to hate me because I have a spot on my tie?" Diana was taken aback. Maybe she was being selfish about wanting to have Jim look his best for her family. "I'm sorry, Jim, I shouldn't have mentioned anything. You're right, no one is going to care about your tie." This did not satisfy Jim. He went into a speech. "You know, I swore to myself that I would never let myself get involved with another nagging woman ever again. One time around the block on that one is enough. I can't stand a nagging woman. I never could. I am a hardworking man. I am not a magazine model. I have a few stains on my ties. Big fucking deal. I wasn't even crazy about going to this damn wedding, but I did it because I knew it was important to you. Now, I'm pissed off. I don't even feel like going. Maybe you would like to go by yourself, and when your relatives ask you where I am, you can tell them, 'I bitched to him about his stupid tie, so he stayed home.' That would be nice and embarrassing, wouldn't it?"

After Jim finished his tirade, Diana was shellshocked. She could not believe he had unloaded on her like that. She flashed back to the conversations she overheard Jim having with his ex-wife. He spoke to her in that very tone. Diana used to assume that Jody deserved it. Maybe not.

All of the information Diana needed to understand Jim's dark angry side was there. She passed it off and ignored it. She even supported and encouraged it.

In Diana's case, what I did not tell you in the story above is how many times she thought about some of her other divorced friends who did not have the same trouble as Jim and his ex-wife. Diana reasoned that some people had rough divorces and some had relatively easy ones. Another constant thought for Diana was "it takes two to tango." After all, what kind of conflict was all one person's fault? Diana merely thought that whatever Jim's contribution was, it could not possibly have been as great as his ex-wife's. He had painted her out as such a witch. This, by the way, was another source of nagging discomfort. Jim was more than willing to paint his ex-wife as a witch. How could that be 100 percent true? At one point in time, Jim and his ex-wife were in love enough to get married. It was a scary thought, but every once in awhile Diana thought that if she and Jim got married and they had problems, would he consider her a witch, too?

Increasing Anger Awareness: The First Critical Path

Increasing your awareness for the presence of anger, the type of anger, and the theme that anger is communicating is the first "lesson" or critical path in this program. There is no complicated or "hidden" message in Diana's vignette. The main point of the story is easy to see. If Diana had been more careful to notice how angry a person Jim was and not assumed that all of his anger was a result of his prior relationship, the choices she might have made would have been quite different. As it turns out, Jim is the sort of person who believes that the women he chooses are actually the "bad guys." They victimize him with unreasonable demands and nagging. In Jim's selfish and predatory mind, he is just a helpless, nice guy who can't take the grief that women dish out to him. It's no wonder he blows his top when he can't take it anymore. Even though he is an angry, aggressive person, he chooses to see himself as being victimized by women. "It's in their nature to be bitches," Jim would tell his friends.

Acting on what we see can be a very difficult thing for people, especially when we want our lives to be happy and blissful. The disappointment that comes from being clubbed over the head by reality is at the very root of angry behavior. That is why I consider the process people must engage in to learn how to deal with anger as a *mastery* process. The word *mastery* implies dedication and focus. It requires a type of concentration that comes from effort that is more than just an acknowledgment, but a decision to make conflict management a high personal priority. Every major life change requires dedication of this type. Have you ever tried to lose a lot of weight? You can't do it just by reading a book. You have to do it by making changes that you think about for much of each day. In doing so, you have to become a zealot of sorts, much to the annoyance of your family and friends who may not want to eat grapefruit, soy, protein bars, or whatever it is you are doing to lose weight.

At the same time that I am telling readers of this book that dedicating yourself to the kind of mastery over anger will help you become happier and less stressed, I am also saying that it is completely unnecessary to rush yourself in the process. You might be in a hurry to lose 20 pounds in five weeks so that you can look good in a bathing suit, but there's no reason to rush with this program. Success is a process that builds every time you take a new step forward, even from the first day. Deepening and strengthening that success comes over time. Plus, I'll let you in on a preview of what you will learn a little later in this program, which is that rushing and time pressure creates frustration, and frustration is a major cause of uncontrolled anger.

Critical Paths

I use the term "critical path" to describe each phase of mastery over anger. This is not a term you must embrace with any particular passion. If you don't like the term "critical path," you can think of each part of this program as a lesson, module, phase, or anything you like.

I do think that the term "critical path" is a helpful shorthand for people who discuss the concepts of this book in groups. You can say, "I am on the first critical path," or "I am on the third critical path," and the people who you are speaking to will know what you have considered or examined in your life and will be able to relate accordingly. On the other hand, you don't have to talk to or relate these ideas to anyone but yourself. Your journey along the critical paths can be a walk you take in the privacy of your own mind.

So having given these few fundamentals as background, the first critical path on the road to mastering calm is called "Increasing Anger Awareness," and if you have read this book chapter-by-chapter so far you will find it relatively easy to begin the mastery process because the first two chapters contain half of the information you need to finish the first critical path.

From Mastery Content to Success Milestones:

Five Steps to Completing Each Critical Path

Mastery content is the first step of each of the six critical paths that people learn in this program. Mastery content is information about the psychology of people that is helpful in understanding the main ideas of each critical path. There are four other steps, which make five steps for each critical path altogether. Here is what the entire first critical path or lesson of "Increasing Anger Awareness" looks like in outline form:

First Critical Path: Increasing Anger Awareness

Step One: Mastery Content—Understanding what maintains anger in the angry lifestyle.

Step Two: Coping Strategies—Acknowledging angry lifestyles.

Step Three: Communication Skills—Communicate more positively by observing and understanding more and saying less.

Step Four: Affirmations—Challenging your anger maintaining presumptions.

Step Five: Achievements that lead you to pursue the next critical path.

After you are finished with these five steps, you are ready to move on to the next critical path, and so on until you feel you are through. There are no tests or formal assessments unless you are taking the course to earn a certificate. You can move on to new critical paths when you feel that you have accomplished as many success milestones as you can. You can always come back to any critical path to reemphasize the mastery portions of each. Do not think of doing this as a "demotion" of any sort. Instead, think of it as becoming smart enough to know that it is better to go back and revisit a critical path than it is to fool yourself into thinking you know all there is to know. There is no harm in that at all. In fact, there is a good deal of maturity in those that can go back and regroup before moving forward. Remember, there's no rush.

Another way that people can go through the program is by reading through the entire book and absorbing all of the information first, then moving through each critical path in a more intense and detailed manner. This would probably be the way that self-help groups would go through the program, or the way anger management courses would be taught when using this book as the main text for the curriculum. Courses and groups might be more time limited, so making everyone familiar with all the steps first is a perfectly fine way of using the material.

> ✓ **Check Point**
>
> *"Increasing Anger Awareness" is the first of six **critical paths** presented in the Mastering Calm program. Each critical path contains five steps that you must master in order to complete the path.*

I have already tried to make things a bit easier for you by providing the first portion of the mastery content for the first critical path in the first two chapters of the book. By reading the book straight through to this point, and by learning about the different types of angry behavior that people use (frustrated and predatory), you have already completed half of one step (in other words, half of the mastery content for the first critical path). For those who need a quick review, I will summarize some of the important concepts in the first two chapters before we move on to the next portion of mastery content for Increasing Anger Awareness.

Quick Review

Excessive anger is the predictable result of people operating under one of two (or both) conditions. The first condition is chronic frustration. People who become so frustrated with life's demands and disappointments ultimately lose their ability to properly decompress or "let off steam." As a result, they are always operating in a state of discomfort and displeasure. Every little annoyance brings them past the point of being able to cope and their anger is a way of communicating pain and hopelessness.

The second condition, which results in chronic or excessive anger, is what I call "predatory anger." Predatory anger is maintained by a set of life circumstances where people's anger has actually created beneficial outcomes. The results of angry interactions have brought them rewards such as money, increased social power, and better jobs. People who show predatory anger do not necessarily seem grumpy and irritable the way frustrated angry people often appear. Predatory angry people may have good social skills. They are more likely to be manipulative, controlling, competitive, self-centered, and insensitive to the pain they cause others.

Chronic anger is maintained by presumptions or beliefs about how the world operates. I have called these beliefs AMPs, which stands for "anger-maintaining presumptions." There are thousands of AMPs that people subscribe to. I listed just a few in the first two chapters. AMPs keep the imaginary container where people store their frustrations almost full, almost all the time. That is the difference between a chronically angry person and a person who merely gets angry once in awhile, and in ways that do not typically affect his or her life. Filling your container with AMPs keeps you in a constant state of readiness to express anger. Identifying your AMPs and the AMPs of others will be an important ongoing task for everyone who goes through this program.

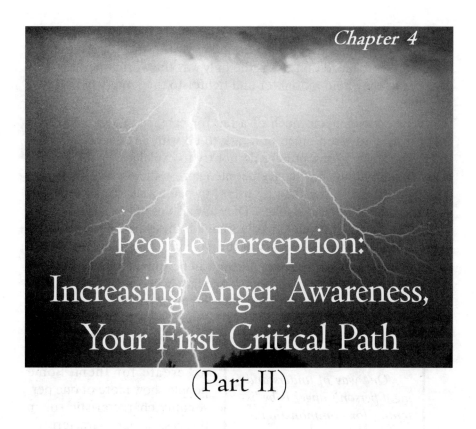

Chapter 4

People Perception: Increasing Anger Awareness, Your First Critical Path

(Part II)

Two main types of anger have been the subject of our discussion so far—frustration-driven anger and predatory anger. In this section I am going to try to help refine that knowledge a bit more by talking about "styles" or "themes" of angry expression. If you don't like the terms "style" or "theme" you might relate to the notion of asking yourself "What broken record does an angry person play over and over when they are expressing their anger?"

A "style" is another way of saying a regularly occurring type of behavior. Many chronically angry people focus or concentrate their anger on one or a few repetitive themes. "I am angry because no one appreciates me," or "I am angry because people are always trying to hurt me." Angry people live their entire lives looking for circumstances that validate the themes they express. Each time they find evidence for the complaints they have about the world, they become more and more convinced that this is the only way the world operates, and as a result they hold on tighter and tighter to their angry beliefs and behaviors.

I have never been much of a fan for categorizing behavior because it is always too much of a task to do with any degree of accuracy. The styles I present here do not try to explain everything there is to explain about how angry people express themselves. They are presented because they can be useful to paint a picture of anger in people with very broad strokes. They are also useful as ways of holding up a mirror to ourselves to determine if these are the themes that we use to keep ourselves angry at the world.

Of course, not every angry person can be summed up as a "type" of angry person. A problem that immediately arises when we try to organize anything as complicated as human behavior into themes is that people are not always true to the cubbyholes we create for them. Some people show more of one personality characteristic (or in this case, anger characteristic) than others. Some people are a mix of one or more. Some people may show characteristics of one style at home, and another at work. If that is the case, why name them at all? Identifying styles or themes of anger does have its advantages. As long as we are willing to admit that naming something merely gives us a common platform for discussing our observations, and does not give us a right to judge or engage in prejudicial activities, identifying something by giving it a name can be helpful.

> **✔ Check Point**
>
> *One way of understanding a person's anger is by listening for common themes and complaints that make up an angry person's "style."*

Sometimes Accurate Observing Can Help Us Avoid Troublesome People and Situations

One obvious value of being able to identify certain types of angry people from others is that there are some angry people who would be better off avoided altogether. The predatory types of individuals are more dangerous (more prone to intentionally physically and emotionally hurt others) so it would be a good thing if we could identify predatory types of behavior and steer clear of them.

The goal of trying to decide what behavior is dangerous or harmful so that we can avoid it is reasonable but not always that easy. One way to approach this difficult task is to determine what theme or style of anger a person is expressing, and then try to determine what purpose it serves. It is actually the second step that determines whether a person might be more prone to acting in a way that is designed to cause intentional harm, a hallmark of predatory anger. Here are some simple observations you can make to tell whether a person's anger is predatory and potentially harmful to you.

Check Point

If I mention it 100 times in this book, it will not be enough. The best way to deal with predatory types of people is to do your best to avoid them altogether. Never make the mistake of thinking that you will be treated "differently" than anyone else in that person's life. This advice can quite literally save your life.

Behavior That Can Signal Predatory Tendencies

1. The person openly defies authority, and may even start fights with police.
2. The person brags about being tough and "not afraid to fight."

(List continued on next page.)

3. The person has a history of getting in trouble for aggressive conduct.
4. The person has no problem breaking or circumventing the law.
5. The person enjoys making other people "squirm."
6. The person prides themselves on being intimidating.
7. The person is overly focused on controlling the people around him or her.
8. The person looks as though he or she enjoys being in conflict with other people, just so he or she can brag about it or tell stories about it. Every day is another fight or battle.
9. The person is often very consumed with ideas of revenge and retaliation against people who have hurt or threatened him or her.

Being Honest About Your Own Hot Buttons

Observing a style or theme in a person over a period of time is a good way of knowing where a person's "hot buttons" are. Similarly, if your goal is to learn how to control your *own* anger and angry responses, being honest with yourself about what it is that starts your own angry episodes is essential to becoming in better control of yourself. For instance, some people may show a great deal of tolerance for being poked fun at. They can take a joke. That same person might react in a particularly angry way to feeling unappreciated or misunderstood. Other people might not care so much about being unappreciated, but may get extremely angry if they feel they are being made fun of.

Knowing what themes raise the level of tension in a person to the point where they become excessively angry, is a very important part of knowing the person in general. Being able to communicate your particular sensitivities to the people who you are close to can be a very important part of maintaining healthy relationships with your boss, partners, parents, children, and friends.

What Message Is Being Broadcast?

When someone goes into a tirade about how no one appreciates her, what else might she be saying? "Don't bother me, I am in too much pain. I have had too many disappointments and I cannot take the thought of even one more. I'm disgusted with people," is what the frustrated angry person might be telling the world.

The predatory angry person may voice the same complaint, but broadcast a different message. That message is, "Don't get in my way, or I will hurt you. If you don't appreciate what I am doing for you, maybe you will learn to appreciate it if I show you that I can also hurt you."

Knowing whether the message is "I am in pain," or "I am dishing out pain," is an important distinction when you are trying to get to know someone. Once you have an idea as to what message is operating, developing a strategy for managing your interactions with the people who communicate those messages should become easier. More importantly, knowing which message *you* are broadcasting becomes a very important piece of information to confront, accept, and ultimately change as a part of your mastery process. For instance, is it really necessary for you to push people away when you are frustrated? There might be some way for you to communicate your disappointment in a way that will make the people closest to you more likely to reach out and interact with you in a more pleasing way. Or if solitude is what you want, perhaps you can get it without having to fight for it. Similarly, if you punish the people who disappoint you as way of keeping them under your control, ultimately, will the end result be the destruction of the relationship and a life without anyone who is willing to be close to you? There are other ways of trying to meet your needs without having to hurt the people you value. Learning how to communicate when you are frustrated and angry has a lot to do with the things you are telling yourself about the world.

Listen for the AMPs

Knowing something about what maintains and stokes anger is an important key to learning how to deal with anger in ourselves and others. Beliefs and presumptions about the world (which I have called, anger-maintaining presumptions, or AMPs) are important ways to discriminate between anger that is maintained by frustration, and anger that is maintained by predation. In the last chapter, we learned that our perception of the world can often take up valuable space in that frustration-holding container that the top blows off of when we become angry. When people express themselves (verbally or through their behavior), it is sometimes possible to tell whether their anger-maintaining presumptions stem from frustration and disappointment, or a desire to manipulate, control, compete, and dominate. If you want to understand the nature of your anger as well as the angry behavior you may encounter, it is important to be able to identify the more frustration-driven anger as well as predatory anger. The frustrated individual views the world with grumpiness, pessimism, and with presumptions that include notions such as:

- "There are some lucky people and some unlucky people. I am one of the unlucky ones so nothing good will ever come of me or my life."
- "What good is being nice to people. Everytime I have tried I have been burned or disappointed, so I might as well stay away."
- "There is no point in putting on a happy face. People who do that are phony."
- "Most of the people I deal with are unreliable. Those that are unreliable turn against me. In the end it would be better if people left me alone."
- "Most people will never take the time or trouble to truly understand me or my needs."

The frustrated person acts out in angry ways as a way to aid his or her isolation and as a way to communicate pain and displeasure. The predatory individual views the world competitively, opportunistically, and with an eye toward eliminating threat. The presumptions that maintain this type of angry behavior are:

"If I don't like the way someone looks at me or treats me, I am going to stop them from even the possibility of hurting me."

"By intimidating weaker people than me, I will show everyone else what is in store for them if they threaten me."

"I may have to hurt or intimidate people for their own good. If they don't learn a lesson from me, they will learn a more difficult lesson from someone else."

The predatory angry individual acts out in angry ways to make himself feel better about himself, to reinforce feelings of self-importance, and to reward himself with feelings of dominance, power, and control. While we are referring to one type of anger as "frustrated," both the frustrated angry person and the predatory angry person are frustrated. Predatory angry people are frustrated and set on edge by threats to their dominance. Frustrated angry people are chronically frustrated at a disappointing world.

More Common Themes That Motivate Angry Behavior

In the following sections, I will describe some major themes or styles of angry behavior. In most of the themes I will try to give examples of the predatory angry person and the chronically frustrated angry person. As a way of exercising your brain, after you read the description of each style or theme, try to imagine what AMPs maintain each type of theme. Try to put yourself in the mindset of each angry theme (you may already be in that mindset!). In other words, express your list of complaints about the world from the point of view of each angry theme. Realize that each of these themes is unhealthy because they present a picture of the world that is one-dimensional, oversimplified, and, ultimately, very self-defeating. What makes each theme particularly self-defeating is that the more you look at the world with such narrow

> ✓ **Check Point**
> *The frustrated person and the predatory person might have the same angry complaint. (For instance, "I am mad because no one appreciates me.") The difference between the two is in how they are behaving around that complaint. The frustrated person might just want people to leave her alone. The predatory person, on the other hand, might be announcing that she intends to teach the people that do not appreciate her "a lesson" by hurting them.*

vision, the more you will convince yourself that the negatives you see *are the world.*

Underappreciated and Misunderstood

This theme's point of view: *Nobody appreciates what I do for them, and they never will. I must be an idiot for being so nice!*

For the chronically frustrated person, this theme may reflect past experiences where he or she has tried to reach out to others, and has failed because they were not adequately recognized. The perception that everyone has failed to show their appreciation creates a cynical and sarcastic worldview. The likely reaction to this worldview is to want to be left alone. Anyone who tries to pull a person operating in this theme out of isolation runs the risk of being the target of their disappointment and anger.

For the chronically predatory person, the theme of being under-appreciated and misunderstood is more of a reflection of personal insult. "You did not appreciate how great I am and, therefore, you need to be taught a lesson." Angry acting out includes the need for this type of person to punish those who are not "smart enough" to appreciate him or her.

Perpetually Threatened

This theme's point of view: *I am sick and tired of everybody...looking at me, picking on me, talking behind my back, driving like a maniac, looking for reasons to leave me behind.*

This is one of several themes that highlight oversensitivity to how they are being treated by the people they interact with. All of the threats, criticisms, and adversarial behaviors of others are imagined or exaggerated. For example, take the case of a woman who is part of a bridge club. She is insecure about her level of play and presumes that the other members of the group probably wish that she would not play with them. People cannot look at her without her thinking they are *staring*. People cannot smile at her without her thinking the smiles are sarcastic and poking fun at her ineptitude. Finally, when she can no longer stand it, she throws her cards on the table and says, "I can't stand you people. If you don't want me to play with you anymore, you should have just said so. Go to hell!"

People like this are tortured by beliefs that they are incompetent, unlovable, and unworthy. This, of course, creates a nonstop stream of frustration and keeps them constantly at the point of boiling over. The predatory angry person is oversensitive to threat by definition. "Who are you looking at?" is the common threat-sensitive attitude. When someone bumps into them they would be more likely to say, "Hey watch it!" than "Excuse me." Walking around angry and with the belief that everyone is a threat to you makes it easy to justify angry and punitive behavior. The predatory person who operates on this theme thinks it is better to hurt others before they hurt him or her.

Taken Advantage of and Victimized

This theme's point of view: *Expressed in terms such as these: "You must really think I'm a moron to accept that offer! That crook of a car dealer told me that this piece of crap would get 29 miles to the gallon! He must have seen me coming," or "Just when I take out my coupon for a free weed whacker, those lying sacks of dog meat told me they gave the last one out an hour ago and I would have to wait!"*

There is no deal good enough to satisfy the person who is always being taken advantage of by some company, bureaucracy, institution, or other person. The word *personalization* is used to describe what people do when they believe that whenever anything negative happens it is because someone doesn't like *them*, or someone is taking advantage of *them*. Personalization is a common link in all of the themes we are talking about in this section, but it has particular relevance to the theme of being victimized. The tendency to personalize is such an important concept to anger management that it is its own critical path! Chronically angry people maintain their angry view of the world by holding on to AMPs that convince them that others do not like

Check Point

Falling into the habit of focusing on how negative and disappointing life is ultimately creates a prison for the person who searches for reasons to believe that this is the only way the world operates.

them, that they are easy "suckers," and that they are too nice for their own good.

On the flip side of the coin, predatory people can justify their anger and their aggressiveness in this theme by saying that someone "tried to make a victim out of me and I just protected myself," or "I 'had their number' and taught them a lesson." These are perceptions that justify the predatory person's hunger for getting into fights and hurting others. If the perceptions are wrong and inadequate and someone gets hurt for doing nothing, the behavior is justified nonetheless. "Hey it's a tough world out there; I am just looking out for Number One."

Externalizing Blame

This theme's point of view: *It wasn't my fault, your face should not have been in the way of my elbow.*

For those who live their lives by going far out of their way to avoid taking responsibility for anything they do, outrageous statements such as this are common. Regret over misjudgment, apologizing for error and expressing a desire to correct one's mistakes are very important basic skills for human beings to live cooperatively with one another. When a person does not see these things as necessary, or if a person sees apology, regret, and shame as "weaknesses," excessive anger is used in place of being contrite or sorry.

The predatory individual almost always views accepting responsibility for wrongdoing as a personal fault. "Why should I apologize for anything? Sometimes you win and sometimes you lose. Just suck it up and stop whining about it." This is, of course, unless the predatory individual is the one who is on the losing end of someone else's personal mistake. Sometimes what makes a predatory person most angry is that someone has the nerve to suggest they did something wrong— even when it is obvious they *did*! Whenever a personal flaw is revealed, the predatory person's sense of feeling threatened increases. The natural response is to take the offensive. I am reminded of one particularly predatory person who was fond of exploiting women merely for the goal of getting them to sleep with him. He was married. His wife became suspicious and hired a private eye to follow him. Eventually, she summoned up the nerve to confront him at a motel. He became so angry at his wife for embarrassing him, that he beat her up, and said she deserved it for "violating his privacy."

For the chronically frustrated person, failure to accept blame or responsibility is more of a function of overload than it is a need to take the offensive. The frustrated angry person knows he or she is wrong, yet may not be able to admit it. Eventually, when the anger subsides it might be possible to engage the chronically frustrated person in a conversation where he or she accepts responsibility and admits blame. The predatory person will not even permit the notion that he or she might be wrong to enter their minds.

Always Correct and Always Critical

This theme's point of view: *Why can't you ever do anything right? Don't you know that the reason why I care about how you do things is so that you don't look like an ass all of the time?*

There are people that just have to be right all of the time, and when they are challenged, become very angry. It is easy to see how, for some people, being challenged is a personal insult. They become angry that you would even dare to suggest your point of view can be valid if you are doing something a different way than they would do it, or expressing a different point of view than they would. When someone has such a strong need to be unchallenged, they usually also have a need to pick at or criticize everything around them, even things they are not personally involved in. The following vignette describes this exact person.

Chronically Critical Kevin

When Kevin walked out of the house this morning, he noticed new trees on his block. "Those idiots who work for the town aren't even using the right trees for this area. Oh, well, the trees will be dead in a month, and my taxes will go up. Such incompetence," he thought to himself. As he walked past his neighbor's house, he glanced in the driveway to see that his neighbor got a new car. "Hmmph, piece of crap foreign junk box. He is such a moron, doesn't even read *The Consumer Reports*." Kevin walked up to the train on his usual way to work. He was feeling a little chilly. If only his wife would look out the window in the morning. She could have done the sensible thing and left out a warmer jacket. "Sweet, but stupid. I guess you can't have everything. Oh well," Kevin thought.

The train came into the station and Kevin saw the people he usually rides to the city with. A few of them mumbled their "good mornings."

Kevin called out to one of the other riders, "Hey, Jim, what happened to your fairy-ass Rangers last night? They got their asses kicked by Toronto." A brief discussion ensued where Kevin and Jim disagreed about the Rangers' chances for making the playoffs. "Ah, Jeez, Jim, get your head out of your ass. You don't know what you are talking about, as usual." Before he left the train, Kevin didn't forget to mention that Mary, another rider looked like she had put on a few pounds. "Get back to that treadmill, we're not spring chickens anymore, are we?"

When Kevin got to work, he assembled his group of salespeople for their weekly call-out on the carpet. He doesn't know where the company got these lazy, incompetent people. If they would only listen a little bit, maybe they would learn something about selling. Today was a little different though; his salespeople didn't really care much about the fact that he was telling them how their numbers were off. Today was Kevin's last day. He was moving to a downtown office. His coworkers were so happy, they threw a party in his honor—the day *after* he left.

People have the need to control for many reasons. The chronically frustrated person is motivated to have control because so much of the world he or she experiences is frustrating and disappointing. Oftentimes people try to control others as a way of expressing a need to protect them from discomfort. "You don't know what is in your own best interests. I do. Let me do that for you. Take my advice, it will be easier if you do." In many instances, this behavior is condescending and infuriating to others, but if you do not let this person have control, they will become insulted that you do not respect their superior knowledge and get angry with you. If you are using the wrong tool to fix the sink, he will jump in to help, offering a "better way" to do it. If you disagree, you are wrong and incompetent. This type of style not only produces angry and critical behavior on the part of the person who it is an issue for,

> ✔ **Check Point**
> *One sure way of stimulating an angry rage in people who are chronically predatory is to dare to insist that they have done something wrong.*

but it also produces anger, resentment, and frustration in the people who they interact with.

The predatory person controls for entirely different reasons. The predatory person controls and criticizes because that is one of many ways he or she dominates the environment. The predatory person sees any resistance to acknowledging that he or she is in control of the environment as a threat. This is demonstrated in this employer's angry speech to his employee who tries to show initiative by doing a job just as efficiently but differently: "You don't want to do it my way? You think you know better? Go out and start your own business. You obviously don't want to work for anyone; you want to be a boss. There is only one boss here, and I am it. If you don't like it, get packing." For the predatory person, controlling other people is a way of managing threat. As long as I can control you, you cannot be a threat to me.

Revenge

This theme's point of view: *Every score has to be settled. I am going to make you pay for what you did to me. Nobody messes with me.*

When anger is a chronic difficulty for someone, they can remain attached to the source of the anger for a very long time. Angry people have difficulty "letting go" of hurt feelings and the perceived insults and injuries caused by angry interactions. As a result, they consume themselves with revenge. This is one of the most self-sabotaging aspects of out-of-control angry feelings. Fantasies of revenge can take up so much room in a person's mental workspace that there is little room left for anything productive. Vengeful people create entire "mental movies" of their revenge fantasies. When life is so consumed by revenge, enjoying anything else is difficult. As a result, all a person is left with is the angry plan one makes to secure retribution. Here is a vignette that shows how ridiculous revenge can be.

Bertha and Brumhilda

Bertha and Brumhilda were thrown together by the chance event of having become next-door neighbors, each with a penchant for rose gardens. As a matter of fact, both were planning on entering a very prestigious competition during the next season. At first the two approached one another as friendly competitors, joking about their secret recipes for plant foods, and showing off their prize-winning hybrids.

While Bertha's grandchildren were playing in her yard, a wayward basketball crushed some of Brumhilda's beautiful plants and effectively eliminated her from the competition. Bertha was apologetic, but apparently not enough for Brumhilda. The following week, after Bertha returned home from grocery shopping, she found that several of her bushes were wilting and tipped over. The plants had been poisoned! Cross words were exchanged when Brumhilda did not like the fact that Bertha insinuated that the only person around who could have poisoned her precious plants was someone who "knew their way around roses." As the years went by, there were many mysterious "accidents" that kept Bertha and Brumhilda out of many more competitions. Bertha never caught Brumhilda, and Brumhilda never caught Bertha (even after installing $5,000 worth of infrared night surveillance equipment), but both spent many a sleepless night thinking about more and more devious ways to put an end to the other's competitive spirit, *permanently.*

The story is silly, but the point is how all-consuming desires for revenge can get and how long lasting they can become. In my work as a psychologist who helps the courts decide custody cases, the stories of revenge are vicious and literally murderous sometimes.

Consuming oneself with thoughts of revenge will always keep an angry person a mere hair away from flooding over in other angry ways. The same is not always so in the personality of the chronically predatory person. Revenge for the angry predator is careful, calculated, and likely to be well executed. Revenge for the angry predator is a response to feeling personal or emotional injury. It is often not important to the psychology of the angry predator whether the damage done to them was intentional or unintentional. Payback must always be of equal and, whenever possible, greater consequence. This is important to know because entering into any longterm struggle with someone who is intimidating, controlling, or bullying will result in motivating the predatory individual to fight and harass until he or she gets the last word or moves on to a more significant and time-consuming battle.

Aggression

This theme's point of view: *When I am disappointed, I do my talking with my hands and with my actions.*

Anger is the emotional response that accompanies aggression. As a general rule, aggressive behavior (pushing, screaming, physical violence, bullying, intimidation, and passive aggression) is always accompanied by anger, but simply feeling the emotion of anger does not always produce aggressive behavior. Remember, when we talk about anger problems in this book, we are talking about an angry *lifestyle*. Getting angry from time to time is a normal human emotional process. When excessive anger becomes a person's preferred emotional state, that is when it leads to problems in someone's personal life. When aggression is the preferred way of expressing anger, and anger is the most typical and frequent emotional state of an individual, this is a very dangerous combination. That is when you have a person who is angry all the time, and who feels that violence and other forms of aggression are acceptable ways of showing that anger.

A second point I would like to make under this heading is that you should not assume that the only angry people who utilize aggression as a way of expressing their anger are predatory types of people. Do not forget the very strong link between frustration and aggression. I am not fond of keeping snakes as pets because they eat live mice, and I don't enjoy watching that interaction. However, many snake owners will tell you that a feisty mouse who is given no path of escape when placed in a small environment with a snake, will kill the snake as a result of the surge of aggression that is built on a foundation of fear and frustration.

The difference between the frustrated angry person and the predatory angry person is that aggression is often the reaction to frustration in the frustrated angry person's psychology, whereas aggression is more often used as a means to achieve dominance and control in the predatory person's psychology. Aggressive behavior from the frustrated angry person is often an attempt to "push away." That doesn't make this type of person any less dangerous to be around, however. Predatory aggression is intended to hurt, control, and dominate.

Always Harsh and Always Insensitive

This theme's point of view: *I love you, but you're an idiot. Wise up for your own good and stop being a loser.*

There are some people who may have the best of intentions when they communicate, but because their personal style is so heavily influenced by anger, even their positive communications can come across as angry and hostile. People who show this theme have poor anger control and poor social skills. For instance, listen to what Jackson Jackstone says about his reasoning for raising his children with an "iron fist."

Jackson Jackstone

(Jackson speaking:)

My children do not understand that when I push them it is for their own good. I tear them down because that is what the world will do to them once they leave my home. I called my son a 'sissy' the other day because I looked at him and wondered what would happen to him if he acted like that outside of my house. I try to set an example of self-reliance and strength, but he just doesn't get it. He would rather do things the easy way. My wife can't stand it when I say things like that to him. Her standards are not as high, and I think that will make the kids weak. She can bake them cookies. I will make my kids productive members of society. If they are successful and hate me in the end, at least I know I have made them successful. I hated my old man, but at least he made a man out of me.

People like Jackson Jackstone have always fascinated me. Their hearts seem to be in the right place, and, at least in his case, he really wants to "toughen up" his kids for the rigors of life. What Mr. Jackstone lacks is balance. He can't seem to figure out that you can have high expectations for your children but be warm and sensitive to their needs at the same time. If I had to guess, I would say that Mr. Jackstone tried to seek that balance at one point in his life, but was frequently frustrated. He is so frustrated that the only compliments he can give his children are nasty, left-handed compliments such as, "It's about time you've figured out that dropping the sissy earring and weird clothes would get you a decent-paying job. You're finally a man now. Keep it up and you won't end up on the unemployment lines with your loser friends."

While Mr. Jackstone may mean well, but is still too rough around the edges, his predatory counterpart is not well-meaning in the slightest. The predatory angry person is insensitive because he or she is just plain mean and enjoys being that way. The predatory person pokes fun, expresses prejudice, and thinks so much of his or her own opinion, that he or she feels that people should be privileged to have the opportunity to hear it. The predatory angry person "crosses the line" with a harsh style as a means of looking for people who will challenge him. That is one of the many mechanisms predatory people have for identifying a potential threat.

Always Impatient and Always Inconvenienced

By the time we reach this theme we can see how there is some overlap and similarity between them. For instance, the theme of harshness and insensitivity is similar to the theme of being overly critical. As I said at the beginning of the chapter, some people may show more than one theme in their behavior. People who are critical might also be harsh. Some people might be critical in a smooth and socially acceptable way but still be cutting and hostile nonetheless. People who show the theme of always being impatient and inconvenienced can show the chronically frustrated aspect of the theme, or the predatory aspect of the theme, and can do so in combination with several of the other themes (critical, harshness, always right, and so on).

When a person is expressing this theme it is like saying, "Why doesn't anyone ever want to take care of me? When I have to adjust to doing things for myself it's just too difficult!" The resulting anger and aggression may come from a history of being disappointed by those trusted to take care of them. Overly angry responses can happen in any situation where they are not being taken care of, which they then take as a personal insult. You can observe this theme in people who are never happy with the way people treat them in stores, restaurants, or other situations where they are supposed to be "tended to,"and will make a big stink in a very public way, then tell the story over and over with pride about how they put someone "in their place."

The always impatient person who is chronically predatory also views inconvenience as a personal insult. However, the predatory person reacts much more strongly and looks to flex their muscles by creating a "consequence" for those who disappoint and insult them.

The difference between the chronically frustrated, impatient person and the chronically predatory, impatient person can be seen in the difference between the responses of two people who have to wait in an extremely long line at the supermarket checkout. The chronically frustrated person complains angrily at the person behind them or at no one in particular, *"I can't understand how the manager of this store expects to keep business when*

> ### ✔ Check Point
>
> *Some people do not realize that a rough and angry style of communication, even when it is for someone's own good can be taken the wrong way. You can communicate by being strong and sensitive.*

he makes his customers wait so long." The chronically predatory person walks up to the managers box and starts to rant, "What kind of so-called manager are you? I have been waiting in line for 15 minutes. Give me the name of your supervisor and district manager. I am going to start writing some letters. I am in a hurry. Get two more cashiers out there instead of letting them take their breaks when the store is full."

What Is the Point of Knowing About These Themes?

I started this section by explaining that the difference between people who have chronic problems with their anger versus those who occasionally become frustrated and angry, is that the people who have chronic difficulties predispose themselves to anger problems because of the way they view the world. Each theme in the sections above shows the kind of negative beliefs and ideas people attach themselves to. Getting to know someone is often an exercise in learning to live with their pet peeves and idiosyncrasies. For the chronically angry person, these life themes are more than just pet peeves, they are anthems—very rigid and predictable modes of behavior. If your goal is to gain a greater understanding of yourself and the people who you interact with, becoming sensitive to the themes around which they organize their views of the world is important. If your goal is to gain a greater understanding of yourself, confronting the themes you use to maintain a negative perception of the world is vitally important to your growth and development. These themes are what keep us in a constant state of irritability.

Changing our tendency to live around these themes can be difficult. Negative perceptions provide a benefit to the people who organize their lives around them, even though, ultimately, they are self-sabotaging. The benefit is a life without surprises. Maintaining yourself in a state of constant negativity is easy because there are so many problems and imperfections to concentrate on. Living an optimistic life is much more difficult. We often have to *work* to be happy. It is often a lot easier to complain than work. We will look at this idea in more detail later.

> ✓ **Check Point**
>
> *It is important to explore themes that you organize your behavior around. Confronting a rigid and negative view of the world is essential to understanding and controlling anger.*

Going Forward

Congratulations! You have just finished the mastery content portion (or the first of five mini-steps) of the first critical path, "Increasing Anger Awareness." The next chapter will present the next four of five mini-steps and lead you to the completion of the first critical path. Remember, take your time.

Chapter 5

Further Down the
First Critical Path

Learning the mastery content (which, for the first critical path is contained in Chapters 1 through 4 of this book) is step one down the first critical path, toward the ultimate goal of mastering control over anger in yourself and others. This chapter will introduce you to the second, third, fourth, and fifth steps which will help you complete the first critical path (remember there are five steps in *each* critical path). In the chapters that follow, each step will be explained in its own chapter.

Step Two on each of the critical paths is learning coping strategies for dealing with anger. One way to describe a coping strategy is to say that it is an approach or plan for dealing with a difficult issue. When you pick up a crab, if you don't want it to attack your fingers, you've got to know that a good approach to doing so is to hold it from the back, behind the claws. Once you know that this is the best general strategy, the rest pretty much falls into place. We will be moving on to Step Two in this chapter, but first I will describe a little about the other steps so we can get used to how things are organized in the program.

Step Three on each of the critical paths also assists coping, but from a different angle. Step Three teaches communication skills. In this program, communication skills are the things we say to (a) center and focus ourselves in tense and frustrating situations, and (b) de-escalate angry interactions so that we can solve problems without anger and aggression.

Step Four on each of the critical paths is yet another type of communication called affirmations. Affirmations are reminders or communications to yourself. Affirmations are statements that contradict the anger-maintaining presumptions (AMPs) we have been talking about up to this point. They are the "anti-AMPs."

> ✔ **Check Point**
> *Affirmations are the things we say to ourselves to actively dispute negative messages we have programmed ourselves to believe. Think of them as being anti-AMPs.*

We rely on affirmations because if anger can be fired up and maintained by certain complaints and viewpoints we hold about the world (for instance, the themes we looked at in the last four chapters) anger can also be quenched by opposing viewpoints. Cognitive psychologists have long known about the powerful effect that "self-statements" have on mood and beliefs, and that is why I have made them such an important part of this program. Step Five is your check-out step. At the end of each critical path you will decide whether you should go on to the next step or move back for a refresher course.

Unfortunately, we live in a very competitive society that places a high value on being promoted, moving forward, graduating, and moving up in ranks. Moving ahead is not always a measure of smarts. Knowing what you don't know can be very smart. My advice about moving ahead in this particular mastery process is: "If you want to grow, move slow."

Let's look at the first set of coping strategies.

Increasing Anger Awareness: Step Two

Coping Strategies

Acknowledging Angry Lifestyles

"What kind of aggravation is the world ready to dish out to me today?" Does that sound like a familiar first thought of the day? For some people, this type of pessimistic thought is the beginning of a nonstop mental tape recording that focuses on the harshness of the world, the stupidity and inconsideration of people, the unfortunate string of bad luck that has results in daily misery, and the lack of potential for anything to improve.

If you maintain this mindset day after day it is a safe bet that you wake up "preparing for battle." The focus of the battle

> ✓ **Check Point**
> *Change is something that you can accomplish without punishing yourself or criticizing yourself for "how you used to be."*

may change from day to day, but it is always something. Monday might be the day to battle the neverending saga of moronic drivers. Tuesday might be another round of battle with the idiots in the Information Technology department at work. Wednesday might be another installment of the epic tragedy of the mother-in-law who won't go anywhere else but your house on vacation. And the list goes on, because there is no shortage of difficult situations one might encounter in a world that revolves around chaos and hard times, where the only experiences one looks forward to are those that are going to cause the next round of problems.

Back to Fill–Hold–Release

In Chapter 1, I pointed out that anger and frustration are linked because everyone has an imaginary container where frustration and other emotional debris that come from displeasure and disappointment are stored. When that container becomes full enough, we blow the top off of it. That is one way of visualizing the emotion of anger, and the mechanisms that cause it to leap out of control. The difference between a person who expresses anger versus the person who lives an angry lifestyle is that the person who lives the angry lifestyle keeps that container close to being full all of the time. The elements of frustration that keep that container full almost all of the time are presumptions about how the world operates, what it takes to survive in a world where things are more likely to go more wrong than right, and how to cope with the fact that the future will most likely get worse instead of better.

> ✓ **Check Point**
>
> *It's always a good idea to have a plan for how to deal with a difficult issue. When you dedicate yourself to developing a "coping" plan, you are always much better prepared to deal with situations that are likely to produce intense emotions. That is the primary focus of the second step of each critical path.*

I have been calling these presumptions AMPs, or anger-maintaining presumptions. This step, Step Two of the first critical path, requires that you acknowledge and examine your general view of the world. Notice I did not say that you had to *change* it, just look at it. Changing negative, angry, pessimistic, or predatory points of view comes at the end of the program, after you have looked at anger from many different perspectives, and that is a long way off.

Questions That Start Raising Your Level of Awareness

- How many sarcastic comments did you make today?
- How many times did you get a cheap laugh at someone else's expense?
- How many times did you call someone a name under your breath or described them as a "jerk" or "asshole" to someone else?
- How many times did you argue with someone just for the sake of arguing?
- How many times did you make someone's life more difficult when you could have just as soon made it easier?
- How many times did you wish someone was dead?
- How many times were you inconsiderate to another driver when you were driving your car?
- How many times did you criticize someone when you could have just as easily left them alone?
- How many times did you raise your voice to someone?
- How many times did you directly threaten someone, or tell someone you were going to do something negative to someone else?
- How many times were you rude when you could have "killed with kindness" instead?
- How many times did other people ask you if you are in a bad mood?
- How many times did you speak to someone and while they were talking, your "inner voice" was screaming at them to "shut the hell up"?

A lot of people can say, "That's me, *all the time*." For some, these behaviors occur, but when they do it, it is out of character. For others, the behavior described above is their character. As a matter of fact, because we live in a very angry world, these thoughts, behaviors, and expressions can become an acceptable way of dealing with others, depending on the crowd of people or environment you are operating in. Unfortunately, as acceptable as they have become, people often pay the price for them. Excessive anger takes its toll on physical and emotional health. Not to mention the social consequences of heavily investing in an angry lifestyle, which can lead to problems with the law, and loss of important friendships and love relationships.

Specifics for Mastering Step Two

In order to raise your awareness of the extent to which you (or others) have developed an angry point of view, or an angry lifestyle, I suggest that your approach or coping plan for mastering Step Two include the following:

Coping Plan for Increasing Anger Awareness

1. Acknowledge the extent to which you view the world as a negative place with little possibility for change. Identify the anger-maintaining presumptions you hold about the world.
2. Acknowledge the extent to which you act out the themes described in Chapter 4 which include:
   - Being under appreciated and misunderstood.
   - Being perpetually threatened.
   - Being taken advantage of and victimized.
   - Externalizing Blame.
   - Being always correct and critical.
   - Revenge.
   - Being always harsh and insensitive.
   - Being always impatient and inconvenienced.
3. Describe the portion of your life that you devote to clinging to angry views of the world, and draw a conclusion as to the actual portion of your personality connected to, and invested in, the expression of anger.

(List continues on next page.)

4. If you cannot comfortably determine the extent to which you lead an angry lifestyle, try to observe how those qualities and behaviors look in others. Compare those angry lifestyle features that you see in others to those things that remind you of how you cope with life.

5. Finally, begin asking yourself whether your angry lifestyle is more of a response to frustration, or more a function of a need to compete, dominate, and succeed, even at the expense of hurting others.

Increasing Anger Awareness: Step Three— Communication Skills

Communicate More Positively By Saying Less in General

Mental health professionals often tell us how important it is for us to express our feelings. This is only somewhat true. Speaking out about your feelings is a concept that is both overrated and misapplied. This is especially true about expressing anger. It was once commonly assumed that expressing anger was a "cathartic" experience. In other words, if we let ourselves get furious and spill our guts, it is better for everyone. This is not so. As a matter of fact, it is more likely that the act of being angry and acting out anger actually *increases* angry feelings and behaviors. Instead, there seems to be much more wisdom in the old adage, "If you do not have anything nice to say, don't say it at all."

 Check Point

The term "expressing your feelings" doesn't give you permission to verbally bash someone. In addition, erupting in a verbal tirade won't necessarily "cleanse you." It will often make you feel more angry.

People who are chronically angry are usually oversensitive also. The frustrated angry person is more sensitive because he or she is in a high state of irritability from being constantly disappointed by life. The predatory angry person is sensitive because he or she has a heightened sense of threat. In this critical path, the aspect of mastery that we are trying to achieve is increased awareness of anger in ourselves and others. One benefit of becoming more aware is that if you can learn to tune in to your own anger, you will find it easier to detach yourself from participating in situations where you are likely to express your anger in a nonproductive way.

The next step of this critical path is about becoming better at communicating. Sometimes learning to communicate better means choosing to communicate *less*. In this first critical path, I will be making a suggestion that is incredibly easy to understand, but very difficult to follow. That suggestion is: *Be quiet more of the time.* The emphasis on this path is to be more aware and observant. Nothing increases awareness like putting yourself in a more passive role. Here are some specific suggestions:

Ways to Say More by Communicating Less

1. Talk less, listen more.
2. Try to withhold your opinion.
3. When you do have to give an opinion, try to give a neutral opinion.
4. Do not offer advice if it is not directly asked for.
5. Pass your opportunity to give an opinion to another person in the conversation by saying, "I'd like to think that over a bit. Let's hear what Jane has to say."
6. Observe others in conversation, paying particular attention to how people react to people who offer advice, always have an opinion, and dominate the conversation with their points of view.

You might find that by practicing these skills, people confide in you more, trust you more, and assume that you are attentive to them. As a result, people might even disappoint you less. There is a lot that we can communicate when we do not say anything. The most important thing that we can choose to communicate is interest. As we will see in some of the following chapters, an essential skill in managing the anger of others is de-escalation." Keeping silent until another angry person you are interacting with runs out of steam is sometimes the best way of getting an angry situation under control. Of course, if you are showing nonverbal behavior that is impolite or sarcastic, the situation will escalate nonetheless. Don't worry, you don't have to be silent forever. Try it as an experiment. As a matter of fact, you can alternate between being your old, pushy, talkative, complaining, or grumpy self and being a more soft-spoken, wise, confident and accepting person to see which one people like better.

Increasing Anger Awareness: Step Four— Affirmations

Developing and Practicing Statements That Tune You In to Your AMPs

"I can't believe what I sound like sometimes!" People who hear themselves on recordings are often shocked at what they sound like. I can assure you that if it were possible to listen to some of the messages you play over and over inside your head, it would be even more shocking.

Step Four on all of the critical paths is practicing *affirmations*. Affirmations are messages you can repeat to yourself or practice to reduce stress or to change your mindset. At first you will probably think that it is a ridiculous exercise to repeat things to yourself. One reason it might seem ridiculous is that it seems like it's too easy to change your behavior by repeating something to yourself. The fact is that a lot of human behavior develops because of the beliefs we attach to them. I spent the better part of the first four chapters of this program describing how angry behavior is maintained by the beliefs we have about how the world and the people in it operate.

The reason that people have trouble with anger relates to the fact that they *hate* being controlled or influenced by anyone. Part of that dislike extends to having to hear from other people about how to control their anger. The great thing about working with affirmations is that what they boil down to is advice you give *yourself.* You know that it is often said that people who are chronically angry are their own "worst enemies." What I am suggesting is by practicing good coping techniques and using affirmations, you can start becoming your own best friend. It's worth a shot. The affirmations in this chapter and the following chapters offer a less extreme way of observing the world and interpreting what happens in it. Remember, the main function of an affirmation is to redirect and counteract anger maintaining presumptions (AMPs.)

> ✓ **Check Point**
>
> *It might sound like a stupid idea to practice "talking to yourself." However, reminding yourself of what it takes to cope with difficult situations and difficult emotions is often an extremely effective way of changing the beliefs that are connected to angry behaviors.*

For instance, let's take look at the AMP "All people are assholes," and the unspoken conclusion that comes after it, which is, "and that is disappointing and makes furious." The purpose of the first critical path is to try and get you to acknowledge that if this is a perception you endorse, people will perpetually upset you. Now let's modify this statement a little bit by saying: "Sometimes it seems like all people are assholes, but I know this isn't really true. It is what I tend to say when I am having a bad day or when I am frustrated and on edge."

In developing statements or affirmations to modify the AMPs that form the basis of negative perceptions of the world, it is important to focus on the natural human tendency to think and act in *extreme* ways when we are upset or disappointed.

When the world becomes that much of a burden, people tend to perceive it in extreme terms, and that is when AMPs express negativity about everyone, everything, every day, every time, and so on. Sometimes it can be a relief just to be reminded that there is no general rule that applies to everyone or everything. Let's look at a few more AMPs and a few AMP-fighting affirmations:

Examples of AMPs and AMP-fighting Affirmations

AMP	AMP-fighting Affirmation
Nobody gives a shit about work quality.	*I sometimes have a hard time getting people to perform up to my expectations. I can get a better quality of work by learning how to motivate and persuade people better.*
People turn into morons when they get on the road.	*I am better off when I let crazy drivers pass or move around me. It is less irritating to be done with them.*
Cops have attitude problems.	*Some cops get carried away with their authority; others are dedicated to saving people's lives.*
All lawyers are snakes.	*All lawyers are snakes.*

The last one is a joke! All lawyers are not snakes. Wait until you really need one. A better affirmation would be, "Good attorneys may be hard to find but they are worth their weight in gold."

Creating Your Own Affirmations

Creating your own affirmations is not that difficult. You must develop a sensitive ear to your own AMPs. That is the whole point of the first critical path. If you are stuck on how to identify your own AMPs, sit down and write a list of everything you hate about the world. What are your pet peeves? What do you hate about people? What do you hate about work? What are the habits and quirks of people that drive you insane? Don't be afraid to use the same kind of language you use in everyday speech when you identify your AMPs. People say bad words. One of your goals might be to use less colorful or rude speech, but I have used all of the words angry people use when I wrote this book, because some of those words reflect people's angry perceptions of the world. If you refer to a dozen people every day as "asshole," it is more than likely you have an angry notion of the world and the people in it. When constructing your affirmations, a good start would be to find another word to work into your vocabulary when you are talking about people in general, or people who annoy you in particular.

Affirmations: Step–by–Step

You can follow this step-by-step sequence to develop AMP-fighting affirmations.

> **Turning AMPs Into Affirmations**
> Example: *I hate everyone.*
> 1. Find the extreme, rude, nasty, and colorful language.
>   **How you can modify the AMP:** *"Hate" is an extreme term by itself, and "everyone" implies that you are reffering to the whole world.*
> 2. Try to soften it.
>   **How you can modify the AMP:** *Maybe I don't hate people, they just get on my nerves.*

3. Find the statements that contain superlatives. Superlatives are words such as *always, everywhere, everyone, no one, nothing,* and *everything.* They are words and terms that imply absolutes.

   How you can relate it to the AMP: *Maybe it's not the whole world that gets on my nerves, but just the people I happen to be dealing with today.*

4. Create new statements that note that there are excepions to every absolute.

   How you can relate it to the AMP: *The people I am dealing with are getting on my nerves. Maybe I should rely on the people I trust a bit more today and avoid people and situations where my patience is limited.*

5. Go out and notice those exceptions. Look for ways to disprove your own rules about people.

   How you can relate it to the AMP: *There are good people out there. Sometimes it takes time and patience to find them, and there will be days when they are few and far between.*

6. Reduce it to an affirmation. Get to the fundamental concept of what you are trying to cope with in as few words as possible.

   How you can relate it to the AMP: *Sometimes people get on my nerves, and when they do, I will try to remember that there are people out there worth knowing and interacting with. The difficult ones are not worth breaking a sweat over.*

Increasing Anger Awareness: Step Five—
Success Milestones

Finding Success

If you have practiced everything in the first four steps of this path, you should have a keener sense of how angry you are, not to mention how much angry company you have in the world. Hopefully now that you have developed this sense, you do not like what you see enough to want to change it. Moving on to the next critical path requires that you have achieved success in several areas. In this program we call each type of success a "milestone." Here are the success milestones for the first critical path, "Increasing Anger Awareness."

**Success Milestones for the First Critical Path,
"Increasing Anger Awareness"**

1. You know the difference between expressing anger and a chronically angry lifestyle.
2. You can explain how anger is maintained.
3. You can understand and identify the two types of anger.
4. You have observed how you and other people focus on particular themes that support their angry lifestyles.
5. You can describe and discuss your own AMPs and the AMPs of others.
6. You can construct your own affirmations, and you have considered the possibility (just the possibility for now) of adjusting your worldview.

Remember, in this first critical path, you do not have to do anything drastic to change yourself—no makeovers, no homework assignments—just raise your level of awareness.

The next critical path will require a little more active participation and experimentation with new behavior than the previous one.

Reading books such as this one and accepting guidance from professionals is like being coached through a series of experiments. These experiments will always require fine-tuning and adjustment to your own personal style and comfort level. Sometimes people look at a suggestion and say, "That's not me, I could never say (or do) that." That's fine. However, before you completely eliminate any new style or behavior, try it first.

Chapter 6

Consequence Forecasting, the Second Critical Path

Step One: Mastery Content

Let's Take Some Photos

Tell me which of these situations is more likely to bring you great bodily harm:

Situation One: *Going to the zoo and photographing lions from behind a protective embankment.*

Situation Two: *Going to Africa and photographing a hungry lion in his own habitat with a necklace of pork chops dangling around your neck.*

That was a no-brainer, right?

If all you are looking to achieve is to get a picture of a lion, while minimizing your risk of bodily harm, you are going to the zoo. Forecasting or predicting relative risk is easy. Now, let's change the circumstances a little bit. I am going to pay you $10 for a picture of a lion from a zoo, but I am going to pay you a million dollars for a picture of an angry, hungry lion in its own habitat. For a million dollars, many people will accept the risk, even if it is higher, in order to gain the reward. The risk might be the same, but there is a benefit attached to it and that alters the perception of the desirability of the behavior.

> ✔ **Check Point**
>
> *In the second critical path, we learn the importance of how the decision to behave in a certain way today, has a profound impact on what happens to us tomorrow.*

So far, once again, my observations of human behavior are less than earth-shattering. Very few intelligent people would foolishly risk their lives to get a picture of a lion, if the picture had no other value. Some people might be courageous enough to take a picture of a hungry lion in a dangerous environment, but only if there was an incentive for doing so.

We all have the same view of the world so far, right? Especially when all that needs to be applied is a little common sense and some logic?

There are times, though, when these commonsense principles do not seem to apply. Let's look at Fearless Felix's life for a moment.

Stuck in Time: Fearless Felix

On the way home from a rough day in the city, Felix Arriverderci was settling into his driving routine and looking forward to a nice relaxing evening listening to opera and paging through catalogs of expensive designer shoeware (yes, while driving). His happy thoughts were disrupted by motion in his rearview mirror.

Another driver was weaving wildly back and forth in traffic, apparently in more of a hurry than Felix. "Look at this crazy bastard. He's driving like a fucking animal. He better not come anywhere near me." Felix went into an immediate state of high alert.

(One of Felix's AMPs was that there should be "payback" for those who cause him any kind of discomfort). It wasn't long before the driver was right on his tail, looking for an opening to move into another lane. There was no opening, so the driver flashed his lights so that Felix would move over. "I can't believe this guy. What the hell is his problem?" Felix would not move over. He rolled down his window and gave the guy the finger. The other driver became furious. He pulled up next to Felix and shook his fist at him. For Felix, the world was empty of any other person besides him, and this offensive man who was trying to pass him on the highway. "Maniac!" Felix screamed at the man. "Screw you and your mother," the guy screamed back, as he swerved around Felix, jumped in front of him, and then hit the brakes, causing Felix to nearly hit the back of his car. "Oh, yeah. We'll see...." Felix was out of his lane and jockeying with the offending driver for position. Felix was going to get out in front of the other driver and slam on his brakes to give him a taste of his own medicine. The driver in front of Felix moved over, and so did the next driver. Felix did not realize that other drivers had noticed both of them and were getting out of their way. When the driver realized that Felix could get ahead of him, he began to tailgate the driver in front of him, so that Felix would not have enough room to cut him off. He was unsuccessful. Felix cut him off and then tapped the brakes. The driver of the other car, who was now in back of Felix, did not seem to care, because he kept coming closer and closer to Felix's bumper. Soon, the driver began tapping Felix's bumper at more than 60 miles per hour. Felix became even more furious. He stepped on the brakes harder and harder. The two cars seemed to be locked together at their bumpers. Felix accelerated to get away. At this point, he would gladly have ripped off his bumper and the other guy's bumper to prove he would not let someone else get over on him. Felix never got the chance. All of a sudden, Felix lost control of the car. His car swerved out of control and into the side of a concrete pedestrian bridge. He was DOA at the hospital.

Felix was "stuck in time." He could not see how his behavior failed to take into account the risk he was placing on himself. This is one of many poor coping styles that extreme anger causes—failure to appreciate the consequences of one's behavior, and failure to see how what you are doing right now can cause a problem in the future. Felix did not perceive the danger of the situation he was in. He could not comprehend what would happen if he continued to escalate his behavior. While he could have chosen to break off his end of the conflict, he contributed to the ultimate outcome, his own death.

Unlike the example of photographing lions I started with, there was no tangible reward to be gained for Felix's behavior—at least none worth the potential consequence. The lion photographer who snaps the picture in the wild is thinking about how great it will be to sit on the verandah of his new million-dollar home, polishing his expensive new camera equipment. For Felix, the only possible reward fantasy available was him being able to go to bed that night saying that he didn't let another angry driver "get away" with passing him on the highway. The risk does not justify the reward. Everyone who drives knows what kind of risk there is to "teaching someone a lesson" on the road. If you don't know that there is risk associated with that, you should not be driving. Nonetheless, aggression on the highway is a common fact of life.

Instead of focusing on the social phenomenon of road rage, what I find more relevant is the decision-making process of angry people, on the road or whenever and wherever it occurs. In the example above, the road rage isn't as important as how Felix handled his angry feelings. Felix "lost track of time." The only time Felix was aware of was the present moment, and the level of rage he experienced in that moment. He lost all awareness of how the future would be affected if things escalated in the present.

We All Consider the Future in Light of the Present, but Not When We are Angry

Why do I write on the days that I don't feel like writing? The answer is when I do not do what is in my own best interest I start worrying about what will happen. Maybe I will sleep instead of work. I will become lazy. I will get fat from being lazy, sick from being fat, and die! Some of us are more sane than that, but the point is that most of us assess our present by thinking about how our "now" behavior will influence the future. We work because, without work, life becomes more difficult in the future. Anytime we give no thought to the future consequences of our behavior, life can get substantially more complicated, difficult, and more often than not, dangerous.

The same logic applies to uncontrolled anger. Maybe you can get away with giving someone the finger out of the window of your car once or twice, but if you do it every day without thinking of the consequences it could have, someone is going to start in with you. You can be nasty, grumpy, and obnoxious to people without catching an attitude in return, *sometimes*. Someday, however, you will be nasty, grumpy, and obnoxious to the wrong person. You can push someone, shove someone, slap someone. One day, you will shove the wrong person. The harder you work at maintaining an angry lifestyle, the faster you run out of time before it comes back at you some time in the future.

In this second critical path, which is called "Consequence Forecasting," we learn how anger distorts your perception of time. It locks you so firmly into the here and now that you lose your ability to think about the consequences you are creating for yourself in the future. Felix was so locked into his battle with the other driver, he forgot to consider what might happen if he continued steering 2 tons of moving steel in an erratic fashion. He didn't care. He only cared about "teaching a lesson" to the other driver that he would never forget. He wasn't thinking that maybe he would kill the other driver and have to spend the rest of his life in jail. He wasn't thinking that a cop might see the both of them and arrest them for reckless driving. Excessive anger short-circuits your ability to look into the future because anger and aggression cause people to focus on the threat that is in front of them *now*. For cavepeople, this was a bonus because any reasonable threat to them was a threat to everything about their future.

Check Point

Feelings of intense anger and rage can cause you to "lose track of time," thus disabling the ability to see how your actions now can cause problems later.

For modern people, this type of concentration in response to *perceived* threat is far from a bonus. It can actually kill you if the threat is out of proportion to the angry energy you are investing to ward off the threat. Failure to adequately forecast the consequences of angry behavior can be seen in examples that are far less deadly than Felix's story. It can simply make life uncomfortable and disappointing. Look at the next story about Rita the meter maid:

Rita the Meter Maid

If there were awards for people who took their jobs seriously, Rita would have gotten more than her fair share. Eight years on the Noble Township Bureau of Parking Enforcement and she has single-handedly brought the people in this quiet little hamlet to their knees—at least when they beg her not to write a ticket for a meter that just expired the moment they approached their cars.

"Parking violators are like other code-breaking social misfits who try to take advantage of the town. They deserve their tickets," she would say. (Note: For those of you who are watching for AMPs, this was one of Rita's.) She would sit in front of parking meters with only five minutes left and wait for the little red flags to tick off a violation. Many times, people would be crossing the street just as the meter was going off and the people would try to convince Rita not to write the ticket. "Nope," she would say. "If your car is in the spot and the flag is up, it's a $25 fine." Pleading did not help. "What the hell did you do for me today fella?" was her standard reply.

One day she started writing a ticket for a car she knew was owned by a new doctor in town, parked in front of a storefront with a residence above it. When the apartment door opened and the doctor saw that Rita was about to write a ticket, he said politely, "I hope you are not going to write me a ticket. I just did a good deed. I delivered a baby upstairs, a cute little guy."

Rita remained stone cold. "You delivered a baby? Woop-de-doo. Why don't you go out and rob a bank to celebrate? You are illegally parked. I am supposed to give tickets to illegal parkers. Here is your ticket. Have a nice de-cay." That was Rita's favorite sign off to people who shot their mouths off about getting a ticket. She would say "de-cay" instead of "day." Oh, it cracked her up every time she said it.

Rita had a passion for baseball. She was athletic and loved to play. She desperately wanted to coach little league, but she had heard the town just filled the position with someone new. "What the hell," she thought to herself. Maybe she would ask if they needed an assistant coach. Rita walked up to the field and approached the man who was talking to some of the kids. "Hey, coach! I just came down here to ask if maybe you could use a little help with these young Baby Ruths." The coach, also the new doctor, turned around and met Rita with the same smile he showed when he saw her in town most days. "I'm sorry, Rita, but I do not think we would work very well together. Have a nice day."

What Goes Around, Comes Around

People do not always remember when others do something nice for them, but when someone pisses them off, memory magically improves. I have seen this work to my disadvantage many times in my own life. The old saying about "what goes around, comes around" is very true with respect to negative, angry behavior. Anger is contagious. It creates a tit-for-tat kind of competitiveness that requires people to escalate their behavior to make a point. To what end? Sometimes it is because one person does not like the way another person looks at them. Or it may be because your neighbor built a fence 2 inches over the official property line. You may not like the sound of the way someone spoke to you. You may not like the way someone looked at your boyfriend or your wife. If someone could assure you that after you shot back a dirty look, cursed someone out, or threatened to beat someone up, you would never encounter that person, or any person related or known by that person, it might be worth venting. Unfortunately, that is not the way life works. Anger has a way of finding its way back to its source.

✔ **Check Point**

Human memory is a funny thing. People will sometimes forget when you do them a favor, but when you go out of your way to do something nasty to them, their memory becomes a lot better.

In this critical path we are forecasting the consequences of anger. I will be trying to convince you that every angry act has the potential for creating some kind of difficult event for you in the future. If you don't want to call for help, do not shoot off a flare. If you don't want a life full of pissed-off people giving you a hard time, don't go out of your way to piss people off. It's as simple as that.

Re-prioritizing the Anger Response

There is often no benefit to angry responding. Sometimes, there *is* a benefit, especially for predatory angry people who find that by expressing their rage, people may fear them, or comply with their demands. Pushing people around does pay off from time to time. For chronically frustrated people, angry responses are signals for people to leave them alone. This pays off too because, if what you really want is to be left alone, being angry and acidic is an effective way of accomplishing that. There are ways of achieving the goals of success and acquisition if you are motivated to compete, and there are ways of achieving the goal of solitude if what you want is to be left alone. Both can be accomplished without using a chronically angry or aggressive style of responding, with the added payoff that it won't come back to you later on.

Every angry episode carries with it a considerable amount of risk. Even the most predatory criminals know that there is no such thing as a risk free crime or act of aggression. There are sweet, little, old ladies who brandish shotguns behind the cash counters at convenience stores. Sometimes it is not so easy to predict which people are going to take your anger and which ones are going to fight fire with fire.

With so much risk associated with road rage, starting a fight with a stranger, or mouthing off to someone who may know someone else who can cause trouble for you, why don't people think more about future consequences before they act? If we go back to the first few chapters, one way of answering this question is to say that when the container that holds frustration and rage is ready to blow, releasing angry energy becomes a priority within the human emotional system. After an incident of angry responding, people often wish they had controlled themselves, but by then it is too late. People who are chronically angry or

> ### ✓ Check Point
>
> *Why don't people think more before they act in angry ways? The way angry people think actually encourages angry acting out. In order to get anger in check, we must learn to think much differently. For instance, we need to think about the future consequences of angry behavior.*

frustrated are always so close to the point of needing to release, that self-control evaporates. It's as if the need to behave in an angry way becomes such a priority that it eliminates the ability to look into the future and predict the consequences of what we are about to do.

There are ways of re-prioritizing the need to respond and regain the perspective that comes when we allow ourselves to look into the future and to predict the possible outcomes of angry actions. Step Two on this critical path offers a technique for doing just that. It is called the "L.A.S.T." technique. The L.A.S.T. technique is a way to re-prioritize angry responding by asking the essential question: *What kind of boomerang is my angry behavior throwing out that is going to come back and hit me in the side of the head later?* Answering this question and going through the L.A.S.T. technique is a way to remind yourself about the consequences of angry behavior, which is why I call this process "consequence forecasting."

Consequence Forecasting: Step Two—

Coping Strategies

Coping Strategies: Listen, Assess, Stop, Turn Away

The coping strategy or approach to managing anger that I will concentrate on in this section is something you can remember with a simple memory aid. The coping strategy itself is a four-step process that I call an "action sequence." It is designed to address the angry act while it is occurring and to force you to look at the future consequences of the angry behavior. There are two ways to remember the names of the action sequence. The first way is to simply use the first letter of each step, which spells the word *last*. The second way is to remember it as a sentence: *Listen, Arthur, just Stop and Turn Away.* With all memory aids, the first thing you have to do is remember the cue and what it's related to. To practice, remember that L.A.S.T. and *Listen, Arthur, just Stop and Turn Away* are cues that help you focus on the consequences of your actions and break off angry behaviors before they become problems.

Listen

Now you know at least two ways of remembering a skill that will help avoid the consequences of impulsive angry behavior (either the word *last* or the sentence *Listen Arthur, just Stop and Turn Away*), let's look at each individual part of the action sequence and start to practice it. The "L" in L.A.S.T., or the *Listen* in the *Listen, Arthur* sentence, stands for "Listen to Your Body Signals". Listening to your body's signals is the first part of making yourself more aware of the type of actions that occur before you pull the trigger and let out anger excessively.

Boiling. Seething. On fire. Trembling. Flipping out. These are the terms that describe the body sensations we feel when we are about to lose it. Everyone has their own way of describing what their body feels like when they are experiencing intense emotion. Ironically, our bodies feel very much the same when we are in love, in a rage, or scared to death. It is just the circumstances around those sensations that change. The term for the general state of being that we are in when there is intense emotion is *arousal*. Some people say it feels like butterflies in the stomach; some say it feels like trembling. During a fit of anger, it feels like the body heats up, because oftentimes that's exactly what the body does. Anger activates a part of the nervous system called the *sympathetic nervous system*. The sympathetic nervous system acts in sympathy with stress and gets your body ready for "fight" or "flight." During this process, the muscles receive more blood. That is why some people say they feel "pumped" when they get angry. Heart rate increases. Pupils dilate. Concentration becomes keener. In really bad cases,

> ✓ **Check Point**
>
> *Tuning into your body's signals and sensations is the first action you can take to make yourself aware that you might be reaching a point where you are going to do something you regret later on. Curiously, the body responds very similarly to all sorts of emotional arousal, whether it is positive (like being in love) or negative (being angry or scared). It's the circumstance around the feeling that often determines whether it is positive or negative.*

smoke starts pouring out of your ears and fire comes out of your nostrils. No, that only happens in cartoons. I am sure you get the point. Your body *tells* you when you are angry. The first step in forecasting the future consequences of your anger is to know when you are starting to boil over.

Assess

After listening to the body's signals, we can start to think about the impulse that is connected to the sensation. After we feel anger in our bodies, we start to think about what we are going to do: "I'd like to punch that asshole right in the face." "I'm going to give that good-for-nothing guy a piece of my mind." "I'm going to slap my kid's behind so hard he will be black and blue for a week." These thoughts can occur more than once, or for more than just a moment. They can become "broken records," or "endless loops" of obsessive thinking. The more we repeat these thoughts and fantasies over and over in our minds, the more we commit to acting on them. Visualizing the angry response or

Check Point

The more we visualize and obsess over what we would like to do to someone when we are angry, the closer we come to acting in ways that bring bad consequences to us later.

obsessing over what we would like to do to act out anger can lead to desensitizing ourselves to the things we might do when we are angry (and regret later).

The "A" in L.A.S.T. or the *Arthur* in the *Listen, Arthur* cue asks you to do an assessment of what your angry impulse is telling you to do. In the stage of assessing, begin to ask yourself if the acts you are visualizing in your head will actually affect the situation positively and put an end to the problem. In this part of the L.A.S.T. or *Listen, Arthur* action sequence, look at the immediate future. In particular, consider whether your angry response will actually end the problem. As a point in fact, most angry responses *prolong* problems.

Stop

After you listen to your body signals and assess whether the angry response is really the end of the problem you are facing, *stop* to consider the longer-term consequences of the actions you are taking.

For instance, if your anger is directed at someone you love, is this going to be one of those fights that becomes an ongoing battle between you and your partner? If your anger is at a person who plays an adversarial role in your life, will your behavior lead to an escalation of hostilities? If your behavior ventures into criminal or illegal ways of expressing anger, can you see yourself going to jail, spending money on a lawyer, possibly losing your job, all for the sake of being able to physically punish someone who is pissing you off? If you find yourself visualizing or mentally practicing the angry or aggressive act, visualize the worst-case scenario after you commit that act. For instance, is slapping your child in the face worth the possibility that the child may dodge you, accidentally fall and hurt himself badly, and have to go to the hospital? Once at the hospital, can you see yourself having to answer questions about how the injury occurred? Can you see yourself having to speak to representatives from the Department of Social Welfare and defending your right to continue raising your own child? Most people will conclude at this point that it is not worth it.

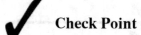

Check Point

"Stop" to think about the long term consequences of the way you are about to express your anger and frustration. Visualize the worst possible outcomes.

Turn Away

Removing yourself or turning away from situations where you know you will regret the way you behaved in anger is a very wise, but very difficult, action. It takes practice and it takes an extreme amount of courage. Breaking off contact with the things that make you angry is not about breaking off contact with the person or situation that is making you mad. It is actually about winning a fight or struggle with yourself.

The expression of anger is a process that gains momentum as it moves forward; the more time that passes, the harder it becomes to stop or short-circuit angry behavior. The bigger problem is, the more we express anger, the more the act of expressing anger keeps us in a state of wanting to be angry. Breaking off an angry mode of behaving requires that you stop that momentum, and that can be a task akin to stopping a runaway train.

When you turn away or break off an angry pattern of responding, you are not losing an argument with another person, as much as you are succeeding in a battle within yourself.

As with the other steps in the L.A.S.T. or *Listen, Arthur* action sequence, it is important to focus on how, at the moment you are expressing chronically angry behavior, you are also determining your own future. As you look for reasons to break off from the momentum that is building, ask yourself what the expression of your anger is worth. Is it worth ending a relationship with someone you love? Is it worth spending a night, a week, a year in jail? Is it worth losing your job? The answer to these questions is almost always "No."

Check Point

When you "turn away" or break off an angry pattern of responding, you are not losing an argument with another person, as much a s you are suceeding in a battle with yourself

Finally, it is helpful to reframe the experience you are going through. Angry interactions are almost always seen as "them versus me." Consider yourself the adversary as part of your sequence to turn away from the anger-promoting or anger-inducing event. What you do to other people when you are angry is bad, but what you do to yourself in terms of ruined opportunities and future aggravation is worse.

The following box shows some examples of what not "turning away" produces in terms of future consequences. It shows how doing what your anger dictates will almost never end an angry interaction, it merely makes life difficult in the future.

What You Feel Like Doing When You Get Angry vs. the Probability That It Will Actually Accomplish Anything Useful

What you feel like doing: "I'd like to punch that asshole right in the face."

Where it usually leads: That's not the end of an angry interaction, it is the beginning of a night in jail, a lawsuit, or a physical altercation that might result in your own injury.

What you feel like doing: "I'm going to give that good-for-nothing a piece of my mind."

Where it usually leads: That doesn't sound like the end of a problem either. It sounds like the beginning of an argument, unless the person you are yelling at refuses to speak to you in which case, your anger and frustration will probably get worse.

What you feel like doing: "I'm going to slap my kid's behind so hard he will be black and blue for a week."

Where it usually leads: What this sounds like is the beginning of a child wailing at the top of his lungs, or potentially a visit from the local child abuse authorities.

Consequence Forecasting: Step Three—

Communication Skills

Verbalizing Your Desire to End Angry

Interactions Before They Escalate

The following conversation takes place after a fender bender, where the first person was driving down the street and the second person was pulling out of his driveway.

Fender-Bender Talk

First Person: *I can't believe you didn't see my car when you were pulling out of your driveway.*

Second Person: *I didn't see you because you were coming down the street too fast.*

First Person: *Not correct. You weren't paying attention.*

Second Person: *Don't tell me I wasn't paying attention, you can't drive.*

First Person: *Look. I don't like your attitude. This is going to turn ugly.*

Second Person: *Don't be stupid, I'm just trying to straighten this mess out. Why aren't you listening to me?*

First Person: *Who are you calling stupid, and why are you raising your voice?*

Second Person: *Don't pull that shit on me. I'm not raising my voice. Next thing you know you'll be screaming for a cop and saying I pushed you. I know your type.*

The "triggers" or "buttons" in this conversation are obviously the personal statements made by the people arguing—the insinuations about stupidity, the comments about bad driving, and so on. Each person is also focused on what the other person was doing and what the perceived fault is as opposed to the responsibilities that are connected to their own behavior.

The conversation takes a decidedly angry turn when the first personal insinuation is made (when the first person tells the second person that he wasn't paying attention). From there, each person makes the same anger mistake: becoming more and more personally insulting. Neither person can break off that line of communication with the other because that would constitute showing personal weakness, and that would be showing fault. This is the point at which the argument becomes more of a battle of each person with themselves. Think about it. Nothing productive is going to come out of each person insisting that they were right. The fact that each person was going to continue to insist that they were right was established very early on in the conversation. Yet, both parties continued, probably knowing that their communication would fail to persuade the other party to admit they were wrong.

Let's rewind the tape and take it from the top with a slightly different focus.

Fender-Mender Talk

First Person: *I can't believe you didn't see my car when you were pulling out of your driveway.*

Second Person: *I didn't see you because you were coming down the street too fast.*

First Person: *Not correct. You weren't paying attention.*

Second Person: *I'm not sure I can agree, but there is no point in arguing. I'm going to go back to my car to make a police report, and the insurance company will straighten it all out. You might want to do the same thing.*

In this version of the interaction, both people express normal human frustration, and both protect their own point of view. This might not always be helpful, but it sure is normal. The first person is shocked that his car was damaged, and the second person responds defensively. By the time the first person gets edgy and says, "Not correct. You weren't paying attention....," the second person has decided that if the conversation continues it will escalate. The decision is to break off the interaction and seek another solution.

Human interaction occurs on many levels. The con man who insists he wants to help his victim win money in Three-Card Monty says, "Hey, man, you look like a smart guy. Come over here and play a game with me. If you are as smart as you look, you might make some money." Is that what he is *really* saying? Well, if you accept the words literally, then that is what he is saying. The literal meanings of the words are the *content* of what he is saying. The *process* of what happens between two people as words are being exchanged is quite different. The process can be translated as follows: "Hey you look like you might fall for my scam. Let's see if you are stupid enough to let me try to con you out of some money."

Setting aside those times when people misinterpret the content of what is said, conflict often escalates when the *process* of what is happening creates frustration or the perception of threat. We already know that both frustration and the perception of threat lead to angry ways of responding. Let's go back to the original conversation and translate some of the process that is going on between the first person and the second person in the scenario that started off our discussion in this third step of the second critical path. Look at the content and process parts of the following conversation:

Content Approach

First Person: *I can't believe you didn't see my car when you were pulling out of your driveway.*

Second Person: *I didn't see you because you were coming down the street too fast.*

First Person: *Not correct. You weren't paying attention.*

Second Person: *Don't tell me I wasn't paying attention. You can't drive.*

First Person: *Look, I don't like your attitude. This is going to turn ugly.*

Second Person: *Don't be stupid. I'm just trying to straighten this mess out. Why aren't you listening to me?*

First Person: *Who are you calling stupid, and why are you raising your voice?*

Second Person: *Don't pull that shit on me. I'm not raising my voice. Next thing you know you'll be screaming for a cop and saying I pushed you. I know your type.*

Process Approach

Second Person: *Shit...someone just hit my car. Now, I've got to go through insurance and become inconvenienced. I wonder what kind of person I am dealing with.*

First Person: *Shit...this jerk just came flying out of his driveway. There was no way I could have avoided him and now he is probably going to blame it on me.*

Second Person: *Okay I'm dealing with a moron. He's going to give me an attitude.*

First Person: *Okay. I'm dealing with a moron. He's going to give me an attitude.*

Second Person: *I should let this kook know that I am not going to take any shit, or he will try to swindle the car repair costs and a few bucks in his pocket.*

First Person: *Cute. He hits me and I have the attitude. This guy is an asshole.*

Second Person: *I knew it. I'm not backing down. If this guy wants to go at it, I think I can take him. This is not a good day to screw around with me.*

First Person: *Oh, so that's the game. He starts in with me and then plays the victim. He's wrong, and he's paying for my damage. I'll kick his ass.*

When you talk to someone, consider both the content and the process of communication. For the purposes of resolving angry interactions without having an even bigger problem in the future (remember, the main goal of this critical path is "consequence forecasting"), you need to win the struggle within yourself first. That is done by breaking off the angry interaction between you and someone else before it escalates. Tuning into the process of what is happening can bring you to a point of better decision-making. Let's look at how this operates in a second scenario between Person One and Person Two:

Content Approach

First Person: *I can't believe you didn't see my car when you were pulling out of your driveway.*

Second Person: *I didn't see you because you were coming down the street too fast.*

First Person: *Not correct. You weren't paying attention.*

Second Person: *I'm not sure I can agree, but there is no point to arguing. I'm going back to my car and I'm going to make a police report. The insurance company will straighten it all out. You might want to do the same thing.*

Process Approach

Second Person: *Shit...someone just hit my car. Now, I've got to go through insurance and become inconvenienced. I wonder what kind of person I am dealing with.*

First Person: *Shit...this jerk just came flying out of his driveway.*

There was no way I could have avoided him and now he is probably going to blame it on me.

Second Person: *Okay. I'm dealing with a moron. He's going to give me an attitude.*

First Person: *This will lead me nowhere and waste my time. In the end I am just going to get into a shoving match with someone who I should not be giving this much importance. Let me walk away before this gets physical. I'll let a cop deal with it.*

In this scenario, the conversation is much shorter. The second person chooses to terminate the interaction because he knows it is only going to get worse from there.

There Is Little to Be Gained by Having Angry Interactions

Children, spouses, boyfriends, girlfriends, bosses, and coworkers can all be pains in the rear end. Daily contact with these people desensitizes you to their faults, flaws, and annoying behaviors. Hopefully, in most of these instances, there are positive points that outweigh the negatives. Over time, the flaws in the people we deal regularly with can get to the point where they reach a flash point and we engage in conflict. In good relationships, the conflicts are managed and the relationship improves. In unhealthy relationships, the conflicts are not managed well and the relationships deteriorate. This explains the ups and downs of established relationships with people we know. When people occupy important roles in our lives, all emotions intensify. We love them more; we hate them more.

None of this explains why many chronically angry people are willing to engage in excessively angry interactions with complete strangers. Why would anyone want to risk going to jail, getting hurt, or making themselves look foolish in public with an individual who is just "passing through" our lives? The answer to this question lies in the stories of people like Felix Arriverderci who we met earlier in this chapter, and in the lives of people who endorse certain angry themes such as the ones we discussed in Chapter 5. When we permit ourselves to feel *threat sensitive*, we make everyone we meet important enough to determine the future of our lives.

Picture yourself walking down the street in the wrong part of town, through dark alleyways, late at night. Picture a large man with his hand shoved into his jacket pocket as though he were holding a gun or weapon, speeding his pace behind you. Your heart races. You start to sweat. You start to picture him poking the gun into the small of your back and demanding your money. You wonder whether he will let you live after he robs you. Now, picture your relief as he crosses the street and ducks into the local rectory because he is Father McNulty, the nicest man in town.

There are times that it is appropriate to feel worried or threatened. When signals are ambiguous, you must tighten your focus to assess whether there is something in your environment that can hurt you. As we saw when we talked about themes of angry living in Chapter 5, there are some people who are chronically and inappropriately threat sensitive. As a matter of fact, they may perceive threat all the time, and they may perceive it from people who they have only casual and fleeting acquaintance with.

For instance, Mr. P doesn't like the way the man walking out of the bank brushed by him. He was offended enough to comment on it. Ms. J doesn't like it when people try to get on the highway in front of her. Even when there is plenty of room to let someone on, she would rather speed up and let them think there is not enough room to get on, rather than slow down and be courteous. She will lean on the horn to show her displeasure when someone merges ahead of her. Mr. L doesn't think the cashier in the food store understands he is in a hurry. She obviously doesn't like men, in his estimation. She is purposely slacking while it is his turn to be checked out. Mr. Q, an 18-year-old who likes to play basketball gets pissed off when someone is on "his court" at the park. He will look for a reason to start a fight. He knows he has no real right to get annoyed, but does anyway.

Ironically, people whom we engage in angry interactions with can become very important strangers to us. One would think that when we meet people who are rude, obnoxious, arrogant, or inconsiderate, the biggest favor we could do for ourselves is pass up the opportunity to interact with them in the future. When we engage in combative and hostile interactions with people, they often become central figures in our lives because of the complaints they file, the lawsuits we become involved in with them, or the physical contact that gets out of control and winds up injuring or killing us or them. When we disengage ourselves from angry interactions with people, we greatly reduce the probability that we will have to deal with them in the future.

Mini–Review

In the third step of this critical path, I have discussed four important points:

1. The importance of disengaging angry interactions so that they do not escalate into problems that will negatively affect your future.

2. The importance of focusing on the process of the angry interaction versus the content of the angry interaction.

3. Becoming aware of themes (and AMPs) that contribute to your threat sensitivity.

4. The self-defeating aspects of creating angry interactions with strangers who you can just as easily let pass.

Taken together, these points form the basis for disengaging angry interactions before they escalate. Now, let's look at some practical communication skills.

Saying the Words Is Not as Hard as Deciding to Say Them

The decision to disengage is the difficult part of reducing the odds that angry interactions will continue on into the future. Learning the words to do it is the easy part. All you have to do is communicate that you no longer wish to continue your part of the interaction.

Magic Words to End Angry Interactions

- "I wish there were some way we could continue this more productively, but there isn't. I need a break."
- "I do not see that there is any point in continuing this discussion if we both disagree so strongly. I'm leaving."
- "I have heard what you are saying. I can't agree. There's no point in either of us becoming more bothered by this."
- I do not see that there is any point in us continuing to piss each other off. I'm going to stop.

There are many other variations of this type of communication. The important parts are (a) I've had enough, and (b) I'm not doing this anymore. There will be times when you can walk away from an argument easily, and times when it will be more difficult. For instance, what if you disengage, and the person you are involved in the interaction with continues to harass you, or follows you, or walks after you screaming and cursing? For some people, if you were angry before you were decent enough to disengage, this sort of ongoing pestering might become infuriating. It might lead to the type of reasoning that says, "Okay, I was patient. I walked away. Now, this idiot gets what he or she deserves." To me, that would be like saying you have two tools in your toolbox: a screwdriver and a sledgehammer—anything you can't fix with the screwdriver, you smash to bits with the sledgehammer. If you do try to disengage from angry interactions, and you say all of the right things, and you cannot physically remove yourself from the situation, you will need to try to de-escalate the conflict in other ways. This is exactly what the next critical path entails.

Consequence Forecasting: Step Four—

Affirmations

Developing and Practicing Statements That Tune in to AMPs

The nature of angry responding is that hostility between two people in conflict grows until it disables one or both of them. You may succeed by yelling, screaming, belittling, criticizing, bullying, or other forms of anger, but your success will more than likely be temporary. The long-term, or future consequences of an angrier, aggressive lifestyle are that people may avoid you, fear you, and they might not like you. You may want that for some reason, but also understand that aside from avoiding, fearing, and not liking you, someone out there will eventually want to hurt or punish you because you might have hurt them or someone they care about. Anger and retribution (revenge) are self-perpetuating. The negative energy created by anger becomes the driving force for the payback that follows, and so on.

Following are some affirmations that start with one of the most basic of all clichés.

Affirmations That Help Focus on Future Consequences of Angry Actions

- "What goes around comes around. (I had better be careful.)"
- "My decision to hurt someone physically, socially, or emotionally will ultimately have consequences that are not worth the energy I spend attacking and hurting."
- "The person I hurt may not hurt me back but may have a support system that will respond in a way that will try to punish me."
- "It is always better to ignore the casual idiot who does something I do not like, but whom I will never see again."
- "It is better to allow someone to identify themselves as a jerk than to display a side of me that will only cause others to identify both me and my adversary that way."
- "It is easier to prevail in every argument by remaining calm and letting my adversary self-destruct."
- "I would gladly sacrifice an ounce of pride to avoid a night in jail. Any other choice just spites me and accomplishes the goals of the people who are my adversaries."
- "Anger is poison. When I let those who I do not like get to me, I am permitting them to force me to poison myself."
- "Ultimately, disengaging from an angry interaction is always a win because I protect my future, my freedom, and my ability to express myself in more important ways."
- "There is no point in remaining in an argument just to see how angry I can make someone else. The only thing that accomplishes is keeping that person in my life longer than is necessary."

Think about these and try to construct some that are specific to your life, your AMPs, and the themes that support an angry lifestyle.

Consequence Forecasting: Step Five—

Success Milestones

What to Achieve Before Moving to the

Next Critical Path

By this point in the process you should be very comfortable observing and describing the components of an angry lifestyle. You should be able to describe the anger-maintaining presumptions that trap you into an angry lifestyle. The natural response to this knowledge is to begin experimenting with ways of detaching yourself from angry interactions, and that is what this critical path is all about.

Success Milestones for the Second Critical Path:
Consequence Forecasting

1. Understanding that chronically angry *actions* ultimately brings a regular stream of angry reactions that ultimately lock you into an angry lifestyle.

2. One area of your life where you can easily cut down on angry interactions is in the casual types of contact you have with people you have little or no relationship with.

3. One technique is to simply disengage from the angry interaction. To do this effectively, you must replace the desire to act out your anger with the belief that acting out anger is an invitation to future inconvenience. You can succeed on this path by removing yourself from the little scuffles, comments, and arguments that you have with virtual strangers.

4. You can also succeed on this path with people you must deal with regularly, although it is more difficult. To succeed on this critical path you must also be able to identify the difference between *content* and *process* in an angry interaction.

(List continued on next page.)

5. Success on this critical path is determined by your ability to identify the process and discontinue it by excusing yourself.
6. Finally, your last marker of success is to retrain your anger-maintaining presumptions (AMPs) so that you consider it a waste of time to participate in angry interactions that can just as easily be ended by noting your disagreement and walking away.

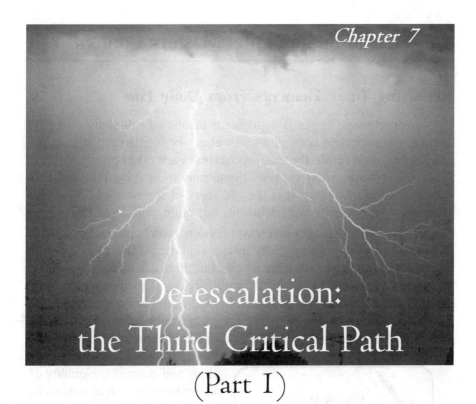

Chapter 7

De-escalation:
the Third Critical Path
(Part I)

In the second critical path, "Consequence Forecasting," you learned to break off angry interactions before they created future problems. This is most useful when you deal with people who are unimportant to you and those you can physically walk away from or avoid contact with.

Sometimes, you might encounter chronically angry people at home, in your family, at work, or in your social environment, where you must interact with them a regular basis and can't avoid them. You may also *be* that chronically angry person at home, at work, or in your social environment, causing problems for others and ultimately creating even greater problems for yourself. That is when it becomes important to learn how to de-escalate angry situations, and that is the focus of this critical path.

De-escalation Step One: Mastery Content

Removing Toxic Elements From Daily Life

When chronic anger is a problem in one of our daily environments, it is toxic and contagious. An angry boss frustrates his or her employees. As a result, the employees treat each other poorly. After a hard day at work, everyone goes home only to be impatient and irritable with their families. It is the old story of the boss who fires the employee, who hits his wife, who hits her child, who kicks the dog.

In small groups, anger can travel from person to person in powerfully destructive ways, especially in close quarters. The most obvious examples of this are family interactions, but there are many other small-group settings where chronically angry styles cause damage to both business and personal relationships. In high-pressure business environments, small groups of people frustrated over not being able to meet deadlines or production quotas, and other forms of pressure, can quickly reach unmanageable proportions and destroy the quality of life in the work environment. In situations where negotiations can become adversarial or when they start out that way (as in labor negotiations or divorce negotiations), it is easy to observe how frustration as well as predation play extremely important roles. When frustration overcomes the ability to negotiate, or when one party in a negotiation resorts to bullying or intimidation, things can quickly deteriorate to an impasse, or worse, outright aggression, even in professional settings.

Check Point

In small, tightly knit groups, a buildup of frustration and pressure can escalate anger between people quickly and very destructively.

The next vignette shows how anger interferes with constructive problem-solving between professionals, and how it spreads between them and their divorcing clients.

The War of the Rosens

Divorce negotiations had been difficult from the start. Jane and Wayne Rosen were calling it quits after a 12-year marriage. About the only thing they still had in common was a deep love for their 8-year-old son, Shane. Wayne wanted to spend some time during the week with Shane, and Jane would only agree to share Shane on the weekends. According to her, it would be too disruptive for her son to go back and forth between their homes during the week. Wayne's response to this philosophy was to sue Jane and fight for custody of their child. He was not about to let his soon-to-be ex-wife dictate the terms of seeing his son. He was not an abusive parent. As a matter of fact, he was very involved in Shane's life. Why should he see so little of his son?

Both Jane and Wayne hired big-name attorneys who were known for their aggressive styles. The attorneys agreed to a conference to negotiate custody. Jane's attorney started the meeting by saying to Wayne's attorney, "My client is willing to make your client a very generous offer regarding your client's boy. She is willing to let your client see the child every other weekend and once per month for dinner." Wayne's attorney snorted, "Okay, if that is such a 'generous' offer, your client will certainly not mind if that is *her* share of the time." Jane's attorney shot back, "You know, that is precisely the type of unprofessional attitude we were hoping *not* to encounter. Look, this is our bottom line. We came here to negotiate. If all you want to do is insult my client, we can put this before the judge." Wayne's attorney replied, "No problem. Let's do it."

Those few interactions constituted the entire first "negotiation" meeting. In total, the cost of the meeting, the letters about setting up the meeting, and the insulting correspondence during the meeting was approximately $3,000—all so the attorneys could pound their chests in front of one another. By the way, the two lawyers went out to lunch after the first meeting and argued about who would pick up the tab.

After the first meeting, the attorneys appeared before a judge who took note of the fact that both mother and father worked, and both were available to the child for approximately the same portion of time. The judge asked Jane and Wayne if they would be living close to one another, and they both said they would. The judge suggested, "Why don't you just *share* your time with your son?" and then proceeded to lecture them on how a long court battle would be costly and contrary to the interests of Shane. The judge's advice went in one ear and out the other, faster then you can say "dwindling bank account."

The attorneys had a second informal conference where Jane's lawyer led off with "an offer that is as good as any offer could ever be," which was for Wayne to have visitation every other weekend and one night for two hours each week. "You can't be serious," said Wayne's lawyer. "You are giving us ice in the winter. Obviously your client is worried about losing custody of Shane, which is exactly what is going to happen if there is a trial." Wayne's lawyer once again replied, "Well we're going to have to go back to the judge." "Fine by us," said Jane's lawyer, and off they went. Wayne's lawyer reminded Jane's lawyer that last time he paid for lunch and, thus, he was owed this one.

Before the next meeting with the judge, Jane and Wayne had an argument over who should pay for summer camp for Shane. At some point during the argument, Wayne said Jane was "acting like a bitch." Jane took that to imply he was calling her a "bitch," which, in fact, he was. When you say someone is "acting like" something, what you are hoping is that the person believes the "acting like" part is going to excuse the "bitch" part, which it doesn't. Jane retorted by calling the man she once swore to love and honor for the rest of her life, "dickless." The argument did not stop there. There was some banging and throwing of objects, none of which were aimed at the other person. "Aim," however, was not the subject of the discussion when Jane called the police and told them that Wayne was trying to kill her.

Wayne was carted off to jail for the evening, only to have his case dismissed for lack of evidence the next day. This, however, did not erase the humiliation of having to spend the night in jail with someone who repeatedly tried to steal his shoes.

Not too long after that, there was an anonymous report made to the Department of Social Services reporting that Jane had abused Shane. Jane did have a minor altercation with Shane during which she raised her voice and poked him in the chest with her finger. The local child abuse authorities interviewed Jane and Shane and determined that there was no abuse. This was a relief to Jane, but most certainly did not erase the awful fantasies she had about her being branded a child abuser and losing access to her son.

The next time Jane and Wayne appeared before the judge, Jane's lawyer made certain to tell the judge that Wayne was vicious and unscrupulous, and Wayne's lawyer made certain to tell the judge that Jane was slanderous and malicious. The judge reminded Jane and Wayne that a trial would be costly and the outcome could go either way.

The lawyers scheduled a third negotiation meeting. By this time Jane and Wayne had spent nearly all of their savings on legal costs and were borrowing from their parents. Shane had started counseling because his schoolwork was suffering. Jane and Wayne had both taken considerable time off from work to attend court dates that were regularly adjourned with no progress. Their employers did not like that. This meeting was considerably longer than the prior two meetings. As a matter of fact, the meeting started at four in the afternoon and went until about 10 p.m. By the end of the meeting, they were exhausted. They had managed to agree on almost everything. The final sticking point was merely one hour of time that Wayne wanted but Jane refused to give in on. Both lawyers reminded one another that this meant they would most certainly be going to trial.

The trial went on for 17 days. Jane accused Wayne of being an alcoholic. That was news to him. The last time he had gotten drunk was the night he asked Jane to marry him. Wayne accused Jane of having a lesbian relationship with her best friend. He made this accusation because he did not like being called a drunk. At the end of the trial, their legal costs were over $50,000 each. The judge's decision was an outcome that was very close to what they had *almost* agreed on—with one exception, which was that he split the hour that they bickered over.

It is easy to read this vignette and say, "I don't believe people would go through all of that over a half hour." After more than a decade of working with high-conflict, hostile families in the midst of angry divorces, I can tell you that this sort of behavior is not only possible, it is *common,* and for reasons more ridiculous than this.

All close relationships require conflict resolution, negotiation, conciliation, and the ability to prevent tense situations from moving past the point of mutual annoyance (which is normal at times) and into the realm of gladiatorial combat. When you live or work with someone in a close relationship every day, there will be emotional highs and lows. In the end, it is the ability to negotiate the lows that keep people happy and functioning smoothly in relationships. I have never heard of a relationship that failed because people were too happy.

Relationships fail because people fight and do not know how to stop fighting.

Uncontrolled anger and hostility are the culprits behind most failed family and business relationships. The key to understanding this is in the word "uncontrolled," because disappointments, anger, petty grievances, and quarrels are part of every close, mutually beneficial or enduring human relationship. Controlling the negatives in close relationships in business or personal settings is much easier to accomplish when people understand something about *de-escalating* conflict. In other words, people move past their disagreements when they learn how to constructively *stop fighting*.

> ✓ **Check Point**
>
> *Family, social, and work relationships often fail for the same reason: poor conflict resolution and an inability to control frustration and anger. Learning how to de-escalate conflict is an essential part of conflict resolution. Not only are you controlling your own anger, you are also managing and controlling the other person's anger.*

De-escalating conflict occurs when at least one person in a heated disagreement discontinues a hostile mode of interacting and redirects the disagreement back to an agenda of cooperative problem-solving. As we will see, perhaps the best benefit in learning how to de-escalate conflict is, when we utilize the technique of de-escalation, we are at the same time controlling our own anger. You cannot be angry and in control of a situation at the same time. A key aspect of this is that the process of controlling anger is always twofold: it is a process of mastering your own angry behavior as well as redirecting the angry behavior of others. De-escalation is the core concept to achieving this mastery.

Goals of Successful De-escalation

When interactions between two (or more) people turn angry, each person promotes, fuels, and advances the *anger agendas* of the other people in the interaction. I get mad at you, you get insulted by my anger, and you become angry at me. We lock horns until one of us "cries uncle" or is otherwise defeated. While kids can brush it off and be friends the next day, it is not the same in adult life. Anger creates resentment and motivation for revenge and retaliation. Angry interactions destroy the more productive agendas of conflict resolution, which solve group problems with some giving and taking from everyone. When interactions between people become angry, resolving conflicts requires *de-escalation* to prevent the predictable outcomes of ever-increasing anger—the destruction of partnerships or, worse yet, physical aggression.

When people disagree and the disagreement turns angry, the focus of communication changes. Instead of solving the problem that led to the disagreement, the agenda becomes destructive. The goal is to hurt or manipulate the person on the other side of the disagreement. There are many kinds of anger agendas. Six of the most common ones are:

Six Common Anger Agendas

1. Wanting to physically hurt someone.
2. Wanting to hurt someone's feelings.
3. Wanting to control someone else's behavior.
4. Wanting to suppress someone else's communication.
5. Wanting to frighten someone away.
6. Wanting to assign blame.

Sometimes more than one agenda can operate at once. In the previous vignette, "The War of the Rosens," both Jane and Wayne brought their anger to an extreme form in order to advance their respective agendas of power, manipulation, control, and the hurting of each other's feelings. The Rosens lost track of their original goal, which was how to share time with their son. These agendas were played out until, ultimately, each person's ability to fight and hurt one another were (at least temporarily) restricted by another more powerful person (the judge). Instead of seeking a mutually agreeable end to the conflict, the Rosens chose to hurt one another more and more.

Escalating hostilities cannot logically solve problems. Regardless of how mean and nasty their fighting tactics became, they were still left with the same fundamental problem they began with, which was how to share time with their child. The more they fought, the more problems they caused for *themselves*.

In this third critical path the emphasis is on de-escalation. Successful mastery of this path requires that you can regularly control your anger and the anger of others by learning the techniques of de-escalation. The main goals of de-escalation are:

Four Goals of Anger De-escalation

1. To prevent angry interactions from escalating to the point where solving the original problem becomes impossible.
2. To reduce the possibility that your own angry behavior will bring you to the point of doing something that will add to your original problem.
3. To reduce the possibility that you will be hurt either physically or emotionally by the person you are engaged in conflict with.
4. To gain control of the angry interactions so that you can most effectively control the outcome, and, if possible, solve the original problem.

The Big Decision

The third critical path requires a major decision and commitment. That decision is to reject the chronically angry lifestyle, either for the purpose of expressing frustration or for advancing one's personal goals in a predatory way. Up until this point, the emphasis has been on looking at anger. Now, the emphasis is going to be on change, and change requires a firm decision.

✓ **Check Point**

Sometimes it is not possible to "turn away" from angry interactions because there is nowhere to go. We need strategies for people at work, at home, or people we are forced to deal with who try to trap us into angry interactions

The Decision to De-escalate

De-escalation is the art of redirecting the focus of a conflict away from personal attacks and back to the original problem, with the goal of solving that problem. The decision to de-escalate conflict-filled situations means that you have adjusted your lifestyle. You now believe it is *always* better to approach a high-conflict situation by de-escalating angry modes of responding, as opposed to escalating the conflict. As we will see later, this is done by substituting conflict-resolving behavior for behavior that would normally escalate anger in yourself and others. When you make this decision, you dedicate yourself to controlling the outcome of angry interactions by directing your behavior and the behavior of the people around you to solve the original problem. Your problem-solving behavior *takes the place* of your own angry acting out. The theory behind this is that if your motivation to resolve conflict is made a priority, the control you achieve in taking this role will reduce your need to gain control of an adversary by acting out in a negative and angry way. You can't be chronically angry and de-escalate conflict at the same time, so redirecting the anger of others permits you to control yourself better.

> ✓ **Check Point**
>
> *The third critical path requires a major decision: to reject the chronically angry lifestyle, saying that you promise to view angry forms of problem-solving to be counterproductive and self-destructive.*

Two angry people promoting their own angry agendas of hurting each other and assigning blame produces chaos. When there is chaos, it is impossible to remain focused on the origin of the disagreement. Even when one person is angry, if there is another person controlling and redirecting the circumstance, there is a greater chance of resolving the problem without it escalating into a circumstance where one party must "win" and the other must "lose." De-escalation requires changing the role you play in anger-generating situations from being a chronically angry responder, to being an active problem-solver.

An Important Mastery Crossroad

You have arrived at a very critical juncture in terms of your progress through this program. This program emphasizes that getting a handle on your own anger goes hand-in-glove with learning how to deal with the angry behavior of others. Angry behavior is a much broader phenomenon than when one angry person makes another person a victim of his or her anger. That is only *one* type of angry interaction, and it is probably the least frequently occurring type. It is more common when one person's angry mode of responding touches off another person's angry mode of behavior—the resulting fight hurts everyone involved.

Let's look at the following vignette to see another example of how anger merely begets anger and draws people into angry interactions.

A Night Out at the Movies

Jack and Jill were settling in for a relaxing night out at the movies. After a hard week's work, this was one night they were both looking forward to. The movie theater was almost empty, which was a treat because it meant that they would be able to relax and get lost in the movie. Jill has a pet peeve about people talking in the movies. It drives her nuts when the people in back of her talk throughout the movie. This nuisance doesn't really bother Jack as much, but it drives him crazy when Jill is being driven crazy, so indirectly the nuisance makes both of them pretty aggravated.

Five minutes before the movie started another couple settled in behind Jack and Jill. Jill gave Jack a whisper indicating, "of all the empty seats in the movie theater...." Jill was hoping that they wouldn't blab throughout the movie. Apparently, they were both quite talkative, but for now it was all right because the lights hadn't dimmed. Sure enough, the woman in the couple giggled and spoke in a regular voice during the trailers and announcements. One of the announcements was that people should be considerate and not talk during the movie. Jill couldn't help but mutter, "You can say that again," when the cartoon character held his finger to his lips and said, "Shhhh!"

When the movie began, the couple was still talking. Jill was "tsking" and turning around, but her admonitions were ignored. All the while, Jack was getting antsy just having to watch Jill get that pissed off, so his patience was running thin as well. Jack asked Jill if she wanted him to say something. Jill told him not to because she knew if

Jack said something, it would not be subtle. Jill told Jack she would try to ignore the couple. At one point Jill asked Jack if he wanted to change seats. His reply was "Screw that! Why should I have to change seats so these two inconsiderate morons can keep talking through the entire movie." Jack said it loud enough so they (and the people five rows ahead) could hear them. Still, there was no relief. Jack turned around and stared directly at the two people and scowled, "Do you think you two chatterboxes could give the rest of the theater a five-minute break from your talking?" The argument began and ended up going on until the manager and two ushers came over. Even after their interjection, the argument continued like this:

Jack: *Who do you think you are talking to asshole? Do you want to take your problem outside?*

Couple: *Sure, I'll take it outside. What's the point of staying in here while you and that stupid, woman you are with are talking through the entire movie?*

To make matters worse, Jack's car was parked right near the other couple's car in the lot. At that point, the altercation became physical, and both gentlemen were treated to an appearance ticket in the town courthouse for disorderly conduct.

One of the major themes of this program is the *contagious* nature of anger. Jill's frustration and discomfort at the talking of the couple behind her was a particularly frustrating pet peeve of hers. Jack's frustration and irritability were less a function of his feelings about people talking in the movies, and more a function of his frustration at having to hear Jill complain about what was making *her* so upset. Jack just wanted to end Jill's reason for complaining because it was driving him nuts.

Another salient point of this vignette is the effect of making a nasty comment to someone, perhaps with the assumption that it is not going to escalate into anything serious. Nasty comments are not always ignored (even though it often makes life easier when they are) and do not evaporate after they are spoken. Anger of all sorts begets, fuels, and encourages anger in others. In today's angry world, insensitive or angry behavior is often met with anger from others.

Conquering Your Own Anger Doesn't Solve All Problems

Let's roll back the tape a minute on the Jack and Jill vignette. Would it have turned out any differently if Jack had not erupted at the man in back of him? Would it have been any different if Jack had asked the man politely to stop talking? There is no guarantee that it would have turned out any differently, unless Jack and Jill would have simply gotten up and moved.

Conquering your own anger does not relieve you of the burden of having to cope with anger from others. Any person who deals with their own anger but cannot cope with handling the inappropriate angry behavior of others may very well turn back to the angry lifestyle he or she left behind. By learning how to deal with anger in others and by dedicating yourself to de-escalating angry interactions (including getting out of situations where angry confrontations are likely to escalate), you ultimately reduce *your* own need to rely on angry modes of responding. There are other benefits as well. You become less threat-sensitive and less frustrated when you have the confidence to know that you can avoid, control, or redirect angry behavior; therefore, you are less apt to be hovering close to the point of explosive, angry behavior all the time. This is how we release ourselves from the burden of being chronically angry.

>
> **Check Point**
>
> *De-escalation is a process where you become less interested in what is personally insulting to you and more interested in solving the problem at hand.*

It is difficult to foster and contribute to angry interactions when you focus your attention on de-escalating angry interactions. Being angry and trying to de-escalate are too contradictory to occur at the same time. One of the best ways to avoid reliance on chronically angry modes of responding is to become better at solving the problems that lead to conflict, and that is what de-escalation does. It redirects the focus of the disagreement from escalating personal attacks, back to solving the original problem.

Making Mistakes Along the Way

Learning the skills and techniques of de-escalating conflict is extremely important. Placing yourself in the role of *wanting* to de-escalate conflict as opposed to feeling the need to blow off steam or release anger, is a separate skill. That skill comes with patience, dedication, and practice, and it would be very difficult to transition from the role of someone who escalates conflict by angry responding, to a person who de-escalates and redirects angry behavior. It's hard to go from a person whose first impulse is to want to punch someone who gives you a hard time, to a person whose first impulse is to redirect and de-escalate angry interactions. Therefore, as you dedicate yourself to this transformation, you will probably make a lot of mistakes.

> ✓ **Check Point**
>
> *When you make De-escalation a priority, it has a tremendous impact on your ability to control your anger because you changed the goal of your behavior from "winning the fight" to "solving the problem."*

Human beings are prone to making mistakes. There will be times when emotions run high and it will be impossible to bring yourself to a point where you can redirect angry behavior and use effective problem-solving. Fatigue, frustration, and lapses in judgment all contribute to keeping you in an aggressive, conflict-escalating role, as opposed to moving into a role that de-escalates conflict. There is no shame in succumbing to any of these processes. Frequently, there are opportunities to correct those mistakes. Most of the time, all it takes to correct a loss of temper is an apology, but apologies can be very difficult to make by people who are chronically angry. In the more advanced critical paths, the mastery process involves forgiveness and blame acceptance, so there will be plenty of opportunity to explore the additional success you can gain by a complete understanding of each of these. Expect failure. Those interactions you cannot de-escalate because of your own temporary personal failure, you can and should rehabilitate after the fact.

De-escalation Step Two: Coping Strategies

De-escalating on Both Sides of Conflict

The four main coping strategies for de-escalating conflict were first mentioned as goals of de-escalating conflict in the mastery content of Step One. They are worth repeating here:

Four Goals of Anger De-escalation

1. To prevent angry interactions from escalating to the point where solving the original problem becomes impossible.

2. To reduce the possibility that your own angry behavior will bring you to the point of doing something that will add to your original problem.

3. To reduce the possibility that you will be hurt either physically or emotionally by the person you are engaged in conflict with.

4. To gain control of the angry interactions so that you can most effectively control the outcome, and, if possible, solve the original problem.

Achieving these goals is easier if you follow a plan or outline that cues and reminds you of ways to cope with anger when it escalates. Creating an effective strategy for keeping your own anger under control while redirecting someone else's anger back to the problem (the process of de-escalation) is not as difficult or unfamiliar as you might think. In the second critical path, "Consequence Forecasting," the Step Two coping strategy used a memory aid to focus you on a method that encouraged looking ahead at the consequences of angry modes of responding. The memory cue or aid was L.A.S.T., which reminded us of the action sequence, *Listen, Assess, Stop, Turn Away.* In this critical path, we will be using some of the same techniques and building on them to form the foundation for de-escalating angry situations. The memory cue for this critical path will be L.A.S.H., *Listen, Assess, Stop, Hand Out Help* or *Listen, Arthur, Stop and Help*, and should be easy to remember because the ideas are very similar.

Moving From L.A.S.T. to L.A.S.H.

You can avoid having a moment of angry behavior turn into days or weeks of aggravation by effectively handling and then turning away from the annoying, incidental interactions you encounter with people who do not play any significant role in your life. The guy who jumps in front of you in line, the woman who looks at you as though she knows you and is annoyed at you, and the maniac on the motorcycle who bobs and weaves in and out of traffic are all people who should come and go in your life. You should not develop long-term relationships with people that stem from and revolve around angry interactions. The cost to you in terms of aggravation, lawsuits, and nights in jail are not worth the loss of control and whatever fleeting feeling of release comes from attacking them, either physically or verbally.

> ✓ **Check Point**
> *In the second critical path, "Consequence Forecasting," the action sequence,* Listen, Assess, Stop, *and* Turn Away *was important to remember when dealing with people who come and go in our lives and who are unimportant. There are times when it is not possible to ignore and turn away from people because they may play more important roles in our lives.*

In this critical path, we direct our attention to those people we have to deal with regularly, those who push our buttons, and those whose buttons we push at home, at work, and in our communities. These are people we cannot turn away from. In the mastery content portion of this critical path, I emphasized that in order to successfully handle interactions that may bring out the worst in us, there must be a conscious decision made to enter conflicts and differences of opinion with a mental attitude that remains focused on problem-solving and not additional problem generation.

This critical path teaches that we can adapt the same basic process with a few modifications to learn de-escalation strategies in situations where we just can't turn away. The action sequence in this critical path is: *Listen, Assess, Stop, Hand Out Help,* or *L.A.S.H.* The process of de-escalation starts with a decision to switch from the role of angry combatant to the role of someone who controls the situation by redirecting the focus of a conflict or disagreement back to the original problem.

In this critical path, we are going to use three of four cues used in the second critical path. We are going to *Listen, Assess,* and *Stop.* The fourth step is going to be *Help* and involves first offering and then soliciting help to solve the original problem. The next sections show a more detailed description of the L.A.S.H. technique for gaining control over situations that turn hot.

Listen

An important goal of de-escalating conflict is to remove yourself from the role of *conflict producer* and reposition yourself in the role of *conflict resolver.* In the second critical path, "Listen" meant listening for your body's signals of anger arousal: tight muscles, pounding heart, body heat, and so on. In this critical path, listening is used as the same type of cue or coping strategy, but now you are going to try and listen to, and look at the same bodily cues in the person who you are engaged in a conflict with, as well as your own.

Angry behavior tends to be imitated during a conflict. When conflicts escalate, one loud voice creates another loud voice. When one person becomes insulting and critical, the other often follows suit. If one starts cursing or swearing, so does the other. With each insult, anger grows because the more someone insults you, the more threatened you are likely to feel. If your goal is to de-escalate conflict, you will have to stop matching angry behavior with angry behavior and respond not from a position of threat but from a position of control. To accomplish this you must be able to listen to yourself and the other person and "catch" yourself either escalating or mirroring the anger in the person you are involved with.

Ultimately, instead of participating in the conflict, you will be countering angry behavior with neutral or positive behavior. There are two reasons for this. The first reason is that expressing anger in response to anger sets the stage for continued loss of control of your own temper. Anger creates anger. Escalating anger never leads to reasonable problem solving because the agenda is to create physical or emotional hurt in the other person and not to solve the problem at hand. Also, as you have seen on the second critical path, there are negative future consequences to escalating angry behavior. When you engage in angry interactions at home, at work, and in your community, you put your job and relationships with friends and family members in jeopardy. And of course, when anger gets way out of control, you often sacrifice your freedom.

The second benefit to moving from an aggressive strategy to a conflict-management strategy is that neutral behavior places you in control of the situation, and assuming control ultimately reduces anger. That is because anger is often nothing more than a hurtful attempt at gaining control of a situation. If you already have control, you will have less motivation to remain angry.

The following is an example of a segment of conversation where both parties are escalating one another and neither directs the conversation to a productive outcome:

How Anger Escalates in a Conversation

J: *I can't believe you would do that after I told you not to.*

P: *I can't stand listening to you when you raise your voice like that.*

J: *I have to raise my voice. You never listen.*

P: *That's right. I "never" listen. "Never." I love the way you make me into this horrible person who never does anything right.*

J: *Did I say you were horrible? Why do you exaggerate?*

P: *I exaggerate because I am horrible, just like you said.*

J: *Dammit! I didn't say you were horrible. What you are is a pain in the ass.*

P: *Oh, that's much better. I'm not horrible, just a pain in the ass.*

I purposely omitted the issue that these two people are fighting over because, by this point in the conversation, it is irrelevant. By the time people reduce themselves to merely insulting one another, the conversation is driven by pure anger. Both people are more interested in the fight than the resolution. Here is the same segment with one person de-escalating by keeping the responses neutral and focused on the problem.

De-escalating Anger

J: *I can't believe you would do that after I told you not to.*

P: *You are raising your voice, so I know you are upset.*

J: *I have to raise my voice, you never listen.*

P: *I'm listening right now. I'd like to talk, but without the shouting. When you shout it is distracting, and if this is important to you, I want to be able to concentrate without hearing you raise your voice. Can we start again? How did I upset you?*

"P" de-escalates the situation by a technique sometimes referred to as *active listening*. She lets "J" know that she is paying attention, and acknowledges his emotion when she says, "You are raising your voice, so I know you are upset." What she is saying is, "Okay. I know you want me to listen to what you are saying. So I am listening." By the same token, she does not want to be badgered or yelled at either. She is willing to talk, but she would like to do it in a more civilized way. What she is communicating here is that she knows things will break down if they just yell at one another. Instead, she wants the opportunity to talk it out. You can see how the conversation is gently moved and directed by her comments. The ball is in "J's" court when she asks "How did I upset you?"

One of the things you might have noticed about this segment of conversation is how "P" manages to discuss the *process* of what is happening between her and "J." Switching from *content* to *process* is one of the techniques we learned in the second critical path. In the first example, "P" joins the angry process and lets "J" know that she doesn't like being spoken to in a loud voice. She barbs and punishes him with criticism and sarcasm. This escalates the argument because she matches his antagonism with her own antagonism. This is a very common example of how people (especially couples), infuriate one another. When one person doesn't like how the other person is speaking, the impulse is to *punish* rather than *persuade*. In the second example, "P" persuades

"J" to start over by telling him she would like to listen to him and is open to discussion. This reduces "J's" motivation to keep pushing and needling her. "P's" comments in the second example are as much of a cue to herself as they are to "J." She is "listening" to the anger that wells up in her when she is yelled at, and she is acknowledging that "J" is angry as well. Instead of diving right into the conflict, she acknowledges "J's" upset and tries to move the conversation back to a productive place. She is switching her role from aggressor to mediator.

When people talk about trying to calm themselves from being angry or frustrated they talk of "taking a deep breath." The idea behind this commonsense strategy is that a pause or relaxing breath will help quiet the sting that accompanies an impulsive and angry reaction. In the second example, "P" simply describes what is going on. She says, "I know you are upset because you are raising your voice." She could have said, "Why the hell are you raising your voice at me? Who do you think you are talking to?" In the second example, "P" leaves her ego out of her response. She simply acknowledges "J's" irritation. Remember, anger feeds anger. In this case, even "P's" rather neutral response did not stop "J" from continuing to attack her by saying she never listens. I set the example up this way to show you that de-escalating a situation does not occur with a single neutral response. It is a process of ongoing persuasion. As a general rule, if one person is neutral and another person is angry, the angry person will be more motivated to come down to the neutral position. This is especially so if you continue the entire L.A.S.H. process as I continue to explain it in this chapter.

Warning

Please be advised: there are times when a person is hell-bent on raging, and the anger will escalate regardless of what steps someone takes. There may be nothing you can do to de-escalate this type of process. When this occurs, it is best to walk away or terminate the interaction. Rage cannot be reeled back in and redirected. When a person is raging, the only satisfying outcome is to hurt someone else. How do you know when de-escalation is impossible? When a person's anger escalates even after you have returned to a calm state and are willing to listen to reasonable conversation. It is best to end the contact rather than risk an aggressive physical interaction or make yourself subject to being emotionally abused.

Assess

The *Listen* step in the action sequence for de-escalation prompts us to take note of the set of reactions occurring in ourselves and people we are engaged in conflict with. The *Assess* cue prompts us to evaluate events that increase escalation and shut off avenues of de-escalation. A more practical way of understanding this is to ask two questions. They are:

1. Am I promoting an anger agenda, or trying to solve a problem?
2. Is the person I am having a conflict with promoting an anger agenda, or trying to solve a problem?

Earlier in the chapter I described some common anger agendas.

This list can be expanded to include any motivation that replaces problem-solving with personal attacks.

Motivation That Replaces Problem-Solving With Personal Attacks

1. Wanting to physically hurt someone.
2. Wanting to hurt someone's feelings.
3. Wanting to control someone else's behavior.
4. Wanting to suppress someone else's communication.
5. Wanting to frighten someone away.
6. Wanting to assign blame.

The assessment of your own anger agenda, as well as the agendas of people you interact with, is important because it is these agendas that pull people out of a problem-solving mode to begin with. I have mediated thousands of family conflicts in hostile custody disputes. Problem-solving efforts that begin with the goal of how to manage the lives of children after divorce quickly erupt into angry tirades between the parents. When this happens, I interrupt parents to ask what they would like to see happen at the end of their argument. Specifically, I ask, "What event could make this argument stop right now?" The responses I receive usually sound like this:

- I want to him to see how selfish he is.
- I want her to see how unreasonable she is.

- ◆ I want him to apologize.
- ◆ I want her to stop taking advantage of the situation.

These are typical examples of how people focus on the personal insults caused in angry conversations as opposed to the underlying problem that caused the disagreement in the first place. None of these statements address the issue of how to solve the problem of managing the children after divorce. All of the statements seek to advance the agenda of "I want to teach him (or her) a lesson," or "I want him to see how wrong he (or she) is."

Let's look at the meaning of each of the previous statements with respect to how they operate in the context of angry arguments. Below, the left column represents the actual words. The right column represents some expressions that serve an agenda of anger more than it serves an agenda of problem-solving:

Actual Communication	How It Serves the Anger Agenda
I want him to see how selfish he is.	The world must know he is selfish.
I want her to see how unreasonable she is.	The world must know she is unreasonable.
I want him to apologize.	The world must be told he is wrong.
I want her to stop taking advantage of...	The world must know how manipulative she is.

The previous example suggests that if your priority is to prove something to "the world" about your adversary, that is not getting to the root of the problem. People are not always willing to learn the lesson you think they should learn, and, moreover, people are not in a "learning" frame of mind when they are upset. On the other hand, when the original problem is solved, people are often far more motivated to look at their behavior and be apologetic about it.

Teaching someone a "lesson" about their behavior is a more polite form of insult than outwardly mocking them or criticizing them, but it is insulting nonetheless. Parents teach children lessons. It is a natural consequence of the difference in power and control between parents and children. In a dispute, if you treat an adversary as though you are a parent and they are a child, you will insult them and appear condescending. You are also placing yourself in a position of power in the dispute and disputes do not settle when there is an inequity or imbalance in power. Everyone must feel as though they have a say in the outcome.

Even if you could persuade a person to accept blame or fault, the original problem often remains unsolved. If assignment of fault is important to you, a very effective way of getting back to the source of the problem would be for *you* to make the first move in this area by admitting to your own mistakes and shortcomings. I will discuss the value of this in some of the forthcoming critical paths. For now, your assessment must help guide you to the point of asking yourself what you want from the interaction you are involved in. Do you want *retribution* ("payback"), or *resolution* (a fair end to the conflict)? Some people want both. They want a fair end to the problem, *and* they want an apology for perceived hurt and past insults.

The Habit of Self-Review

Getting to the point of successful conflict resolution requires that you assess what you want the outcome of your participation in an interaction with someone to be. There are specific behaviors you can look for in yourself and in those who you are engaged in adversarial disagreements with. Below is a list of behaviors that will almost always escalate conflict:

- Bringing past hurts and insults into a conversation.
- Getting up in someone's face.
- Refusing to allow someone to express themselves.
- Sarcasm.
- Belittling remarks.
- Suggesting that someone who doesn't agree with you is mentally ill.
- Giving someone the silent treatment.
- Demanding the other person accept all or most of the blame.
- Threatening to hurt them physically or emotionally.

Your ability to concentrate on whether you are acting in any of these ways requires dedicated practice and *self-checking*, and that is a difficult task. We are usually very unaware of the things we do when we are angry and unreasonable. That is because we are usually so focused on being "right" that we tune out how demanding, unreasonable, and insensitive we become as we demand to be recognized for being right.

The main purpose of self-checking is to develop a habit that competes with the impulse to act out when we are angry. To go back to some of the language I presented in the first few chapters of this book, angry responding is a group of habits that keeps us locked into a *chronically angry lifestyle*. The more we learn to interfere with these negative habits by replacing them with more positive habits, such as de-escalation strategies, the less angry we become in general. I will take the opportunity here to remind you that devoting some serious time just to achieve the skill of self-checking is part of the reason I refer to this program as a mastery program. There are a lot of people who engage in many or *all* of the behaviors previously described. Abolishing any single behavior may take months or even years to accomplish. Changing long-standing habits and tendencies to be chronically angry takes time. Removing your angry habits is the ultimate success. There are smaller, but very significant successes to enjoy along the way. Every time you short-circuit your anger response to anything or anyone, you have achieved success. For instance, just being able to hear someone criticize you without getting even angrier and escalating the conflict is a major step in the right direction.

I have found that one way of becoming better at interfering with behavior that supports a chronically angry lifestyle (such as those conflict-escalating behaviors previously listed) is to practice reviewing your "normal" mode of behavior when you are not engaged in an angry interaction. These will be your first signs of long-term success. Here are some practical tips:

Tips to Help Self-Review Your Behavior

1. See if you can catch yourself unfairly criticizing people you know as well as how often you put down or insult people you do not know.

2. Check to see if when you are speaking to one person, you have a need to put down or criticize mutual friends or acquaintances.

(List continued on next page.)

3. Review your "non-angry" conversations with people and try to assess the extent to which you make sarcastic comments, or your tendency to poke at other people in a mean and hostile way even as a form of exercising your sense of humor.

4. For a single day, count the number of times you refer to people as "stupid," "inept," "lazy," or "worthless."

5. Listen to what people tell you when they are involved in minor arguments with you. Do they think you are controlling, mean, unfair, or bullying?

6. Ask a person you trust and love to point out these behaviors when they see them. Develop a code word or phrase so that you do not have to listen to a speech or a lecture. If you are the friend or loved one who is pointing out these behaviors, try your best to do it in a gentle way. If you find that this is causing more problems than it is helping, step away from the job.

After you have become better at reviewing your behavior after the fact, your natural tendency will be to notice your behavior when it is occurring. When you can catch yourself in "real time," you can start redirecting conflicts to more productive outcomes.

Stop

When feelings are hurt, and defenses go up on both sides of an angry interaction, how do you tell someone, "I want to stop fighting now." In other words, once you have raised your own level of awareness about your contribution to the conflict, how do you stop the escalation and redirect the focus of the dispute? In Step Three of this critical path, I will suggest several types of communications that you can use to accomplish this, including many different variations of simply saying, "I want to stop fighting now."

Another technique that you can use to successfully de-escalate many conflicts is to say nothing, and just listen to the other person talk themselves out. Allowing a person to express their side of a conflict without interrupting can be a very effective form of de-escalation. As a matter of fact, it is probably one of the most effective ways of de-escalating a hostile situation. Often the people we engage in conflict, or who engage us in angry interactions, are frustrated and merely want to be heard. Conflicts can escalate very quickly when both sides are convinced that they are not being listened to, and both people interrupt one another to make a point. This can lead to a *second* argument about rudeness and interrupting, something I will describe in the next section as an *offspring conflict*. When people feel they are not being listened to, they become frustrated. When people are frustrated, they communicate more strongly, more severely, more harshly, with more volume, and with more pointed words.

> ✓ **Check Point**
> *Putting the brakes on an escalating dispute can often be as simple as saying, "Look, I really don't want to fight anymore," or by not saying anything and letting your adversary talk themselves out.*

Along the same lines, another simple and very effective way of stopping an increase in hostility is to actively encourage a person to keep talking. How would it make you feel if you were in an argument with someone who genuinely stated, "Keep talking. I want to make sure I hear all of your side of the story before I talk." Can you describe whether hearing that from someone would motivate you to be more angry or more reasonable in your approach to resolving the conflict?

Both of these techniques are effective ways of putting the brakes on an escalating conflict. They are good ways to "stop" the escalation of the conflict so that you can redirect the flow of the interaction back to resolving the original problem. Another technique that you can use to manage your own anger and stop angry interactions from escalating is to refuse to participate in "offspring conflicts." The following sections shows how people create arguments within arguments.

Avoiding Offspring Conflicts

Angry interactions escalate when people permit the interactions to produce *offspring conflicts*. Here is an example of an argument that produces an offspring conflict or an "argument within an argument."

> **How Offspring Conflicts Happen**
>
> **Johnny:** *I do not think you should go out looking like that.*
>
> **Maria:** *Why not?*
>
> **Johnny:** *You look kind of trashy.*
>
> **Maria:** *I do not.*
>
> **Johnny:** *Yes you do, I don't want people to think you are a whore.*
>
> **Maria:** *Screw you. Are you calling me a whore?*
>
> **Johnny:** *Screw me? No. Screw you. Don't speak to me that way. You have a problem. I tell you that I don't like something and you can't accept it.*
>
> **Maria:** *Who do you think you are, telling me what my problem is? I'm leaving. I'll dress whatever way I want. Go fuck yourself.*
>
> **Johnny:** *Leave this house looking like that and don't bother to come back.*

Even in a relationship as obviously dysfunctional as this one, there could have been attempts made to solve the original problem that would not have ended in the kind of breakdown that resulted at its conclusion. Here is a second scenario:

> **Avoiding Offspring Conflicts: Second Scenario**
>
> **Johnny:** *Can I tell you, I feel uncomfortable with you going out in the clothes you are wearing?*
>
> **Maria:** *Why?*

(Dialogue continued on following page.)

> **Johnny:** *Well, you look sexy and great, but the outfit is kind of revealing and I know I will be thinking that other guys will be staring at you all night.*
> **Maria:** *Are you that insecure?*
> **Johnny:** *Maybe.*
> **Maria:** *You have no reason to be.*
> **Johnny:** *That's nice to hear, but I still feel uncomfortable. I'll try to loosen up a bit, but for tonight do you think you can change your shirt?*

I left out Maria's ultimate response so that I could ask you: Do you think Johnny would have had more success in approaching Maria this way? Do you think Maria would have given in? Of course, what I am asking is, if you took Maria's position in the interaction, would *you* have given in if Johnny changed his tone and approached you with the language he used in the second scenario?

The difference between the first and second scenario was that, in the first scenario, one argument ran into another and into another. The anger "followed" each topic and became more intense as it accumulated. In the second scenario, both people showed greater self-control. Johnny was less demanding. Maria was less critical. Whether it worked out to a fair compromise in the end, it did not address Johnny's lack of trust in Maria, or Maria's potential flirtiness or lack of consideration, depending on the whose side you are more sympathetic. One thing is certain, however, and that is, in the second scenario, Johnny and Maria would not let the circumstance escalate, and both made efforts to *stop* the conversation from wandering into off-spring conflicts. This prevented the kind of additional damage that out-of-control anger did in the first scenario. Johnny and Maria have problems in their relationship. Proper anger and conflict management give them the *opportunity* to discuss their problems in a civilized way. Civilized problem-solving is a fundamental element of success in all important relationships, whether they are personal relationships or business relationships.

Let's look at a snippet of conversation between two office co-workers. Trina is Lucinda's immediate supervisor. Lucinda is a far more competent worker than Trina and does not like being directed by someone who she feels is not as intelligent and motivated as she is:

Lucinda: *I'd like to take care of the report you asked me to write, but the folder that has the information I need is in your desk.*

Trina: *I'll look for it later. I have other things to do right now.*

Lucinda: *Later does not work for me. How do you expect me to do my job when you won't give me what I need to do it?*

Trina: *I didn't tell you I wouldn't give it to you. I just said I can't give it to you now.*

Lucinda: *I just don't see why you won't give it to me now. If you would just reach into your desk and give it to me, we would not even be involved in a discussion that has taken as long as this one has.*

Trina: *Maybe that's not the real problem. Maybe the problem is that I resent it when you make your priorities my problems.*

Lucinda: *Excuse me? You asked me to do this. Maybe the problem is that you ask me to do things and then make it impossible for me to do them.*

The problem between Lucinda and Trina is not the item Lucinda will not get for Trina, it is the working relationship between Trina and Lucinda. Trina knows that Lucinda does not think much of her, and Lucinda knows that Trina will put her in a bind and slow her down to make sure that she is not upstaged by her. In order for Lucinda to keep moving ahead in her business environment, she needs to appear as less of a threat to Trina (because of the difference in their positions of power). At this point in the conversation, Lucinda still does not have the document she requested. What she has is an escalating conflict with Trina. The relationship is as tense as ever and both people have reinforced the other's anger and hostility. Here is an example of how Lucinda can try to get her job done without escalating the hostility between her and Trina:

Lucinda: *I'd like to take care of the report you asked me to write, but the folder that has the information I need is in your desk.*

Trina: *I'll look for it later. I have other things to do right now.*

Lucinda: *Well, that puts me in a difficult situation. I know you want that report done, and I want to help you do it. I can't do it without that folder. I can get started on it right now if you would hand me the folder. If you can't give it to me now, you will have to track me down later when I am doing something else.*

Lucinda made it more important for Trina to give her the folder and more of a pain in the neck to avoid giving it to her, preventing Trina from blowing her off and irritating her. She did this by focusing squarely on the problem, and not permitting her irritation with Trina to erupt into a personal discussion like it did in the first scenario.

Hand Out Help

I have already pointed out that once you invest yourself in the process of de-escalation, you automatically assist *yourself* in controlling your own anger. When you are involved in the act of de-escalating an angry conflict, your anger does not get a chance to take off. de-escalation is a constructive process; investing in anger agendas is a destructive process. They are opposites, so they cannot exist at the same time. The same is true of the next step in the L.A.S.H. (*Listen, Assess, Stop, Hand Out Help*) technique for de-escalating conflict, which is "Hand Out Help." The goal of this part of the action sequence is to offer a solution or concession to end the conflict. As long as the concession is reasonable and not insulting, this is another natural way of managing your own anger by

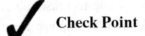

Check Point

An offspring conflict occurs when the process of an argument or conflict creates another conflict. For instance, when two people disagree and one person starts to yell, the person being yelled at starts arguing about the fact that they do not appreciate being spoken to in that tone of voice.

investing something positive into the conflict. This part of the technique is simple to understand, but difficult to execute, which is true for most things that ultimately lead to success in life. If you are offering your help and assistance in reducing conflict, you can often elicit the help and assistance of those who have become your adversaries. While anger begets anger, you will also find that, when angry energy in a conflict is reversed, positive problem-solving often produces more reasonable concessions from someone opposing you in an adversarial situation.

Suggesting an Action

In the final step of the L.A.S.H. action sequence, you attempt to accomplish de-escalation by making the first move to reduce the conflict. This requires more than words; it requires that you suggest an *action* that you would be willing to take to reduce the conflict. There are times when people will not accept reasonable solutions to conflicts, but these times are in the minority. Most people engage in arguments to learn how to push other people's buttons and drive them crazy. Their "prize" is the emotional breakdown of the other person. In order to succeed at mastering the ways of positively influencing the outcome of angry interactions, you must shoot for a different prize. That prize is gaining the opportunity to change the energy of the situation from volatile to reasonable.

Favorable solutions are never guaranteed, but they do become more likely when one person is willing to drop the sword. People who engage in angry arguments place "winning" the argument as the highest priority. Winning is usually defined as the other person admitting wrongdoing or breaking down to a point where he or she cannot argue anymore. If the person you are arguing with is a family member, friend, lover, coworker, or boss, you may achieve short-term success, and win the argument. But if you prevail in an argument by overpowering someone with anger, you may be destroying whatever long-term potential there is in the relationship. On the other hand, the long-term survivability of the relationship may not be important to you. Some people may irritate you so much that your anger is used purposely to end a relationship. Becoming intensely angry is one of the most common ways that people end relationships, because sometimes it is easier to feel angry than it is to feel hurt.

Getting to the end of a conflict without "scorching the earth" is always more beneficial in the long run. Even when you must end a relationship, there is absolutely no benefit to you to leave on adversarial terms with the worry that the person you were involved or interacting with will operate with an agenda to "settle the score" at some point in the future.

The "Win–Destroy" and "Destroy–Destroy" Outcomes

When people engage in de-escalating conflict, they operate toward a win-win or win-compromise solution. When there is no motivation to de-escalate conflict, the natural course of angry interactions can conclude in only one of two scenarios: the "win-destroy" scenario, and the "destroy-destroy" scenario. The win-destroy dynamic produces an end to a conflict by destroying an adversary's ability to fight. It is the classic threat issued to soon-to-be ex-spouses who are separating in a hostile and combative way. The sentiment expressed is, "You hurt my feelings, and you violated my trust. Now I am going to make the rest of your life more miserable than you ever thought it could be." It is the relationship equivalent of the big-business threat: "I'll make sure you never work in this town again!"

Motivation for win-destroy outcomes in angry interactions can come from frustration or predation. The chronically frustrated person wants to destroy the source of frustration in order to prevent it from causing any future pain. The chronically predatory person reinforces their need to feel powerful by observing the results of the pain and destruction he or she can cause and actually feeling good about it. In either case, the strategy is severely flawed. Winning a conflict by destroying an adversary produces motivation for revenge, if not by your destroyed adversary, then by the agents or sympathizers of the adversary. Second, it may induce sympathy for your adversary in people who were previously supportive of *you*. Take the case of the gentleman who suspects his wife is cheating on him. He hires a private investigator, and the investigator takes pictures of his wife and her paramour holding hands and kissing in the park. Before he can confront his wife with the pictures, the wife confesses and tells her husband she is no longer in love with him. Not content with the wife's admission, and still stinging from the breach of trust, the husband publishes the pictures on the Internet, and sends copies of the pictures to his wife's family and friends. As a final act of rage, he even shows the pictures to his children. It is hard to continue to sympathize with the husband when he is going so far out of the way to exact his revenge.

I evaluate my relationships with people in part by watching how people I am involved with treat others. If I see that someone has a vicious streak in them, I will start to wonder if there will ever come a

> ✓ **Check Point**
>
> *Most people want to see their adversary "break down" at the end of a heated argument.*
>
> *A much more productive outcome to any argument is to induce a more reasonable response from your adversary— preferably one that permits you to gain something you didn't have before the argument started.*

day when that viciousness will be turned on me. Unless you operate in a group that values and promotes the expression of uncontrolled anger, most people will evaluate win-destroy behavior as frightening, unnecessary, and unflattering. On the other hand, people who can take charge of a situation and guide it to a positive and fair conclusion without "scorching the earth," are generally considered confident, reasonable, and intelligent.

Being on the winning end of a win-destroy outcome is not always a guarantee of freedom from future conflicts. Unfortunately, this is an easy point to prove considering the rising incidence of terrorism in our world. One nation is in conflict with another nation. Tensions escalate. Eventually one nation overpowers another in retaliation for aggression on a smaller, sneakier scale. The psychology that dominates is a psychology of revenge and retribution, not conflict resolution. Both sides assume the other side is incapable of understanding what is "right," so all sorts of destructive outcomes are justified. When both sides operate under the presumption that the only way to communicate is by destruction and death, the outcome can never be favorable and will always escalate.

Dealing With Personal Terrorism in Domestic Violence

What can a person do if their true desire is to de-escalate an angry or hostile interaction, while the other person or people in the interaction promote win-destroy or destroy-destroy outcomes? One area where this is a difficult and serious problem is in the area of domestic violence, where victims may be stalked, assaulted, or have their privacy invaded. It also happens when the people are "set up" to look like the aggressor by someone who merely wants to get them in trouble. Both scenarios happen in very high frequencies in domestic disputes.

The out-of-control aggressor in domestic violence disputes has a lot to risk. Courts are enacting newer and tougher laws for dealing with domestic partners who commit aggressive acts. Today's court system is stepping up investigatory practices, and imposing harsh criminal sentences on perpe-trators of domestic violence, and also on people who use the system in a manipulative way. Victims of domestic violence are all too familiar with the dynamics of win-destroy and destroy-destroy motivations in adversaries. Attempts to break off contact with abusive partners often results in the partner vowing to remain a part of the victim's life forever, as a stalker or violent abuser. Strategies for dealing with this type of anger require a sup-port system. Once you are convinced that de-escalating the conflict is not a possibility, it is crucial that you connect yourself to as many resources as possible. Here are the general steps you should take:

Steps to Take for Victims of Domestic Violence

1. Contact your local police and ask them to refer you to a domestic violence victim resource center or hotline.

2. Get counseling from a qualified mental health profes-sional who has experience working with victims of do-mestic violence.

3. Enlist the aid of family members and friends. Make sure that there is always someone who knows where you are and how to get in touch with you.

4. Set up a "code word" that will alert people that you are in trouble. If you cannot call the police or are trapped, they can do it for you.

5. If you have a cell phone, learn how to use one-number dialing or speed dialing. This way, if there is an emer-gency, you can keep your phone in your pocket or hid-den and press one key that will call an emergency number of someone in your support system. You will not be able to talk, but you can use the phone to "broadcast" your message to whoever is on the other end.

6. The National Domestic Violence Hotline Telephone Number is: 1-800-799-SAFE (TDD: 1-800-787-3224).

Being the Angry Person in a Domestic Dispute

If *you* are the person who is stalking or is aggressive to a present or former partner, or you cannot stop fantasizing about hurting or injuring a former partner, *you need immediate help.* You will also benefit from surrounding yourself with a support system. Connect yourself to a domestic violence or abusers counseling group. If you cannot find one in your area, ask your local priest, minister, or rabbi to help you find a referral. You may also ask your family doctor or inquire at a local mental health clinic. You may even get help at the emergency room of a local hospital. If you own weapons or firearms, give them to someone for safekeeping. Drug and alcohol abuse are problems that greatly intensify aggressive behavior. If you are using either drugs or alcohol, seek additional help for these problems. While this program is geared at helping people control their angry behavior, this book alone is not enough to help you through a crisis where you feel as though you could physically hurt or kill someone else.

You can help yourself avoid engaging in win-destroy, and destroy-destroy conflicts by concentrating on the following:

Staying Out of Destroy-Destroy Conflicts

1. Inhibit your impulse to "fight fire with fire."
2. Do not assume that people will believe or buy into whatever the predatory person is doing to malign you. Part of what frightens people about what happens when they are victimized by lies, bullying, and gossip is the fear that false and malicious information will be believed. Give yourself more credit than that.
3. Stifle your fantasies of revenge and retribution, and concentrate on what you can do to make your position and image better.
4. If you have a strategy that you plan on using to counteract what is being done to you, and the strategy is not merely a hostile retaliation, don't threaten or warn about what you are going to do. Simply do it.

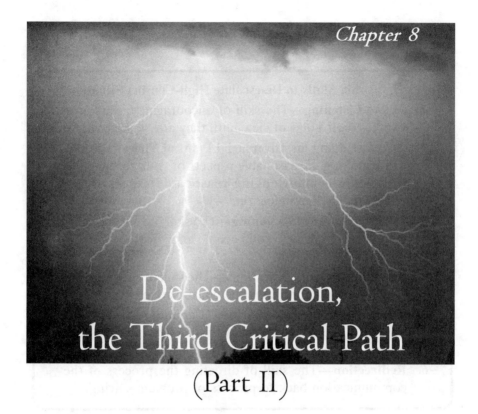

Chapter 8

De-escalation, the Third Critical Path
(Part II)

De-escalation: Step Three—
Communication Strategies

Communicating Strategies for Managing Anger While De-escalating Conflicts

As you start de-escalating a high-conflict situation, you are controlling your own anger as well as the anger around you. Good communication skills are essential to this task. Six important communication skills are mastered in this step of the de-escalation critical path:

> **Six Skills to De-escalate High-Conflict Situations**
>
> 1. **Active Listening**—The skill of encouraging a person to express their point of view until they are "talked out."
> 2. **Acknowledging an Adversarial Point of View**—The skill of identifying unreasonable aspects of your communication while acknowledging reasonable aspects of an adversary's communication.
> 3. **Avoiding Angry Questioning**—The skill of refusing to interrogate people who you become angry with or who become angry with you.
> 4. **Economical Communications**—The skill of communicating without monopolizing the conversation.
> 5. **"De-greasing" and "De-barbing" Communications**—The skill of making your point without implying the other person is a moron.
> 6. **Redirection**—The skill of directing the process of the communication back to process of problem-solving.

Active Listening

Less talking and more listening is almost always the most effective way of de-escalating a situation. It takes two to tango and it is hard to fight with someone when only one person is talking. A common objection to this strategy is, "Why should I just sit there and let someone scream at me?" You may not have to. You may be able to say, "I will not permit you to speak to me in that tone of voice," and then walk away. But there are times when two people find themselves "locking horns," and they cannot separate from one another because there is a problem to solve or because there is no place to go. You then have two choices: (a) scream back louder, matching anger, with anger; or (b) try to get the other person to calm down so that you can redirect the conversation.

In Step Two of this critical path, we discussed that escalating anger leads to very destructive outcomes: either win-destroy or destroy-destroy. When people cannot get to the point of redirecting angry interactions, it is often because they cannot get past the feelings of insult that occur when people are behaving angrily toward them. This feeling of being insulted by another person's anger becomes the first opportunity in every argument to generate *offspring conflicts*.

The following is an example of how it can happen in a very brief conversation:

Generating an Offspring Conflict in Two Brief Messages

Husband: *Mary! What the hell is wrong with you? Why do you get so bitchy when I talk to my brother on the phone?*

Wife: *Your brother never calls unless he wants a handout and by the way, where do you get off telling me that I am a bitch and that there is something wrong with me?*

In close family or work relationships, arguments over things happening in the here and now can quickly move to topics that have been sore spots for a very long time. Here's what happens next as the conversation escalated to a greater level of conflict:

Going From Bad to Worse

Husband: *There is something wrong with you. Your mood changes on a dime. It drives me nuts. What should I do, tell my brother he is a loser and hang up the phone on him?*

Wife: *Well, someone should tell him what a loser he is. I'd like to know why I have to sit here and be called a bitch because you have to deal with your lazy brother.*

Husband: *Because when you act like a bitch you make a difficult conversation with my brother that much more impossible.*

(Dialogue continued on next page.)

> **Wife:** *Sure, I'm your wife and I live with you and deal with you, and I am a bitch. Your brother, who wants money and will take the food off our table gets your full attention without the attitude. You should ask your brother to come over here and cook you dinner.*
>
> **Husband:** *Comments like that cause me to say you are acting like a bitch.*

In this example, neither person understands what the other person is really trying to communicate. The husband doesn't understand that his wife is complaining about much more than his brother. She is complaining about the way he speaks to her and interacts with her *in general*. The wife does not understand that her husband is uncomfortable talking on the phone to his brother, and that her behavior makes him even more uncomfortable. Both spouses are too busy promoting their agendas to hear that there is a problem in their relationship that goes beyond what has just happened. As long as each concentrates on their own topic, the tension and anger in the conversation will escalate, as it is further fueled and supported by past insults. For anything productive to come out of the situation one of the people has to *stop and listen* to what the other person is saying. I'll show it to you both ways. Here is how the wife attempts to make the first move to de-escalate the conflict:

> ### Wife Making the First Move to De-escalate
>
> **Husband:** *There is something wrong with you. Your mood changes on a dime. It drives me nuts. What should I do, tell my brother he is a loser and hang up the phone on him?*
>
> **Wife:** *I am sure you find yourself in a very difficult position when your brother calls you up looking for money. After all, he is your brother. I'd like to be more supportive, but I can't do it when you call me a bitch. Tell me what's on your mind. I would like to hear what is upsetting you, but please do not do it in an insulting way.*

In this instance, the wife tries to de-escalate the tension by acknowledging the discomfort in her husband. She also lets her husband know that she cannot be supportive of him when he is calling her names. She is shifting the focus of the conversation by going *to* the problem and making the insult less of an issue. The next request she makes of her husband is that he keep talking. There is no guarantee that he will, but she is not going to keep adding to the anger. She has made a firm decision to de-escalate.

Here is an example of how the husband might have gotten his original point across without insulting his wife:

Husband Making the First Move to De-escalate

Husband: *Dealing with my brother is a real pain in the neck, Mary. I know you don't like him, but he's my brother. It makes things so much more difficult when you make faces at me and criticize me while I am talking to him.*

Wife: *Well, someone should tell him what a loser he is instead of just offering him a free ride every time he complains about having no money.*

Husband: *I can see why you would resent that. Maybe I haven't listened to you tell me how much it bothers you. Talk to me about it some more.*

In this example, the husband's initial complaint is much less antagonizing although it still doesn't produce the most sympathetic response from his wife. What it *does* accomplish, however, is the prevention of offspring conflicts. When the wife responds by calling the brother a "loser," the husband doesn't take the bait. Instead, he acknowledges her resentment because that is what she feels. The husband may not like the way she feels, but there is no denying that she feels it, so he acknowledges it. This is a key component of active listening—to acknowledge whatever emotion a person is feeling without saying (or implying) they shouldn't feel that way or that they are "sick," "stupid," "unfair," or "insane" for feeling the way they do.

Some might look at the husband's statement as wimpy or henpecked. Marriages do not thrive on people "winning" fights. They thrive on love, and on tolerance for a partner's faults and misgivings. Disagreements in any important relationship are not competitions that award the winner with a trophy that says, "I am right." Yet people often behave as though they are. Disagreements are unpleasant periods that disrupt the people in the relationship from having more successful interactions. Winning is not a desirable end if the consequence of the "win" is hurt feelings, resentment, or mistrust. The outcome of an argument between two people who want to remain in a close relationship is to resolve the dispute and get back to the aspects of the relationship that are pleasant.

In the second scenario, the husband exerts a positive type of control over the situation. If his wife is looking for a fight, she is not going to get it. In both scenarios, where would this conversation end if *someone* didn't exert some control over its escalation? Most likely it would have ended in a larger fight. Eventually both the husband and wife would have become even more upset with one another. Continued fighting would not make the husband feel better about his wife's negative reactions to how he deals with his brother. It would also not make the wife feel any better about the brother placing stress on her relationship with her husband. Whatever problems there are in the relationship, at least, in this scenario, the husband was not going to let the argument at hand add to them.

Some couples develop their entire "normal" mode of interaction around fighting and bickering. The topics may change, but the underlying issues are usually frustration, disrespect for one another's feelings, and disappointment in the partnership. Many marital and "love" relationships often become the source for the chronic frustration that carries into the way people in those relationships treat the rest of the world. When you can reduce the number of angry interactions in important work and family relationships, you are much less likely to interact with the rest of the world in a frustrated and angry way.

Here are other examples of using active listening as a means of addressing potentially antagonistic situations, without escalating the circumstance to a point where conflict and out-of-control anger take over. The following examples first present an insulting *barb*. Think of a barb as an inflammatory statement or an example of verbal "button-pushing." People can respond to barbs by either escalating or de-escalating the situation. Here is an example of how it is possible to react with a response that either "takes the bait" or de-escalates the situation.

> **Escalating vs. De-escalating**
>
> **Barb or Antagonistic Statement:** *I can't stand the way you leave the bathroom when you know I have to come in after you. You are a slob.*
>
> **Escalating Response:** *You really don't have to try too hard to look for reasons to get on my case before I leave the house in the morning, do you?*
>
> **De-escalating Response:** *It sound's like you are pissed off. Let me hear what you think I could have done differently.*

The de-escalating response shows an amount of patience and kindness that you might believe the antagonistic person may not "deserve." People often reject the notion that they should respond in a civilized way to people who approach them in an uncivilized way. They see it as "taking shit." I know it is a crass way of saying it, but that is how it is commonly described. As a matter of fact, to connect it to the notion of AMPs or anger-maintaining presumptions, a very common AMP is: "I don't have to take anyone's shit." In other words, you should not have to be the subject of anyone's nasty or inconsiderate behavior. Well, it would certainly be a better world if everyone was considerate, but they aren't. The more realistic point of view would be to develop a set of skills that takes people out of your face as soon as possible. Fighting anger with anger doesn't do that. It does the opposite. It keeps people in a defensive and stubborn frame of mind. It requires point and counterpoint, and that is another way of saying it forces disagreements to escalate. Failing to respond angrily to someone else's antagonism, impatience, or insensitivity puts you firmly in control of the situation.

A key to developing the skill of active listening is to stop yourself from considering your role in the conversation as "shit-taker." This does not mean you have to keep yourself in relationships where you are at the mercy of someone else's inconsideration. What it means is that for the moment the interaction is going on, de-escalating by actively listening gives you the freedom to get to the end of that conflict as quickly as possible. In addition, it also keeps you from getting snookered into an angry verbal or physical argument. This is not taking shit. This is being smart. When the interaction is *over*, you will have all the freedom in the world to decide whether you want to remain in a relationship with an inconsiderate partner, or remain in a job where you have to hear people complain all day. You will also have the freedom to forgive those people who you love or who you were certain were having a rough day. The following examples represent skills involved in active listening:

Skills Involved in Active Listening

1. Talk less, listen more.
2. Acknowledge emotions such as frustration, irritation, anger, and disappointment in the person expressing them to you.
3. Do not imply that a person is stupid, sick, or otherwise horrible because they have a particular feeling.
4. When you can, ask a person to keep talking so that they can see you are willing to listen to their side.
5. Don't assist the formation of "offspring conflicts."
6. Remember, responding to angry statements with active listening and other de-escalation strategies doesn't require that you allow yourself to be abused. It merely brings you to the end of an interaction more quickly so you can decide how to handle the rest of the relationship without any additional grief.

Acknowledging an Adversarial Point of View

Arguments often take a nasty turn for the worst simply because of frustration that builds when each side believes the other side is failing to acknowledge that they have a valid complaint.

Here is an example of a conversation that transpires between two business owners. One business is a gas station, and the other business is a dry cleaners next to the gas station. The owner of the dry cleaners is upset because the employees of the gas station park their cars in his lot and that prevents customers from having quick access to and from the dry cleaners.

Failing to Acknowledge an Adversarial Point of View

Dry Cleaner: *I have asked your men not to park in my lot, but every morning when I get here, two or three of my spaces are taken up by those guys.*

Gas Station: *I'll talk to them about it.*

Dry Cleaner: *Bullshit. I've already spoken to them about it, and they ignore me. I am doing them a favor by not towing them.*

Gas Station: *So do you want an award for not towing them? I said I will talk to them.*

Dry Cleaner: *Look. If those cars are still in my lot, I am going to tow them and file a complaint against your business.*

Gas Station: *Don't threaten me. I don't like your attitude.*

Dry Cleaner: *My attitude? You are the one who doesn't give a shit about whether my business is affected by the actions of your employees.*

Gas Station: *You know what? Talk to my guys yourself. Tow them. Do whatever you want. Just don't bother me unless it is MY car you have a problem with.*

Each of the business owners sees the problem as a nuisance. Neither places a priority on maintaining a neighborly relationship with the business owner next door. At the end of the conversation, whatever preexisting tension there is has just escalated.

Now consider what a simple acknowledgment of the other person's position would have accomplished instead:

Acknowledging an Adversarial Point of View

Dry Cleaner: *I have asked your men not to park in my lot but every morning when I get here, two or three of my spaces are taken up by those guys.*

Gas Station: *That is inconsiderate. I don't want my men to disrupt your business. I'll talk to them about it and get back to you after I do.*

Dry Cleaner: *That would be great. I hate to take you away from your work. You've got a business to run, too.*

The gas station owner offers little more than he does in the first scenario, but he acknowledges that the dry cleaner is inconvenienced by the situation. Because the gas station owner demonstrates an appreciation for the dry cleaner's business, the dry cleaner shows the same sympathy for the gas station owner's role as a business person. It does not always work out this cleanly, but when it *can* it *will*. There are a number of ways to acknowledge someone else's point of view politely even when it differs from your own. Here are some examples:

Ways to Acknowledge What Someone Else Is Saying

- I am listening carefully to what you are (saying, proposing, asking, requiring, and so on).

- I understand that is your position, even though I can't agree with it.

- I understand that this is important to you. I am not trying to minimize your concern.

- Even though I do not agree completely, I think you have some valid points.

- Ultimately I disagree, but your points make sense and are well taken. I can appreciate your position even though I do not agree with it. You make some very good points.

Body Language and Mumbling Counts, Too

In conversations in which there is disagreement, one sure way of escalating conflict is to ignore or ridicule another person's point of view. Nonverbal behavior such as rolling your eyes, talking under your breath, or making sarcastic remarks is almost always seen as hostile and insulting, and, as a result, quickly escalates anger. These behaviors all form the basis for offspring conflicts.

Over time, people develop communication habits that become habits of the way they argue and disagree. These behaviors always serve as signals for escalation. Often, we are not even fully aware of when we act out in these ways. Some of these habits include interrupting or talking over someone who is trying to make a point, waving your hand at someone or making faces; suggesting that what someone is saying is "stupid," "ridiculous," or "moronic;" or answering every point by saying, "Right," or "Yeah, sure," in a condescending or irritating way.

An important aid to de-escalation is gaining the ability to acknowledge that a position you have taken in an argument is unreasonable or the result of an emotional reaction. Just as angry behavior induces angry behavior, reasonable or conciliatory behavior induces other sensible behavior. If what you are looking for is more sensibility from someone you are involved in an angry argument with, demonstrate your own ability to be reasonable.

Check Point

Over time, people develop communication habits when they are arguing. These may include rolling your eyes, sighing, shaking your head, waving your hand, and a host of other behaviors that can be seen as rude, and, therefore, escalate conflicts.

Avoiding Angry Questioning

Among the many angry habits people have, one of the most common ones, shown even by young children, is the habit of pummeling someone whom you are angry at with questions. Some of the more common "who, what, when, where, and why" questions are:

Angry Questions

- What's wrong with you?
- What's your problem?
- Why can't you listen?
- Why are you being so stupid?
- Why can't you leave it alone?
- What do I have to do to get it through your thick skull?
- How can you expect me to listen to that shit?

(List of questions continues on next page.)

- Where do you come off speaking to me like that?
- What planet are you from?
- Where is your brain?
- What happened to your common sense?
- Who put a bug up your ass?
- Where do you get off speaking to me like that?
- When am I going to catch a break with you?

Try to think of questions such as these as "invitations" to sarcasm, hostility, other pointless questions in response to these pointless questions, and, most of all, escalating anger on both sides of the conversation.

Questioning someone during an argument in a pointed or hostile way creates defensiveness. Defensiveness "turns on" whatever threat sensitive cues people have for themselves. Questioning is also a way of assigning blame, backing someone into a corner, or insinuating that someone is stupid, as in the "what makes you..." types of questions in the process of escalating arguments. Here are some examples:

"What Makes You..." Questions That Lead to Defensiveness

"What makes you think you are right?"

Also means: "There's no way you can be right because you are so wrong."

"What makes you think you can do that?"

Also means: "I am going to make sure I limit what you can do."

"What makes you think you have the choice?"

Also means: "I am going to make sure you won't have any choices," or "You are too stupid to know you have no other choices."

(List continues on next page.)

> *"What makes you think you are smart enough to pull that shit on me?"*
>
> **Also means:** "You are incredibly stupid and I am incredibly smart."
>
> *"What makes you think you can get away with that?"*
>
> **Also means:** "You are incredibly stupid and I am incredibly smart."
>
> *"What makes you think I care about what you have to say?"*
>
> **Also means:** "You are meaningless to me."
>
> *"What makes you think that people aren't going to let me know?"*
>
> **Also means:** "You are not nice enough for people to be loyal to."

Any one of these questions is insulting enough, but what they carry with them in their implied meanings adds even more fuel to the fire. The fact that angry questions carry a lot of implied insults combines with the fact that, in the course of typical human interaction, questions *generate* answers. In other words, it is normal to answer a question when someone asks; therefore, if someone "bites" you with a question, they are setting you up to bite back. Because the question itself is so insulting, the answer is very likely to be insulting as well. People can quickly escalate arguments by simply answering one nasty question with another nasty question. You can have an entire angry argument with one another simply by answering one question with another:

> ### Arguments That Escalate From the Use of Angry Questions
>
> **A:** *Why can't you get what I am telling you into your thick, cement-like head?*
>
> **B:** *Why are you such a pain in the ass?*
>
> **A:** *What makes you so nasty?*
>
> **B:** *What makes you think you are a fucking walk in the park?*

(Dialogue continued on next page.)

> **A:** How do you live with yourself for being so hostile to me?
>
> **B:** How do you live with yourself thinking you are so perfect?
>
> **A:** How would you like it if I packed up all my shit right now and left?
>
> **B:** Why do you think that would bother me one bit?

If this argument is making you laugh (or cringe) because it is so familiar to you, try asking fewer questions in your attempts to de-escalate conflict. Also, watch your tendency to merely trade off one hostile question with another. The goal of de-escalation is not to interrogate someone into submission. It is to redirect the focus of the conflict back to solving the original problem.

Economical Communications

Even when someone is not using nasty, abusive, or hostile language during an argument, more subtle but equally frustrating aspects of communication can increase frustration and quickly escalate conflict. One of the most common ways that people do this to one another is by making speeches or otherwise overstating a point. When someone is being polite enough to listen to what you have to say, make your point and move on. Do not use it as an opportunity to climb up on a soapbox and destroy whatever progress has been made in the interaction.

The following is an example of a speech given to an ex-husband from the ex-wife when they were brought together to improve their communication regarding their child. This speech occurred right at a point where the usually stubborn ex-husband admitted that he can be somewhat stern and over-critical about the parenting skills of his ex-wife:

Mark, thanks for giving me the opportunity to get this off my chest. It's just that when you confront me about my style of dealing with my daughter, I feel you are hostile and overly critical, and I can't really deal with that very well. I mean, it makes me very tense and very uptight, and it reminds me of some of the other difficulties we have had, where you were completely disrespectful. And there's more than one person who has said to me over the years, 'I can't believe that Mark would treat you like that.' And I would say to them, 'Well it's not always the way it seems on the outside. People are different behind closed doors.' And I would like for things to be better between us, but there is no trust—no trust whatsoever, and even though you are giving me this chance to express my feelings, I'm thinking to myself, "well, you know, how long before the other shoe falls," and "Is this only a temporary thing?" It's kind of like some of the things that happened last summer when I thought things were going well and you wrote me that really nasty letter that started the whole fight that lasted until Christmas where I was the one who finally gave in. But I think you still need to think about that and take some responsibility....

The ex-wife is doing a lot more than taking the opportunity to solve whatever problem she was having with Mark. She is using the opportunity to reprimand him; express hostility and mistrust; and review and rehash older, unsettled problems. Unless Mark can summon up super-human patience and refuse to respond to any of the button-pushing, it is likely that the conversation will escalate from here, even though he was the one who began to de-escalate the situation by apologizing.

The moral of the story is "keep the interaction polite and focused." The purpose of all the de-escalation techniques we are learning on this critical path is to move as quickly as possible back to the original problem, and solve it. The speech above could have easily been paired down to the following:

A More Reasonable Reaction

Mark, I appreciate what you said. It makes me feel better that some of the past problems we have gone through can improve. It still makes me a bit anxious to confront some of these things, but this is the kind of turn for the better I was hoping for.

This much-improved, shortened speech shows that less is more, and that is always a good rule of thumb to follow when trying to de-escalate an argument. It does not hurt that in the second scenario, the ex-wife speaks positively about her hopes for continued improvement.

De–greasing and De–barbing Communications

As we discovered in the last section, communicating to "excess" can involve repeating a theme, bringing up past hurts, and insulting someone by recounting something over and over. To further economize the process of reducing anger and conflict, we need to examine our language for hooks, barbs, and what I refer to as "grease" around a communication. Look at the following statements:

Adding "Grease" to a Heated Argument

- "I am glad you seem to be listening to me *for once*."
- "You are really helping me out *for a change*."
- "Thanks for not beating this one to death."
- "Wow, lightening must have struck on that one. You gave in!"
- "Well what do you know, there's a first time for everything."
- "We finally settled it after only 12 trips to court and $9,000 in attorney's fees."
- "There are people who told me you would never be fair on this one."
- "You see? It wasn't so hard to be a little nice was it?"
- "You see, it's not necessary to be an asshole all the time."

Each one of these statements pairs a compliment with an insult or implies that some good behavior is a once-in-a-lifetime event. If you can get to the point in a conversation where things are moving in a productive direction, one of the quickest ways to ruin progress is to deliver a left-handed compliment like the ones above. This can be a particularly destructive mistake when you are interacting with a predatory person, an intelligent person, or anyone who has "given in" on something begrudgingly and may be looking for a reason to jump into battle.

There are people who have developed such ingrained angry habits that they cannot deliver a genuine compliment. They are always "giving with one hand and taking away with the other." When people point out to them that their compliments are not taken kindly (because of the insults that are passed along with them), their response is usually to make it worse by refusing to acknowledge that someone could be insulted by those types of comments. They will say something such as, "Come on. I was only teasing. Learn how to take a joke." There can be a time and place for teasing, as long as you know the person very well, and you are not in the middle of a conflict or anger-driven inter-action where people tend to be more sensitive and have less of a sense of humor. Inappropriate teasing at any time is usually an aspect of anger that is sneaking out even if you swear you are not doing it to be inflammatory or rude. Also, if you are going to tease or poke fun, be prepared to respond without being defensive when it comes back to you. Some of the people who tease most are the least willing to take a poke in the ribs and will immediately erupt into an angry tirade if anyone were to dare say something they could take the wrong way.

Redirection

The ultimate goal of de-escalating any angry interaction is moving the conversation to the point of successfully solving the original prob-lem. Finding the words to accomplish this is easy. The hardest part is getting yourself to the point where you take charge of the responsibil-ity to do it. That is because some people consider it a matter of pride to "give up a battle." The belief that it is "wimpy" to stop a fight before it is won is a very unfortunate side effect of living in a competi-tive society, where "winning" is placed at a point on some imaginary scale above the notion of cooperation. While being a fierce competi-tor can be a valuable asset, it will never bring you as far in life as learning how to successfully master your emotions and to positively influence the emotions of others.

The ability to persuade someone to stop attacking you so that you can stop attacking them is an awesome ability and useful in any aspect of life that involves interaction with others. For one thing, it is a fan-tastic way of overcoming any difference in size or strength between two adversaries.

Here are a few other ways of communicating to help redirect the topic back to solving the problem that created the conflict in the first place:

> **Redirecting the Conversation Back to Problem-Solving**
> - "I don't like to hear myself talking in this tone. I'm sorry. Let's start again."
> - "This is not achieving anything productive. Can we move back to the original problem?"
> - "I would like to apologize for the way I am handling this. I'd like to approach the problems we are having again from the beginning."
> - "I am not proud of how this conversation is turning out. Let's go back and start again."
> - "This kind of talking isn't getting us anywhere. I'd like to apologize for my insensitivity. Can we try again?"

As with other communication strategies I have advised, do not expect these statements to produce immediate good results. Getting another person to join in the de-escalation process may require that you make multiple attempts. Take for instance, the following circumstance:

You say: "I would like to apologize for the way I am handling this. I'd like to approach the problems we are having again from the beginning."

They say: "You *should* apologize, you have been acting like a complete and total jerk."

Where do you go from here? Well, you can put your sword back up and start slicing into one another again, or you can keep going down the path of de-escalation. De-escalation is not an on/off switch. Just because you have made certain mental decisions to turn the argument in a more productive direction is no assurance that the other person will respond immediately or at all. A few more attempts may be necessary to start bringing the conversation around. Start by going back into an "active listening" technique. Follow up by moving the conversation back to the "process" of what is going on. Here it is again:

You say: "I would like to apologize for the way I am handling this. I'd like to approach the problems we are having again from the beginning."

They say: "You *should* apologize, you have been acting like a complete and total jerk."

You say (using active listing): "I can see you are too angry to accept my apology."

You follow up by saying (switching from content to process): "I would like to solve this problem we are having. I don't want to argue, but I am stumped. Even when I apologize, you still want to attack me. I wish we could just resolve our disagreement without insulting one another."

Notice, I did not recommend that you say: "Yes, I was a jerk." There would be nothing wrong with saying that if it is what you really believed, and if you felt that your behavior was so out of line that you needed to keep apologizing about it. By this point in the conversation, you have already apologized. Continuing to beat yourself up at the request of the person you are arguing with does not seem productive. It may start the kind of offspring conflict that begins when you become frustrated and start to criticize the person you are speaking to for not accepting your apology.

While apologizing is a helpful way of soothing hurt feelings and taking responsibility after an argument, people are not always willing to accept apologies in the throes of anger. Instead, they might insist that you are apologizing just to "shut them up" (which I think is a perfectly good reason to apologize, as long as you still acknowledge your own wrongdoing). Or people may say that you are apologizing insincerely so that you can gain the opportunity to hurt them again. Offering an apology as a form of de-escalation is a very good way of stopping yourself from continuing with some behavior that is increasing anger in the context of a disagreement. It may be a good way of transitioning from "this is all your fault and I hate you" to "I don't like what I am saying and I would like to work this out with you." This type of apology addresses what you are doing *right now* in the conversation. Apologizing for *what started* the disagreement is helpful if the apology solves the problem. If it doesn't, the argument may be resolved, but the problem that started it isn't.

To sum up, you can use a three-step process you can rely on to redirect an angry and escalating conversation back to the original problem:

> **"How to De-escalate" Review**
> 1. Directly state that you would like to stop arguing and go back to the original problem.
> 2. Be persistent in not accepting any invitations to rejoin the argument if the person you are involved in the argument with keeps attacking you.
> 3. Focus on the *process* of what is going on (the argument and how you would like to end it) instead of on the *content* of the argument (your personal insult or reaction to what is being said).

De-escalation: Step Four—Affirmations

Developing Statements for Tuning in to Your AMPs

Communication skills help us manage our emotions *and* the emotions of others. Affirmations are the AMP-defeating statements we tell ourselves inside our own minds to help us gain control of ourselves. In this third critical path, it is essential not only to develop the statements, but to rely on them to stop the escalation of our own anger. The statements also help to control the anger of someone who has placed themselves in an adversarial position. Using self-talk and affirmations to mediate our own angry behavior and control the angry behavior of others is a cornerstone of ultimately gaining mastery over negative and angry emotions and situations.

Affirmations and self-talk are used to "talk yourself down" when you are encouraging angry interactions to escalate. They are also used to stop and redirect others during your attempts to de-escalate angry situations. Because practicing and using affirmations are such an essential part of both processes, I am going to separate the affirmations that relate to de-escalation into three categories. They are:

> **AMPs That Help With De-escalation**
> 1. Noticing the anger in yourself and/or the person you are interacting with.

(List continued on next page.)

2. Noticing the signs of escalating anger in yourself and the person you are interacting with.

3. Becoming insensitive to another person's attempts to de-escalate an angry interaction or noticing the insensitivity of others to your attempts at De-escalation.

These categories represent three distinct points in time in the process of how angry arguments and interactions escalate.

The first point in time is when you notice that you or someone else is becoming angry. This is the point in time in the L.A.S.H. process when you are listening to what your body is telling you about your reactions. It is also the point in time when you may be observing increasing anger in a person or people you may be interacting with. Assessing (the "A" in L.A.S.H.) and Stopping (the "S" in L.A.S.H.) escalation will almost always be more successful sooner rather than later.

The second point in time is when you notice that you are saying or doing things to escalate the conflict, or the people you are interacting with are saying or doing things that are escalating conflict. You may notice yourself raise your voice, or use sarcasm or insults to make a point. Managing yourself or someone else at this point in time is more difficult because you, or the other person, has made a commitment to take the angry argument "to the end," which means winning and not solving the problem.

The third point in time is when you or an adversary have let the anger and conflict escalate to the point where you or both of you have become insensitive to the idea of redirecting the conflict to a reasonable solution. At this point in time, damage has already been done and one or both people in the interaction may have devoted themselves to ending the conflict in a "win-destroy" or "destroy-destroy" outcome.

Starting to Become Enraged and Noticing the Anger of Others

Anger starts off with a number of uncomfortable bodily sensations (irritability, butterflies, muscle tension, and so on), but it is stoked with anger-maintaining presumptions such as:

AMPs That Kick in at the Beginning of an Angry Interaction
- "This person is pissing me off. I am going to have to do something about it."
- "This asshole is giving me a hard time. I am going to teach them a lesson."
- "If this person wants a fight, they are going to get a fight."
- This is insulting. Anyone who insults me is going to pay a price for it."
- "This person is treating me like I am an asshole. We'll see about that."
- "I can't believe what I am hearing. No one is going to get away with shit like this."
- "What's with the attitude? No one is going to give me an attitude like this and get away with it."
- "This person is insulting my intelligence. I won't tolerate it."
- "This person has crossed the line. Now he is going to have to deal with my ugly side."

As you will see in the next critical path, initial feelings of insult are almost always "personalized" responses. These personalized responses cause people to start investing in a conflict. And of course, the more you invest in a conflict, the more you allow it and encourage it to escalate. A personalized response is a response where you assume that any insult or anger-inducing event is done to you as opposed to being an aspect of defect or fault in the person who is irritating you. It is as if you believe that you are the only person who is mistreated by the person who opposes you, as opposed to that person acting like a jerk with everyone.

Affirmations that counter these personalized insults are helpful in de-escalating your need to retaliate:

AMP-Fighting Affirmations
- "Why am I letting this person get under my skin? It is just going to lead to a worse fight."
- "If I respond to the mood this person is in, it is going to cause other, more difficult problems for me to deal with."

Watching a person in the process of "winding themselves up" or escalating their behavior can generate AMPS that sound like these:

AMPs That Kick in When Anger Continues to Escalate

+ "This person is really pissed off. I am going to have to defend myself."

+ "Whatever is happening here, I am not going to take any shit."

+ "This person had better get hold of themselves before they catch some heat from me."

+ "This person had better watch their tone of voice or I will scream right back."

These AMPs show that by watching a person become angrier we start to mirror the angry behavior and prepare ourselves to respond. Any AMP that implies, "If they don't stop, they are going to get it back from me...," is a type of self-talk that desensitizes you and makes you more prone to angry, escalating responses. "Go ahead, push me one more time..." is the type of mindset that looks for a reason to release the frustration that is building by watching another person's anger increase.

Affirmations that fight these AMPs take a forward look and realize escalation will invariably lead to inconvenience:

AMP Fighting Affirmations

+ "I am not going to let this person get the better of me by pushing those buttons."

+ "I am going to bring this person under control so that we are both more reasonable."

+ "Taking the bait that is being thrown at me now is only going to lead to a long and stupid fight that will ultimately hurt both of us."

The most important goal of any behavior during this phase is to be able to promote your own decision to de-escalate the conflict. It is to persuade the adversarial person to join in the problem-solving effort, as opposed to joining the adversarial person's need to insult, injure, and attack.

Listening to Yourself Escalate, and Observing

Someone Else Escalating

If you are unsuccessful at monitoring your own anger early on in the process, you will be drawn into the process of increasing escalation. Sometimes this happens because frustration becomes overwhelming, and sometimes it happens because of habits we have developed that instigate us to match insults with insults, and anger with anger. This type of behavior is driven by AMPs that express these ideas:

AMPs That Start Insult-Driven Conflicts

♦ "I am not going to let this person get the better of me without giving them a piece of my mind."

♦ "If I can't get this person to agree with me, I am going to punish them."

Affirmations that fight these AMPSs concentrate on controlling the damage already done and redirecting efforts back toward problem-solving:

AMP-Fighting Affirmations

"I have made a decision not to let myself get this way during confrontations. I have to force myself to honor that decision."

"It is not necessary to end an argument by hurting someone else. I can still influence this situation positively."

"I am not going to continue being aggressive in this confrontation because it will not solve the problem."

As you dedicate yourself to approaching all conflicts with a priority of de-escalation, it becomes easier to catch yourself engaging in the angry habits that promote escalation. One of the most satisfying progress points on this critical path is when you can hear yourself saying inside your own head, "Hey, what is the point of what I am doing right now?" This is the point at which you realize that you can exert some control over yourself. From that point, controlling the situation is the far less difficult task. Escalating a conflict to the point of hurting someone either physically or emotionally requires an angry investment of two people. When you gain the presence of mind to attempt de-escalation, even if the de-escalation process fails, as long as you do not re-engage, you will retain the ability to walk away. The only time you do not have this option is when a person has made up their mind to physically hurt you. In those instances, when you know beforehand that a person has that tendency, you should never permit yourself to be in a situation where escape is not an option.

Becoming Insensitive to Redirection

Angry conflicts can reach a point where people become insensitive to redirection. This may include a failure on your part to stop yourself from escalating your own anger, or a failure to be able to influence or redirect the behavior of someone who is escalating their anger toward you. There is only one type of self-talk message or affirmation that applies in this circumstance and that is: "This situation has gotten completely out of hand. I must try to walk away and convince the other person to walk away as well."

When people become completely insensitive to redirection, they are not capable of being influenced or persuaded by the type of reason or logic. This is the point at which anger turns to rage. Another way of describing this is to say that this is where people become completely dedicated to promoting the "win-destroy" or "destroy-destroy" outcome. The primary focus of this book is "mastering" circumstances where anger can be controlled. There is no controlling or influencing the anger of some people when it turns to rage. The best way to deal with rage is to get away from it, and end the interaction. Any communication that is attempted with a person who is truly enraged has the potential to increase anger, regardless of how expertly one tries to de-escalate the behavior. I will not try to convince anyone who goes through this program to remain engaged in conversation or interaction with anyone whose anger continues to escalate to the point of rage. This includes situations where you have tried once or twice to redirect the conversation and have failed, and you observe the situation getting worse instead of better.

De-escalation: Step Five—Success Milestones

Becoming a Facilitator

Success on this critical path is a very impressive milestone. Achieving success at this level will break habits that have led you into difficult times. Your home and work relationships should have improved to the point where you are far less involved in angry interactions, disagreements, and "turf wars" and more involved in productive interactions. Hopefully people are beginning to see you as more of a leader and facilitator and less of an adversary.

Moving to the next critical path, which is called, "Overcoming Angry Themes by Conquering Personalization," requires that you have achieved the following difficult set of success milestones:

Success Milestones for the Third Critical Path

♦ You can identify angry agendas in arguments, interactions, disagreements, and problem situations. You use your knowledge of your own anger agendas to focus your attention away from hurting someone either physically or emotionally and toward redirecting yourself and others to the task of solving the problem.

♦ You understand the four goals of successful de-escalation, which are:

1. To reduce the possibility that your own angry behavior will bring you to the point of doing something that will add to your original problem.

2. To reduce the possibility that you will be hurt either physically or emotionally by the person you are engaged in conflict with.

3. To gain control of angry interactions so that you can most effectively control the outcome, and, if possible, solve the original problem.

4. You can prevent angry interactions from escalating to the point where solving the original problem becomes impossible.

♦ You reject the notion that anger-escalating strategies are effective ways of solving problems and dedicate your efforts to de-escalating angry behavior whenever you become involved in conflict.

♦ You can reduce the possibility that your own angry behavior will bring you to the point of doing something that will add to your original problem.

♦ When you fail to de-escalate your own anger, but can repair damage after the fact, you dedicate yourself to doing so.

♦ You have become comfortable and competent using the L.A.S.H. technique for de-escalating conflict.

♦ You have developed the habit of self-review, and utilizing it after angry confrontations. Ultimately, you seek to review angry behavior close in time to when it is happening, so you can act on it before you damage yourself or others.

♦ You can identify angry habits that you have learned in past relationships and have developed as a matter of personal style. These angry habits include:

  * Bringing past hurts and faults into a conversation.

  * Getting in someone's face.

  * Refusing to allow someone to express themselves.

  * Sarcasm.

  * Condescending and belittling remarks.

  * Giving someone the silent treatment.

  * Suggesting that someone who doesn't agree with you is mentally ill.

  * Cursing and swearing.

  * Raising your voice.

  * Demanding that the other person accept all or most of the blame.

  * Threatening someone with even more hostile interaction in the future.

- You understand the concept of "offspring conflicts" and you have learned to avoid generating or participating in them.
- You are comfortable taking the first action or making the first concession in a disagreement, even if someone else started it.
- You do not consider "win-destroy" or "destroy-destroy" outcomes to be reasonable or positive outcomes to solve problems or resolve conflicts.
- You have mastered the art of "active listening."
- You can acknowledge an adversary's point of view, even when you are in disagreement with it.
- You can communicate economically without giving speeches or taking advantage of an adversary's patience to listen to your side.
- You can communicate without barbs or implied insults.
- You can skillfully redirect an adversarial interaction to move toward a problem-solving effort.
- Using your knowledge of the difference between the "content" of a conversation and the "process" of a conversation, you can successfully manage hostile interactions and de-escalate conflict.
- You can make multiple attempts at de-escalating angry communications if your first attempt fails.
- You avoid pointed questioning as a way of communicating during a conflict or disagreement.
- You have identified anger-maintaining presumptions that keep you locked into and escalating conflict as opposed to detached from and de-escalating conflict.
- You have developed a list of effective affirmations that serve as cues and reminders for you to de-escalate anger in yourself and others.

Chapter 9

Overcoming Angry Themes by Conquering Personalization, the Fourth Critical Path

The last critical path is extremely "task intensive," which is just a fancy way of saying that you have to learn how to do a lot of new things to achieve mastery at this level. The fourth critical path requires less technique but is more difficult because it asks you to point your critical eye at yourself and your lifestyle. This course relies on two very different types of learning. The type of learning associated with the third critical path is understanding how you operate in relation to other people around you. This fourth critical path asks you to look at the way you understand yourself.

The primary benefit of learning techniques such as de-escalation is so that every time we practice the technique and succeed, we are learning to choose or substitute a healthy, problem-solving behavior for an unhealthy, angry mode of behavior. As a beneficial side effect of that choice, you will reduce your level of frustration with the world at large. In simpler terms, you don't have to hate the world so much when you can solve your problems without anger or aggression. Also, you don't have to expect the worst of every situation when you become confident that you can direct and manage the outcome without anger. By contrast, choosing angry methods of problem-solving is unpredictable. You can sometimes win and achieve your goal, or you may lose and possibly get physically or emotionally hurt. After mastering the third critical path, you have learned how to use practical skills to get people off your back, out of your face, and when you want to, even closer to you.

In this next critical path we will revisit some of the angry themes and styles people *invest* in. When you apply the mastery content of this critical path to yourself, you will be making your changes from the inside out—not so much in how you operate in your environment, but from what perspective you view the environment in the first place. If the third critical path helped to expand our set of tools for dealing with others, the fourth critical path concentrates more intensely on the craftsman (you), and the attitude that the craftsman brings to work.

Step One: Mastery Content

Returning to Angry Themes and Styles

To start the mastery content of this critical path, we must do a brief review of the angry themes and styles I talked about in Chapter 4:

> **Angry Themes and Styles From Chapter 4**
> - Being under appreciated and misunderstood.
> - Being perpetually threatened.
> - Being taken advantage of and victimized.
> - Externalizing blame.
> - Being always correct and critical.
> - Always seeking revenge.
> - Being always harsh and insensitive.
> - Being always impatient and inconvenienced.

If you recall, these angry themes and styles serve the purpose of keeping people focused on viewing the world in a negative way. There are benefits to looking at life through one of these negative and angry styles. For one thing, life can seem a lot more predictable when we assume that there is something "wrong" with everyone and everything we encounter. Being "mad at the world" can rarely cause disappointment. After all, because few things in life are perfect, it should be fairly easy to find fault with everyone and everything we encounter. Besides, concentrating on everyone else's imperfections makes us oblivious to our own. The task of improving ourselves is far more difficult than giving advice to others on what *they* need to improve. Take it from me, I hate working on my problems so much I teach others how to "fix themselves" for a living!

Living a Life of Disapproval

Living a life of disapproval is the common thread that runs throughout every angry style of behavior. Just think about how you felt growing up as a kid when your mother, father, or teacher was angry with you. Of all the things you felt, probably the strongest feeling was the feeling of disapproval that comes when an important person is mad at you. When you allow yourself to become absorbed by an angry lifestyle, you communicate a perpetual message of disapproval to everyone you encounter, whether they are important people in your life or strangers. The following is an example of how angry lifestyles are broadcast through everyday behavior:

I disapprove of the way you look, the way you act, the way you drive, the way you speak to me, the way you raise your children, the way you work, the music you listen to, and the food you eat. In fact, I disapprove of the way you interact with me. And if you are not interacting with me, I disapprove of the way you are interacting with everyone else.

Of course you have "the right" to approve or disapprove of anything you wish. The problem comes when you believe that everyone was put on this earth for the purpose of gaining your approval, and that those who do not immediately do so are "bad," substandard, annoying, or *angering*—and this is the first trap people set for themselves when they make life an exercise in *personalization*.

Personalization

Personalization is the process by which you become angry at people for being flawed or imperfect. And on top of that, you act as if they are being flawed specifically to displease or annoy *you*. It is the process of taking someone else's faults and imperfections *personally*. The assumption that occurs when we personalize life's discomforts is the assumption that when people are acting in an unpleasant way it is because they want to cause us displeasure, and not because this is merely the way they are. The following vignette is of that behavior:

The Monster in Seat 32A

This story happened to me while I was writing this very chapter on my homebound flight to New York from a business trip in Texas. The flight was a rather long flight, and because I was determined to get this book finished and published, I even bought an extra battery for my laptop, to ensure I would have enough juice to keep me typing my words of wisdom all the way home. As I walked through the jetway and up the aisle to my seat in the back of the plane, I noticed a child of about 5 or 6 years of age with a crew cut and freckles across his nose, kicking my bag walking directly in back of me. Everytime I would lift or move the bag in back of me out of his "range," he would manage to find some way to kick it harder. His father, standing right behind him and observing the entire event, rested his hand on his son's shoulder as the only form of discipline he would offer. No problem. "I love children," I reminded myself. I was just a little highstrung from the three shots of espresso I had in the terminal before boarding.

As I sat down in seat 32A, the seat no more than 4 feet from what I would soon learn must have been the airline's most smelliest bathroom. I settled in and obediently turned my computer off. upon takeoff. As is my habit, I took a quick catnap until we were at altitude. When the flight attendant announced that I could turn on my "approved electronic device," I was startled at how much turbulence we were encountering so early in the trip. I was soon to discover that the source of the turbulence was the little bag-mangling boy who was careening from side to side in the seat in front of me. It was apparent that he was attempting to rip the seat from its bolts and possibly take it home. Mother and father were both leaning as far back as they could in their seats, with their mouths posed in cavernous, fly-catching circles, sleeping. Being the author of a self-help book on anger management, I could not say any of the things I was thinking such as, "Please sedate your little dervish. I cannot make my wonderful contribution to the world with him systematically taking it apart." Nor could I reach over the seat and duct-tape each of his arms to the armrests, as was my impulse.

As luck would have it, one of the parents awoke and took him to the bathroom, which soon thereafter emitted an odor of megacyclonic proportions. As my anger started to percolate, this became part of my internal dialogue: *I can't believe my luck. All I wanted to do was sit down and write peacefully, and now that child is making my trip miserable. Why aren't his parents containing him? Why don't they care about what he is doing to me?*

When I calmed down a little I started to think about what it would be like to be full of so much energy and trapped in such a small space. This kid was obviously uncomfortable in his own skin. His parents were probably exhausted. I only had to sit near the kid for a few hours, and he was driving me insane. What about them? When do they catch a break? Maybe they were able to get a little bit of sleep because he is acting less wildly than he usually acts. Maybe this was a *good* day for him. Then I started to look at how much writing I had actually gotten done. I wrote nearly 20 pages on this leg of the trip, no more or less than I usually write. What did I really have to complain about?

Prior to forcing myself out of my own angry tirade, I attributed my annoyance to what I believed this little boy was doing to "me." *I* was insulted that his parents did not move and contain him for *me*. *I* was aggravated that no one had any supernatural knowledge of what *I* was doing, how important it was, or how it was being interfered with. The more I thought about it, the more aggravated I became, because it wasn't going away and helping *me*. In other words, I was *personalizing* this little boy's behavior. I could not have peace and quiet. What else would I want if it could have been given to me? Well, a first-class ticket would have been nice. Add to that a foot rub, some lobster tails, and everyone else missing their flight. I could be the only one on the plane and surround myself with all the things I think I deserve. What are the chances of that?

Well, the chances of that are exactly the same as the chances of going through life without encountering any annoying, hyperactive, little boys who are more concerned with working off their nuclear supply of energy than they ever will be about wondering if they are interrupting my self-appointed genius. You see, the little boy wasn't annoying *me*. He was merely being himself and operating in his own imperfect manner. The biggest problem that I was having was choosing to personalize his behavior as though it were being directed at me.

I Don't Like the Way the World Is Set Up, and It Is Really Pissing Me Off

It may sound ridiculous to believe that a person could be pissed off because the world doesn't operate the way any one individual thinks it should operate, but this belief and many like it form the foundation for most angry lifestyles. The perpetually under appreciated and misunderstood person does not get enough "thanks" from his world as he thinks he should, and that pisses him off. The perpetually threatened person does not understand what is wrong with the people in the world, who seem to go out of their way to give him a hard time, while everyone else is left alone. That pisses him off because he should be left alone and not bothered by anything. The person who externalizes blame is pissed off because the rest of the world can't see that nothing is ever really his fault.

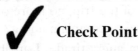

Check Point

The foundation of a lot of angry behavior is the belief that when people are behaving in an unpleasant way, they are doing it just to piss us off.

Anyone who lives exclusively through one angry theme (or alternates between angry themes) is dissatisfied with the world because, remarkably, everywhere they go, everyone acts in exactly the same way, which is against their needs and interests. The end result is that everyone in the world who acts in any disapproved way is annoying, irritating, and *angering*. This can be one of the most difficult AMPs to conquer—the AMP that says, "Anyone who does something I disapprove of bothers me and pisses me off, because they wouldn't be behaving that way if they weren't trying to piss me off." Because chronically angry people who live their lives around angry themes disapprove of just about everything, the world itself becomes a very irritating place. It is a place where no one appreciates *me*, everyone gives *me* a hard time, everyone tries to take advantage of *me*, nobody listens to *me*, nobody gives a shit about *me*, and nobody will listen to *my* better way of doing things.

A Crappy World Is as Good as It Gets—Says Who?

Angry people do not *want* to enjoy life. Enjoying life is too scary and unpredictable. They would rather be searching for the things that validate their notion that "a crappy world is as good as it gets." There isn't a place on this planet where you can put your feet up and not be pissed off about something. Even on your best day, you can find a fault, a flaw, an obnoxious person, an incompetent oaf, a loser, or a moron within a stone's throw. For those who invest in angry lifestyles, *not finding* an offensive person would constitute an utterly disappointing day. It might even force us to look at ourselves to find imperfection. Let's look at another example:

Imbe-cile Phone

Another difficult day commuting from New York has Ron Rager settling into his usual seat on the train and looking forward to a dry martini at home. Just as he is dozing off, he hears the cell phone twinkling tone of *The Lone Ranger* beep-beep-beeping a few seats away from him: "HELLO BOB! BOBBY V! BOBBY VICIOUS! HOW THE HELL ARE YOU! I JUST GOT OUT, AND I KILLED THEM! HEY BOBBY HOW ABOUT MEETING ME FOR SOME BREWSKIES, BUDDY? I'LL BE IN AT 7:15!"

Ron immediately began to fume. "Why is this asshole screaming into his cell phone? Who wants to listen to his conversation?" The phone rang again: "SHEELAH, SWEETIE! WHASSUP SWEETS! BOBBY AND ME ARE GOING TO GRAB THE BUDZ AND SUDZ. MEET US AT MICKEYS? GREAT. LET'S MAKE IT A PAHR-TAY! HEE-YEAH!"

Ron pictured himself saying something to the jerk that would really cut him down, really prove what an inconsiderate idiot he is. He was ruining Ron's ride. As Ron looked around he saw other people making faces. Maybe it was bothering them, too. It sure was bothering him. Part of what is wrong with the world is that no one has the balls to speak up to people like this idiot. God help him if that phone rings again. He would take care of this guy for everyone.

Ring! "HEY JOHNNY OH! WHAT THE HEY, MAN...." Ron could not contain himself. When the man hung up the phone, Ron walked over to the man and put his face right up to him. "Excuse me, but do you have any idea how loud and fucking rude you are? Why does everyone else on this train have to listen to you scream into your damn cell phone?" The man was truly astonished. He had no idea. Ron continued, "Do you actually think anyone gives a shit about you and your beer-drinking friends? You are an inconsiderate ass. Why don't you...."

By the time he could finish his tirade, the conductor was tapping Ron politely on the shoulder and asking him to move to another car. He was frightening some of the passengers. Ron looked around. Everyone was staring at *him* like *he* was the moron.

Ron Rager's problem is that everyone else's problem is *his* problem. He has taken it upon himself to set the standard for all acceptable behavior and to *personally* react to everything that is annoying to him or he presumes to be annoying to everyone else. Ron can't help but react. Everywhere he looks he sees stupidity, rudeness, incompetence, carelessness, ruthlessness, idiocy, lunacy, and those are only the things he sees when he is trying to shut the world out. Ron has a hard time ignoring any of these things because of how it "bothers" him. It makes him cringe to see people acting in a way that is not on his list of "approved" behaviors.

What Ron doesn't realize, is that he has set up the world to disappoint him, and, as a result, the only things he sees are the things he disapproves of. Ron will tell you himself, that he has lost his patience with a world that never seems to get any better, only worse. What he will not tell you is, what he lost way before his confidence in the world was hope that his own life would one day provide the rewards he thinks he deserves. He has worked hard and has not gotten nearly as far as he thinks he should have—all because the world does not value the work he has done or the type of person he is. He is frustrated, and has been for a very long time. That makes him pretty mad, *all the time*.

Life Sucks and Then You Die: How Pessimism Takes the Sting out of Chronic Frustration

It should be pretty easy to make a connection between chronic frustration, the themes of angry lifestyles, and maintaining a negative outlook on life. Retaining a pessimistic outlook helps us stay chronically frustrated. It is what psychologists would call a "maladaptive coping style." This is a fancy term for "coping with the difficulties of life that is effective but has bad side effects." Pessimism and negativity, very important elements of all of the angry lifestyles, are maladaptive coping tools because they abolish hope that life can change for the better. If we abandon hope that life will ever change for the better, we can never be disappointed when things don't turn out the way we want them to.

Retaining the belief that life sucks and will never change is the beginning of developing a chronically grumpy, angry personality. Chronically angry people still have to work, deal

> ✓ **Check Point**
> *A very important belief (AMP) that lies beneath the personality of the chronically angry person is the belief that they live in a screwed up world with screwed up people, and so far nothing has shown them anything different about life. The expectation that life will continue in this fashion, and the loss of hope that it will ever change, allows the chronically angry person to feel like a "victim." Being a constant victim gives people permission to be angry.*

with their families, try to have social relationships, and perform other chores of day-to-day living. Therefore, it is not enough to say, "Life sucks and will never get any better," and then retreat into a corner. You still have to interact with people. Interacting with people is difficult when you believe life is horrible, so you must then include in your perception of life another set of beliefs (AMPs) that sound like this, "I would like to change my mind about this horrible world we live in. It's just that all the people around me are such idiots that they make it even worse." The second belief *(people are horrible)* proves the first belief (the world is horrible), so the chronically angry person is like a mad scientist who seeks to prove every day that the world is screwed up and will never change, and that all of the people he or she interacts with are "proof" that this is so.

This logic is an important part of how people personalize what they experience in order to remain angry and miserable. Ultimately, it translates into a set of AMPs that all sound like this: "I've been alive this long and life hasn't done me any real favors, so why should I have faith in anything?" This becomes the basis for the perception that the angry person is a *victim* of a screwed up world. What is a better way to stay angry than to believe daily that you are a victim? Claims of victimization give people *permission* to be angry. The problem is, through the process of personalization and victimization, we become *selective* about how we experience the world. Like other angry habits, personalization is a process of selective perception. The more we personalize, the more we notice, experience, and search for everything that is annoying, as if it is the only thing that exists in that moment in time.

Four Attitudes Necessary for Conquering Personalization

If you recall, I referred to the process of de-escalation in the last critical path as "task intensive" because it required you to learn a lot of skills in order to master it. Getting a handle on your own tendency to personalize anger-generating aspects of life is easier when you adopt certain attitudes. Doing so requires a reworking of the thoughts and beliefs that mediate or control your behavior. In order to do this, you will not need to rely on very many skills, like in the last critical path. Instead, you will have one major task: to critically examine your *attitudes* about life. This is not a new idea in this program. As a matter of fact, we have addressed the underlying beliefs and attitudes that mediate angry behavior in every section that involves AMPs and affirmations. AMPs are the beliefs that maintain and support angry behavior. Affirmations are the beliefs and self-talk that counteract and reprogram it. In this critical path it will be more important to tune in to AMPs and retrain them with affirmations. This critical path goes to the main gear of the anger-generating mechanism, which is the way people perceive the world, and the way they (mistakenly) think that the negative parts of the world were all put there just to annoy *them*.

The four attitudes that we will concentrate on in this critical path are:

1. Risk-Taking—Replacing pessimism with hope when possible.
2. Expanding the World Viewpoint—Expanding our perception of the environment to include the things that are *not* annoying us, and ignoring the things we cannot change.
3. Empathy—The difficult art of looking at life from someone else's point of view.
4. Forgiveness—Open-mindedness about what we notice as other people's faults.

Risk–Taking

The world is neither predictably "good" nor predictably "bad," because the world, luck, chance, fate, and ultimately, people, are not predictable at all. In order to experience any of the good in life we must take risks. There are a few "nevers" and a few "always," except for the rigid rules we concoct in our heads or the snap judgments we make about people. The quick judgments we make about people can seriously hinder the opportunities we make for ourselves. Have you ever avoided someone because they looked too tough, too nerdy, too manly, too womanly, too stupid, too intellectual, too sneaky, too prudish, too promiscuous, too flaky, too weird, too artsy, too boring, too criminal, or "too" anything else?

Have you ever disliked or hated someone because they gave off "the wrong vibe"? How about this one: Have you ever looked at someone and said, "You know I can tell that guy's whole life story just by the look on his face." (I have, and I am almost always wrong.) Television is a great contributor to the fantasy that villains look a certain "bad" way and "nice people" look a certain "good" way, but they don't. One of the most dangerous people who was ever referred to my office was a sweet, petite, kindly looking woman who had the unfortunate habit of stabbing people she did not like, in public, in plain view of others. She looked "nice." I would have opted to encounter her in a dark alley over say, some 6-foot four man with a crew cut, muscular build, and close-set eyes. Mostly we judge people because they remind us of someone else in one way or another. Heck, most times we don't even do that; we just get a "feeling" or a "hunch."

These feelings or hunches are a natural part of human behavior and it doesn't mean that if you get an occasional feeling that someone is either "good" or "bad," you have an out-of-control anger problem. It probably *does* mean that you have an out-of-control anger problem when you look at *everyone* you know and find something "bad" about them. Chronically angry people have a knack for developing a critical or hostile agenda toward everyone without getting to know them. Or worse yet, after getting to know someone, they concentrate on the negatives and assume any positive characteristic is "phony."

Chronically predatory people make the basic assumption that people are "bad" because predatory people are threat sensitive. In order to justify hurting or victimizing someone, they must operate under the presumption that almost everyone wants to do them harm.

Chronically frustrated people have a long history of disappointment with other people so they may presume all people are bad, as a mechanism to distance themselves from others. In either case, a key to overcoming the burden of having to believe that everyone around you is somehow bad, untrustworthy, unredeemable, toxic, worthless, or stupid is permitting yourself to take a risk. You can only succeed at this risk-taking if you are willing to admit that the "filter" you have developed for screening people is overactive.

Expanding the World Viewpoint

If you have looked far enough into yourself to know that you are selective in the way you view the world, and that all you see is the incompetent and flawed side of life, do not consider yourself either impaired or terrible; merely consider yourself an expert at about *half* of what the world is about. The world is not perfect, after all. I won't try to take that away from you. We have war, poverty, terrorism, corruption, inequality, incompetence—all of the things you have already studied and identified in excruciating detail, especially if you are chronically angry. Now what? *Everything else*, that's what. Life is about variety, and the most ironic and sad aspect about looking at the glass half empty, with a negative, critical, and sarcastic attitude, is that it doesn't make life tremendously less difficult. The individual who personalizes life mistakenly thinks that the world was specifically designed to make things more difficult for them in particular. "Why did *my* car break down today?" "How did *I* get a boss who is such a complete idiot?" "Out of all the people in the whole grocery store, why did *my* cashier's cash register tape crap out when I was in a hurry?"

Expanding your point of view of the world to include the *possibility* that life isn't always as bad as you make it out to be is an important part of the sort of risk-taking I spoke about in the previous section. Making room for that possibility involves allowing yourself to look at life from other people's point of view. That is a skill and an attitude called "empathy."

Empathy

They say that you should never judge a man unless you have walked a mile in his shoes—that's one way of describing empathy. Developing an angry lifestyle that relies on personalization makes it impossible to have empathy, because, if you remember, personalization puts you in a "me-centered" universe. It forces you to think that everything that happens in life has some direct connection to you. Sometimes it doesn't even require a direct connection to you in reality. It can happen in fantasy. You see someone walking toward you. Immediately, they start to "bother" you even though they are minding their own business. Maybe it's the way they look, the way they are dressed, the tune they are humming. *Something* is bothering you. A person you have had no more than 10 seconds of contact with, only through observation is starting to fill your frustration-holding container. Why? The reason why is that you have to feed the monster that maintains the chronically angry lifestyle. When there aren't enough real annoying people in your life, you tend to fantasize and make annoying people out of those you don't even know.

Empathy is the ability to give someone the benefit of the doubt by seeing life through their perspective. It is the art of not assuming that their motivation is evil, hostile, or threatening. Ripping apart someone you don't even know represents a *failure of empathy*. Instead of seeing strangers as people who have families, friends, goals, ambitions, and loving qualities, you see strangers as nuisances, even potential enemies.

Empathy is a skill that can exist in young children or can take a lifetime to master. Our early experiences help to determine whether we are empathic ourselves. As a general rule, the more we are loved and respected as children, the more we tend to cut others some slack. If we grow up around people who are critical, nasty, and mean, that can give us an unfortunate "head start" in perceiving the world in a chronically angry way. Like most behaviors, empathy can be practiced, and in this program it is practiced by examining perceptions of the world and modifying those perceptions when they are rigid, negative, and insensitive.

Looking Back at Yourself Through the Eyes of Someone Else

One of the most challenging forms of empathy to develop is to become empathic ("empathetic" is also correct) to someone who has just experienced a difficult time with you. This is a form of empathy that requires a difficult kind of perspective because it amounts to you saying: "I know it must have been difficult for you to have to deal with me when I was acting that way." You are being empathic to the person's experience of dealing with you when you are not at your best. It is especially important to develop this skill in intimate relationships because personalization is such a common aspect of many lover's quarrels; and when one partner personalizes something, it can bring on a response that is overly personalized, in turn, from their mate. It can become a vicious cycle.

Breaking that cycle requires that one person (both would be better) step outside of the personalized behavior and acknowledge to their partner that they are sorry for taking the issue at hand personally. The empathy portion of that process is to say, "It must have been difficult for you to deal with me while I was having that personalized reaction." Obviously, unless both of you are shrinks, you would not necessarily say it exactly that way, so instead it would be more likely that you would say, "I'm sorry I gave you a hard time," "I'm sorry if I seemed stubborn or unreasonable," or "I'm sorry if I was touchy or angry," followed by, "It must have been a pain in the neck to deal with me in that mood." The empathic portion of the response can go a long way in defusing the situation, because it shows the understanding that you were giving the other person a needlessly difficult time. The following vignette is a typical example of how people who are involved in an intimate relationship with one another can personalize the issue of love-making:

Jane and John

Jane and John, a married couple of six years, have both come home very tired from work. As tired as John is, he would like to "work off his stress" by having sex with Jane, a concept that Jane does not appreciate because her vision of sex is less mechanical and more romantic. Jane gives a halfhearted effort because she is exhausted, and John becomes immediately frustrated and then angry.

> **John:** *Can you tell me what is so difficult about this, or what is so disgusting about me that you cannot bring yourself to make love to me?*
>
> **Jane:** *It has nothing to do with you, John. I am exhausted. I had a hard day.*
>
> **John:** *I had a hard day, too, but it wasn't that hard that I can't have sex for 15 minutes.*
>
> **Jane:** *I'm sorry, I don't feel the same way. It's not you.*
>
> **John:** *Not me? Who is it, then? How come I can't get you to pay attention to me?*
>
> **Jane:** *Pay attention? Is that another way of saying, "make sure you get yours so you can fall asleep"? That kind of pisses me off. Are you saying I should act like a whore just because you want to release your "tension"? I'm sorry. I think I am better than that. I am allowed to be tired. Good night.*
>
> **John:** *I'm going downstairs.*
>
> **Jane:** *Good night. The brothel is closed. Try again tomorrow.*
>
> **John:** *Very nice.*

In this example, Jane and John have personalized reactions, and neither can take the other's point of view. It is easy to see how the personalization aids the failure of empathy. The more you take something personally, the less you can see the other person's point of view.

Ultimately, and predictably, the argument escalates to the point of John sleeping in another room, and Jane makes an insulting wisecrack upon his exit. John took Jane's lackluster sexual interest as a sign of disinterest in *him*. This created frustration and anger. Jane then took John's anger personally to suggest that John expected her to act in a way that was insulting to her perception of herself. The argument could have been avoided or de-escalated by both Jane and

John acknowledging that they were taking things too personally. John might have used empathy to admit that it must have been difficult for Jane to tolerate him acting like he did. Jane could have done the same on her side. At the very least this would have gotten them to sleep without the stress of an open argument, and take a fresh start to re-examining their love life.

Forgiveness

Many people think that the most difficult sentence in the world to utter is, "I love you." I disagree. I think there are two sentences that are far more difficult to utter. I believe the two most difficult sentences to say are, "I'm sorry" and "I forgive you."

This section is about forgiveness, which is a most undervalued and unappreciated behavior. When we think about what kind of characteristics make for a person we want to spend significant amounts of time with, we usually choose the characteristics of "loving," "giving," "intelligent," "charming," "sense of humor," and maybe a few others. For my money, I'll take "forgiveness" as one of the top three. I don't know about you, but I screw up a lot. I need a lot of forgiveness. Actually, most of us do. What we need, and what we are willing to dish out, however, are often not equivalent commodities. The chronically angry person has terrific difficulties with forgiveness. He or she may demand to be excused of all their faults and misgivings but be punitive and harsh when people make mistakes that require their good graces. Sometimes the underlying presumptions (the AMPs) that feed the anger will not permit it. Here are some examples:

> **Anger-Maintaining Presumptions That Prevent Forgiveness**
> - "People who do bad things to me deserve to be punished."
> - "When people make mistakes, the lessons they learn from being punished are for their own good."
> - "People are never sorry for the things they do wrong."
> - "When I make a mistake, it is an honest mistake. When other people make a mistake, it is because they have gotten caught trying to get away with something they shouldn't have been doing."

(List continued on next page.)

- "When I make a mistake at work it is minor. If someone else makes a mistake at work, they do not deserve to work anymore because they are too incompetent."
- "When I hurt someone's feelings it is often unintentional. When someone hurts my feelings it is because they have it in for me."
- "If you forgive people too easily, they will consider it a sign of weakness and walk all over you."
- "If someone does something bad to me, and I make them pay for it, they will think twice about doing it again."

Chronically angry people may see forgiveness as an undesirable trait that makes them vulnerable to looking like a "chump." This would be particularly so in the character of the predatory angry person who, in the worst of cases, has no capacity for either empathy or forgiveness and, as a result, has little capacity for love. Personalization and empathy are opposing forces. The more you personalize a reaction to something, the less you can see from anyone else's point of view or perspective. This is often what causes couples and other people in close relationships to fight with one another. An essential ingredient to ending any conflict is being able to show that you can be sensitive to the other person's perspective.

Forgiveness as a Charitable Contribution

Forgiveness can be a very powerful tool to depersonalize the impulsive, critical, and angry judgments we make about people and about life. If forgiveness is a difficulty for you, one way to develop the trait is to consider it a form of charity. Even grumpy, irritable, chronically angry people will donate a buck or two to charity on the right day. I'll tell you how to save yourself some money and make a more valuable charitable donation to the human race. Make a donation to the PICS Foundation. You've never heard of the PICS Foundation, you say? The PICS Foundation is The People I Can't Stand Foundation, and if you are the chronically angry type, the list of people you can donate to is probably very, very long. The donation you can make is not in time or money, but in patience and tolerance. Consider a "small" donation a day of not ripping apart anyone you don't like, just for fun.

Just forgive them for being imperfect. A "medium" donation would be showing extra patience to someone who is a regular, but harmless, pain in the ass. A "large" donation would be to do something nice for a person who is a large pain in the ass.

Something in It for You: Emptying the Frustration Container

You can practice forgiving people on a number of levels. Forgive those who you don't know and who bother you just by taking up space on your planet. Forgive those who you do know and who you believe were put on this earth to make your life a living hell. It might help to remember that, like most of us, people who "don't get it" or whom we mistakenly assume don't get it, suffer from having to live with themselves, their quirks, and their real deficits. Worse yet, they also have to deal with *you*, and your faults and imperfections! Whenever you forgive someone else, you reap several immediate benefits. First, you take a huge scoop out of that frustration-holding container that contributes to the chronically angry lifestyle. Second, forgiving people deactivates AMPs such as "All people are stupid," "This guy walking toward me is ugly," "I hate men," "I hate women," "I hate people."

An even greater benefit is that, if you continue to forgive people for their faults, eventually *you will forgive yourself* for your own. Chronically angry people, especially those who are frustrated (as opposed to those who are predatory) often do not like their own behavior. They feel self-conscious about being so angry, and as much as they criticize others, they are equally critical of themselves (this is not true of the predatory angry person). They resent their own impatience and intolerance. Like a cigarette smoker who can't give up the impulsive habit of smoking, the frustrated chronically angry person may want to be less angry, but at the same time succumb to the angry habits they have developed over a lifetime of reacting in hostile and impatient ways. The more "permission" you give others to be human, imperfect, selfish, and prideful, the more you will understand these traits in yourself. You will not hate in others what you hate in yourself.

Quitting the angry lifestyle is a complicated process. That is why I say it takes a lifetime of dedication, where you devote blocks of time to conquering certain aspects of anger (these blocks of time are the critical paths). You can't quit the angry lifestyle "cold turkey." You can, however, successfully manage and redirect yourself away from it.

Good, Bad, and Every Flavor in Between

Part of what interferes with our ability to forgive is the tendency for chronically angry people to divide the world into two distinct categories of "good" and "bad." Adding insult to injury, the "bad" category usually contains a lot more entries than the "good" category, and that happens because of AMPs such as "The world is a terrible place to live." With AMPs such as this floating around in your head, much of what you will see will almost certainly be bad. The best you might come across is the occasional "tease" of finding something tolerable in an otherwise miserable existence. When that fleeting moment is over, it is likely to heighten your frustration because it did not last, or was so rare.

Much of what we have been talking about on this critical path requires expanding our inventory categories, and sometimes creating new categories. Here are a few you might not have considered that land between "good" and "bad":

Between "Good" and "Bad"

Good

Good, but having a bad day...

Good in this setting or role; bad in this setting or role...

Good, but could be better...

Good enough to live on the same planet, but I wouldn't want to be his next-door neighbor...

Good enough to deserve another chance...

Not good enough to date my daughter, but with improvement, who knows?

Bad

Bad, but not hopeless...

Bad, but with a lot of work, less bad...

Bad today, but I hardly know him; maybe better tomorrow...

Bad to me, but I have seen better behavior toward other people...

Bad enough to want to avoid; not so bad we have to kill him.

There are a lot more. See if you can come up with some of your own. For angry people, finding the gray area of life requires some creativity and a sense of humor. Some angry people have excellent senses of humor because part of what makes things funny is exaggeration. We will see in the next step of this critical path how exaggeration can be used negatively or positively as a coping strategy.

Like many of the concepts that I promote in this program, I do not expect you to snap your fingers and become more empathic, less prone to personalizing, and more prone to forgiving. All positive change begins with a single thought such as, "Maybe I should consider being a little more forgiving." The thought is followed by an experiment, where you can try acting on what you have been thinking about. Sometimes the experiment is so successful that a change in behavior is almost immediate. More commonly, the experiment takes a lot of practice and must be conducted a dozen, hundred, or thousand times.

Step Two: Coping Strategies

Interrupting Bad Habits

The coping strategies for all of the critical paths are methods and cues to "stop and think" about what you are doing, how you are behaving, and what impulses you are acting on. Whenever we inappropriately express anger, escalate conflict, or personalize what is happening around us, we act on impulses that are fueled by illogical assumptions and snap judgments. Over time, these impulses become *habits* and angry behavior becomes automatic. A person walks toward me with headphones, sunglasses, and a bop in his step. He is singing at the top of his lungs, and obviously doesn't mind drawing attention to himself. He is different than I am. One of my AMPs kicks in: "Anyone who doesn't act the way I would act is a moron." I make a snap judgment: "This guy is an ass." I personalize it: "He is acting this way to bother me." The entire process takes place in a split second and is only one of many more angry interactions that will float through my head in a given day. Because a lot of angry behavior is impulsive, learning how to arrest that impulse and stop ourselves is important. That's probably how the common wisdom of "stop and count to 10" was born. In the prior critical paths we have learned that angry behavior is the result of viewing the world we live in through a set of angry presumptions (AMPs) that make us so infuriated or enraged that we tend to act in one of two ways: (1) to work off some of that frustration in the form of angry behavior because we cannot bear it any longer, or (2) to direct predatory anger against another person because we have decided that is a justifiable way to achieve a goal.

So far the way that we have tried to reduce anger in our minds and thoughts is by practicing affirmations, a key component of all of the critical paths. Affirmations work by training your thoughts to key emotions or your focus to logical, practical, and positive interpretations of life. We all know that the more we repeat certain ideas to ourselves, the more they become true in our minds. This works for "good thoughts" as well as "bad thoughts." Liars can repeat their distorted realities to themselves to the point of believing they are true. It also works in reverse. We can step back into the real, logical, practical world by repeating thoughts that improve our ability to cope. Affirmations are the "big all-purpose tool" for retraining our beliefs and mediating angry behavior, but they are not the only tool. In this critical path, we are going to concentrate on some other tools that help us do this as well.

Untwisting the Logic of Personalized Actions

Before the age of 5 we all develop an uncanny skill for being able to justify selfish behavior by pretending that it benefits someone or something else. Take my 5-year-old nephew, for example. He likes to feed my fish. As soon as he learned that he could only feed the fish a tiny bit of food and only once per visit with me, he came up with the justification that he needed to feed the fish because they were *hungry*. They needed *him* to feed them. For all anyone knows, they could have been hungry; however, it is hard to escape the possibility that my nephew feeds the fish more for his own need than the fishes. A similar type of logic prevails when we personalize what we disapprove of. We convince ourselves that the anger and aggression we are about to display is for the good of everyone (even though it isn't). We sometimes even go a step further by punishing those that offend us.

Do you remember the story of Ron Rager, the guy who couldn't stand listening to another person speak on his cell phone in a loud and obnoxious way? Ron reasoned that he was doing the world a favor by confronting the offensive passenger. He wasn't, even though people might have agreed that the person who was talking on the phone was annoying. He was doing "himself" a favor because the behavior of the guy on the phone was bothering him. He was merely using his belief that he was doing the world a favor to justify his anger. After Ron convinced himself that he was some sort of cell-phone-abuse super hero, it was easy for him to punish the offender. Ron twisted the logic of his actions by allowing himself to believe he was teaching this person "a lesson." This is probably one of the most common ways that people bring themselves to the point of angrily acting out. The mechanism that allowed Ron to act out in an angry way was put into motion by his personalization of the annoyance.

What Am I Responsible for Anyway?

Ron concluded that he was doing everybody on the train a favor when he jumped up and started screaming at the passenger for speaking too loudly on his cell phone, but he did not weigh it against how other people might have felt about seeing two people engaged in a nasty argument. People can be put off when others fight or bicker. Perhaps it would have been different if Ron were saving a fellow passenger from being mugged. Maybe people would have tolerated, even applauded, Ron's ability to confront or attack the offending person. When we engage in personalization, we distort logic to convince ourselves that angry, inappropriate behaviors serve some worthwhile purpose. Excessive anger can fool us into believing that we are responsible for "fixing" and improving the behavior of others who annoy us, not for our own sake, but for the sake of everyone else.

It is no different when we are engaged in a more personal argument with someone we are intimately connected to: a lover, spouse, or family member. In these situations, anger is also used as a weapon allegedly to "teach a lesson," but it is really used as a means of permitting angry actions. This is the very basis for what people call "head games" in a relationship. We often presume that "head games" in love relationships are very complex manipulations. Mostly they are not. They are angry feelings that have been transformed by the twisted logic of personalization. Untwisting the logic that turns selfishness into what is good for the rest of the world is a matter of asking yourself exactly when it was that you were made responsible for someone else's behavior. If you conclude that your intent was noble but your execution was off, ask yourself these questions:

- "Is there another, more respectful way of educating some-one, especially the people you care about?"
- "Is there any other way you can teach people by setting a more appropriate example?"
- "Is this the way you like to be treated when someone is trying to teach *you* a lesson?"

There is nothing wrong with taking on the responsibility to make the world a better place to live in. However, accepting that responsibility means that you actually have to do something that does the world some good, not merely disguise an angry fit by wrapping it up in the twisted logic of personalization.

The coping lesson in all of this is to determine what purpose your angry behavior serves. Examine even more critically those times you believe you are doing the world a favor by teaching lessons to those who make you angry. The best lesson you can teach anyone is the one you teach by example.

Making the Unimportant Important

Personalization inhibits the ability to effectively deal with anger. The thinking behind it goes something like this: *If so-and-so's annoying behavior wasn't bothering me it would be meaningless and unimportant. Because it is bothering me, it automatically becomes important because it is personally insulting and I want it to stop.*

Coping with this type of distorted thinking requires that you ask yourself if it is necessary to believe that everything that bothers you is important. Here is where we need to make an important connection. Let's go back to the container that holds our frustration and disappointment. Those of us who carry around a container that is almost full all of the time can't afford to decide what is important and what is not because *everything* or *anything* can put us over the top. This is a good place to point out that inability to moderate frustration and keep that container as empty as possible places us in a state of readiness to act out in angry ways. It prevents us from properly evaluating what is important and what is not because there is little room to absorb the stresses and strains of daily life, some of which comes from having to deal with annoying people. If you find yourself falling into the trap of reacting as though everything is important enough to become angry over, it is time to look for ways to empty that container. One way to begin is to understand that expressing anger in unhealthy ways is a toxic process. It damages your physical and emotional health. For me to invest in a process that is ultimately going to hurt me, it has to be pretty important. Ask yourself how many people or things are important enough to make you want to damage yourself over.

Step Three: Communication Strategies

Developing Empathy and Forgiveness, and Dealing With Frustration

This critical path emphasizes how you can modify your thinking and perceptions so that you do not feel as though you need to confront everyone who is doing something annoying. There are times, however, when it might be appropriate to confront someone who is interrupting your ability to enjoy something. There is no harm in trying to persuade that person (or people) from stopping what he or she is doing, as long as you are capable of dealing with the possibility that person you are speaking to might not have read this book and might tell you to *go screw yourself*. I don't say this just for effect. I say it to remind you that part of the reason for understanding anger is that it is a very big part of the world we live in; and while it might be your goal to moderate your own anger, there are many people who could care less, are angry, want to stay that way, and will say precisely that to you in their own words or actions. When we encounter people such as this, it is sometimes a very difficult lesson in personalization because, even if you have gotten to the point of not taking the annoying behavior of others personally, it is an even harder task to remain calm when you approach someone politely and they are personally insulted in return. One way to keep your cool is to "inoculate" yourself.

The Inoculation

Okay, you are going to say something. Common sense tells us to be polite; however, while polite behavior may *encourage* politeness from others, it does not *guarantee* it. You must be prepared to deal with the circumstance of a person being offended merely because you entered their personal space and said something they perceive as a criticism. Of course, if you know the person, you might have a good idea of how they might react. If you don't know the person, do not make any assumptions except that the person is *not* going to be responsive to your politeness. In other words, presume the worst and be pleasantly surprised at the best. This way, if your polite approach is met with angry, rude, or obnoxious behavior, you can shrug it off and walk away. (Remember the L.A.S.T technique? If not, you might want to go back to the second critical path and review.)

Preparing yourself for the worst-possible response is a way of inoculating yourself against the sort of shock people receive when they make a request in a polite tone and are rebuffed in a nasty or angry manner. In the following sections, you will find suggestions on how to maximize your chances of redirecting rude or obnoxious behavior without letting anger get the best of you.

P.A.W. at Them

Postulate, Apologize, and *Wonder* are ways of opening your request for someone to change his or her behavior. Postulate means *to inquire*, as in:

- "Do you think I could ask you to turn down your radio a bit?"
- "Do you think you could be so kind as to remove your car from the spot that is blocking mine?"
- "Could I trouble you to clean off your plate?"

Apologies are not necessary in the real sense, but are often considered a polite form of speech. To put a person you are going to make a request to at ease, you might try apologizing for interrupting them from whatever it is they are doing, as in:

- "I am sorry to bother you, but..."
- "I hope you do not find it too much of an inconvenience if I ask you..."
- "Please forgive me for disturbing you, but would you mind..."
- "I wonder if you would mind my asking..."

- "I wonder if it would be too much trouble for you to..."
- "I wonder if it would be all right for me to ask you to..."

These techniques require practice if you are the type of person who is usually gruff or very straightforward. Sometimes a little finesse can go a very long way.

The Presumed Rejection

Asking politely is not a guarantee of a polite response in return. Expecting that people will always return polite questions with polite answers can lead you to form AMPs that only bring you back to the point of feeling frustrated and angry. An example of one such illogical assumption is: "If I take the time and trouble to be nice to someone they had better be nice to me...."

Unfortunately, if you live life with the expectation that every good deed you do will be returned immediately, you will often be disappointed. Your disappointment will build frustration, and your frustration will motivate you to anger. Instead, approach the situation hoping to be pleasantly surprised by the response you receive.

Don't Forget to Say "Thank You"

We forget some of the most basic social skills when we take on the burden of living the chronically angry lifestyle—the "pleases," "thank you's," and "your welcomes," for instance. Whether your P.A.W.s are addressed or ignored, do not be so quick to fly off the handle at how rude someone is for not meeting a polite request. The only thing this will accomplish is to provide the opportunity to engage in an *offspring conflict*. A sign of success in moving through each critical path is that the more advanced you become, the less offspring conflicts you let yourself advance or participate in. When things do not go as you would like, you must be satisfied that you have tried to make life a little easier for yourself (there is no harm in that as long as you do not *demand* it in an angry way), and you may have even encouraged the person you are making the request of to control their behavior at a time when their pride is not on the line.

If your request is honored, a simple "thank you" will do. If your request is ignored or responded to in a nasty or aggressive way a simple, "I am sorry to have disturbed you," may actually cause the person to calm down and (begrudgingly) redirect their behavior. Some people need the opportunity to have a small and childish temper tantrum when they are asked to control themselves. This should give you a very clear idea of what the emotional capacity of the person you are dealing with is.

Communicating Forgiveness With and Without Words

In the mastery content portion of this critical path, I emphasized the value of forgiving people for their imperfections as a way of depersonalizing your response to them. There are many ways to forgive people, ranging from, "I forgive you because I love you" to "I forgive you for being a jerk, because I am aware that, as a jerk, you have no capacity to control your behavior. Therefore, I should not take your jerky behavior personally, and neither will I kick your ass for it." It's not likely that you would actually *say* either of these sentences to someone. Each of them more accurately reflects the internal language we use to control our behavior and reaction to things.

When it is necessary to forgive the people we love, there are often no "best words" to use. The true (and most difficult) forgiveness comes from not giving them a hard time or making unreasonable demands on them. In other words, ignoring stupidity and insensitivity is sometimes the best form of forgiveness we can practice. It makes the world a little better for lack of spreading unnecessary anger; and it is a good form of charity (as we discussed in the mastery content portion). It is also economical. Saying nothing doesn't require fancy brainwork, and snappy sarcasm when things don't go the way you plan. As with many things in life, less is more.

While forgiveness is often something that doesn't require more than just an attitude and willingness to tolerate certain faults and flaws, there are times seeking forgiveness and giving forgiveness in words and actions are important turning points in relationships. Certainly, an important aspect of giving forgiveness to someone we love is to do it freely and with no strings attached.

Because we must often forgive in an atmosphere where we may have been hurt and may still be angry, it is possible to "give with one hand and take with the other" by forgiving someone and then threatening them, for instance, by saying, "I'll let it slide this time but if you ever do it again, I'll...."

Another way that people show their anger when someone is trying to mend a fence with them is to capitalize on the fact that the other person is apologizing and demand what I call "retroactive apologies," or apologies for past hurts that go back to the beginning of time, as in, "Now that you have admitted you were wrong about this, admit that you were wrong about...." If it is your impulse to respond to an apology in this way, it would be much better to take a time-out and cool off before trying to address the apology. A person who is apologizing can feel very vulnerable. Hitting them when they are down might cause another angry argument to erupt and undo the original intention.

It is often sensitive and helpful if we forgive people with words that imply we are no more perfect than they are. When we do this, we can show *empathy* and *forgiveness* at the same time. The following are some examples:

- "I know how frustration can get the better of someone. It happens to me, too. I am going to let it go."
- "It's hard to be patient all of the time. We have both regretted losing our tempers. I forgive you."
- "I wish it didn't happen, but nobody's perfect, me included. I forgive you."
- "I hope this ends with us both feeling better about things. Hearing you say you are sorry makes me feel better. I know how difficult it can be to apologize when you are angry. Thank you."

✓ **Check Point**

Developing the skill of forgiveness is essential to learning how to depersonalize anger and overcome your angry themes. Forgiving helps empty the frustration container that keeps people in a state of readiness to be angry.

Forgiveness is an art, and it is developed with time and maturity. Having something to hold over a person's head is a common theme in many dysfunctional relationships. That makes forgiveness impossible because forgiveness should signal an absolute end to whatever caused the problem in the first place.

Some people are "grudge-holders." Holding a grudge is a convenient way of reactivating personalized feelings from past conflicts. Grudges are reminders

that someone had the gall to do something bad *to me*. Forgiving someone releases us from the burden of having to retain the anger that
comes from the personalized insult. Of all the reasons why it is important to forgive the people we love, the most important reason is
selfishness. It is to be able to feel comfortable asking those same people
for forgiveness when we screw up.

Asking Forgiveness

Asking for forgiveness or apologizing is a difficult thing for most
people to do. For some reason, "owning up" has become something
of a taboo in our society. Nobody does it unless they are pressed
firmly up against the wall. The real problem in *not* owning up is that it
requires so much work. Often, it means remaining embroiled in a
feud. It requires gossiping to other people to gain sympathy and support, and it forces you to present yourself at your worst while you act
defensively and full of self-righteousness. This is all another way of
saying that it requires you to remain attached to your personalized
perceptions, even when you are dead wrong. What's the point of that?
It is often not worth it.

In every conflict there is always *something* to apologize for, and if
you cannot identify the source of your own misbehavior, try searching for whether or not you took anything that happened between you
and the person you are in conflict with *too personally*. From there all
you need to do is acknowledge that you acted impulsively and insensi-
tively and you are home-free. Most "wrongs" that occur in the context of close relationships occur because someone is either (1) selfish,
(2) aggressive, or (3) insensitive. These would be three excellent
categories to explore the next time you are having a fight with someone you are close to, and you would like to do your part to reduce the
anger. Once again, the best words are those that are the most forthcoming and take no more than a few seconds to say: "I am sorry I was
so insensitive." "I am sorry I was so angry and mean." "I am sorry I
was so selfish." "I am sorry that I took it so personally."

Beware of the Un-apology

As simple as these sentences are, they are completely impossible
for many chronically angry people to say. The most some people can
do is provide a lame excuse for their behavior, something I call the
"un-apology." Here are some examples:

Examples of Un-apologies

- "I'm sorry. My blood sugar was low and I just wasn't myself..."
- "I was tired..."
- "I have been under a lot of stress..."

"When I heard the things you were saying I couldn't control myself..."

- "You were provoking me, and I lost my temper..."

When people offer these apologies, what they are really saying is: "I screwed up, but it really wasn't my fault." Acceptance of blame and responsibility are very important aspects of repairing damage done by anger. By refusing to accept responsibility, it is difficult for people to accept your apology. An apology requires that you step outside of your own personal frame of reference and relate to what the person you are apologizing to is feeling.

Here are some modifications that make the previous un-apologies turn back into more genuine apologies:

Turning Un-apologies Into Genuine Apologies

- "I'm sorry. My blood sugar was low and I just wasn't myself, but that is not an excuse to have hurt your feelings. I can understand how you were upset by my behavior, and I will make a better effort to be more sensitive."
- "I was tired, but that is not an excuse to take my irritability and discomfort out on you. In the future I will try to be more patient, and I will keep my temper under control."
- "I was under a lot of stress, but I should have realized that you were under stress, too. Everybody is, and that does not justify me blowing up and getting out of control. That was bad judgment on my part, and I am very sorry for the way I behaved."
- "Instead of concentrating on my own behavior, I was focusing on yours. That was wrong. I'm sorry.

One type of un-apology that is impossible to turn into a real apology because it is an insult takes one of these forms:

> **Insults Disguised as Apologies**
>
> "I should have never let you get me so mad..."
>
> "I should have known better than to interact with you when you are in such a bad mood..."
>
> "I should learn to keep my mouth shut when you are having an off day..."

These statements merely invite more arguing and escalation of anger because what they are really saying is: "I'm sorry for being so stupid that I didn't realize it is pointless to have a civilized discussion with you." The best apologies stay focused on your role, your responsibility, and your desire to make things easier for the person in the future.

Exaggeration and Absolutism

At least for the purpose of dealing with conflict and angry feelings, there are about a handful of words and phrases that should be stricken from the English language. They are presented in the box below:

> **Words That Express Exaggeration, Personalization, and Victimization**
>
> **Definitely**—"I am *definitely* not the one who should be apologizing for your nasty behavior."
>
> **Horrible**—"This is *horrible*. I can't take dealing with you anymore."
>
> **Always, Each, and Every Time**—Why does it *always* have to come down to this, *each* and *every time*?"
>
> **Finally, Nothing, and Ever**—"When will you *finally* get it through your thick head that *nothing* will *ever* get straightened out unless you examine your behavior."
>
> **Everything, Nothing, Zilch, Zero, and Nada**—"You don't get it. I do *everything* around here and I get nothing back. That's right *nothing, zilch, zero, nada*."

These words and phrases and many others like them are words that communicate extremes as in, "You *never* listen to me when I talk to you." It is a safe bet to say that when someone is using these kinds of absolute statements within an argument, what they are saying is, "You have something against *me* and that is why you refuse to listen to me." Extreme statements that use absolutes and exaggerations increase feelings of personalization on both sides of an argument. This kind of "button pushing" escalates anger.

Personalization and Self-Victimization

Anyone who personalizes the negative aspects of life long enough will ultimately conclude that they are *victims*—victims of an unfair world, victims of other people's rudeness and stupidity, victims of bad luck. From the point of view of the victim who falls into this role through personalization, it is easy to justify being chronically angry. After all, once a person reaches the conclusion that *life itself* has been designed to victimize them, what better reason is there to be perpetually angry? If you think back to the themes of the chronically angry person, the majority of those themes are built around lack of appreciation, lack of other people's willingness to understand, and other kinds of imagined victimization.

The sense of victimization brought on by looking at the world through angry themes and by personalizing life's negative events is a function of a kind of chronic exaggeration that angry people frequently engage in. Chronically angry people, whether they are frustrated or predatory, look at life in a very dramatic and magnified way to prove the point that life was either designed to screw them, or that aggressive behavior is the only way to deal with life's difficulties.

Chronic anger is an *attitude*, and attitudes can be healthy or unhealthy in part as a function of how accurately they reflect reality. Attitudes are collections of beliefs that govern and motivate behavior. We have been discussing the beliefs that govern and motivate behavior throughout this book whenever we talk about AMPs. If you carefully study the AMPs presented in this book, you will see that many of the perceptions that form the basis of AMPs are exaggerations. Part of developing affirmations that fight those AMPs is to discover and unearth those exaggerations and modify them to be more reasonable reflections of what happens in the real world. For instance, take the AMP "The world is full of idiots." The way we transform that AMP into something more constructive is by acknowledging that there *are* annoying people in the world, but there are also many good people as well. Taking the exaggeration out of the AMP restores hope that life can change for the better. Allowing the exaggeration to remain merely encourages us to keep looking for the bad in life and ignoring the good.

I'll finish this section by pointing out that using extreme language is one way we reinforce the connection between personalized attitudes and angry behavior. The bigger and more extreme or absolute the word or phrase is, the more justification there is for angry behavior. This is one of the ways people use to "talk themselves into" angry behavior—people hear what they are saying (and the absolute and exaggerated ways they are saying it), believe it, and their words become "proof" of how victimized they are. A more fancy or technical way of saying this is, "absolute and extreme language becomes *self-confirming.*"

Suspension of Belief

Another type of absolutism is *suspension of belief.* Refusing to believe that there is any other explanation other than the belief that the world is horrible, everything is always someone else's fault, and unpleasant feelings are the result of what has been contrived or masterminded to upset *me,* is an indication of personalization. The way this appears in person-to-person communication is in sentences that begin with, "I can't believe...." In reality what these communications invariably mean is, "I refuse to believe...(anything else)" *or* "I can only believe..."

For example the phrase "I can't believe you would do this to me" really means, "I can *only* believe you are doing this to me, because you hate me...." Depending on the context in which it is used, *"I can't believe..."* can also mean:

- "I can't believe you are not taking the full blame for this."
- "I can't believe how poorly you are treating me."
- "I can't believe how stupid you are."
- "I can't believe that you can't see how stupid I think you are."
- "I can't believe that you are not on your knees begging for my forgiveness."

What the "I can't believes" often indicate is refusal to acknowledge responsibility for part of the conflict. "I can't believe..." is often the equivalent of saying, "I deny responsibility for...." Movement along this critical path is about relieving yourself of the burden of personalization and victimization, and, instead, taking responsibility for actively directing the outcome of events around you.

Moderating Extreme and Absolute Language

Using extreme and absolute words and phrases is a habit. People who exaggerate when they are angry tend to overstate themselves in everyday speech, even when they are not angry. Everyday conversations that do not revolve around conflict are a great place to begin the process of retraining yourself toward a more *understated* use of language. When you catch yourself saying absolute words and phrases, try the following instead:

Instead of:

"Every time I go to that gas station I have to wait half an hour before I can get anyone to come over to the car...."

Try:

"Well not *every* time, but it really annoys me when it happens and it has happened more than once...."

Instead of:

"The food in that new Chinese restaurant was *absolutely horrible.*"

Try:

"The food in that new Chinese restaurant was very disappointing."

Instead of:

"The traffic on the expressway was a fucking nightmare."

Try:

"The traffic on the expressway was backed up again."

The reason why I suggest you moderate *all* of your language is that it is easier to commit to recognizing and altering everyday talk because it occurs when you are not necessarily enraged and you are not wrapped up in any conflict. Succeeding in everyday language is much easier at first and will help you to catch yourself when you are exaggerating or overstating yourself in more frustrating, anger-evoking situations.

A second way to moderate your language is to ask someone you trust to point it out to you from time to time. Give them a list of your personal extreme words and absolutes. Just remember, anytime you ask someone to help you with a bad habit, you run the risk of them actually doing the job *well.*

Third, as a substitute for "I can't believe," try saying, "I want to know more about...." Instead of saying, "I can't believe you just said that to me," try saying, "I'd like to know more about why you just said that to me. It's very upsetting to hear and I want to straighten this out." Then, after you say that, just *listen.* It is very difficult to listen without reacting, especially when it feels like you are being attacked or criticized. This becomes easier to do when you are not listening for the words that are personal insults against you, but, instead, asking yourself what is motivating this person to communicate whatever it is they are telling you. This is a time when focusing on the process is much more important than the content. If you encounter someone that calls you an "idiot," their choice of words may be rude and disrespectful, but is there anything reasonable behind what might have gotten them upset enough to say it? Sometimes there is not, and a person who is rude and disrespectful is just a rude, disrespectful person. Sometimes there is something reasonable behind why they have become so angry. Looking at it from a slightly different perspective, if you curse and swear at someone when you are angry, are you ruining the opportunity to express yourself in a way that will permit someone to examine their own behavior and treat you in a more positive way?

Effective Communication Produces Opportunity

In order to succeed at anything in life we must have opportunity. Very few of us are "born lucky," without the need to worry or care about working in some way to direct the courses of our lives. Of all of the things that excessive anger destroys, it has a very serious effect on opportunity. Effective communication can create opportunity. The words we use; the subtle choices we make when we speak and interact with others; and, most importantly of all, avoiding exaggeration, can make the difference between producing good opportunities or destroying them. When we interact with the people we love, communication during problem times creates the opportunity for deepening the relationship. When we communicate effectively at work, it is often a sign of competence and leadership, and that creates opportunity. That opportunity is easily ruined when people insult one another, belittle one another, and harass one another. This is true at home or in the workplace. Whenever you are forced to interact with someone in a tense, uncomfortable, or conflict-ridden situation, you should ask yourself if you are expressing your thoughts, feelings, and beliefs in a way that is creating or destroying opportunity.

People communicate in angry ways often because they do not feel as though anything positive can come out of an interaction that is driven by civilized conversation. When people are cut off from feeling as though they can achieve something useful, they become frustrated. And as we know, frustration can produce very angry modes of responding. When people convince themselves that nothing positive can come out of an interaction, the act of releasing anger and frustration becomes the most positive thing one can achieve. People tend to make this decision prematurely because of assumptions they make about the situation. For instance, in the middle of an argument or disagreement, you may conclude, "This person is a moron, they will never get my point." (Do you recognize this? It is an AMP.) If you have not put enough effort into examining the validity of this presumption you may not be able to cash in on the opportunity that the interaction might present. Is it worth it to write off a potentially good job because you felt put off and angry at your employer in the first interview? Will you cut off a person who may become a good friend or partner because you concluded that they were "bad," "stupid," or otherwise undesirable without exploring the opportunity that might make itself known if you had given it a little more of a chance?

The moment you engage someone in an angry, hostile, and critical way, you destroy whatever opportunity exists in that relationship. Sometimes those opportunities come back to you in very roundabout ways. Recently, I spoke to a college professor who told me a delightful story about a student of his who really tried his patience. The student was unruly, interrupted his lectures, and carried on in an arrogant way. Instead of embarrassing the student, this professor took him aside and told him that he thought he had great potential, but that he needed to develop better social skills. The advice didn't seem to click at the time; the student remained annoying. Ten years later, the student called the professor and remarked that his advice was the best advice he had ever received, although he didn't have the good sense to follow it until after he graduated. Nonetheless, he did follow it, and not only had he matured nicely, he was the president of a multimillion-dollar corporation. He called to thank the professor, and to offer him a six-figure consulting contract with his firm.

Step Four: Affirmations

Looking at Life Less Selectively

Personalization is a process where people permit themselves to feel victimized and outraged by distorting their perceptions of how the world operates. Instead of acknowledging that we all face challenges, unfairness, bad luck, and difficult people, the personalized perception is that the world has been constructed unfairly with the deck stacked against *them.* In order to achieve this kind of distortion, people look at life *selectively*—that is to say they see only what reinforces their perception of the world, and ignore what doesn't. Permitting yourself to believe that the world has been constructed solely to bother you allows you to remain in a pissed-off state. After all, who wouldn't be pissed off living in a world that was created to torture and torment them? Personalized perceptions of life cannot succeed without lots of AMPs that work around the clock to maintain the attitudes of pessimism, disgust, and negativity. Because AMPs are practiced habits, they must be actively disputed with more reasonable beliefs. Let's look at the AMPs that foster a personalized view of the world.

For the most part, none of these things are true of the average person with the average life—they are exaggerations. Obviously, there are people who truly experience catastrophic events and serious illness who feel as though life has been unnecessarily cruel to them. There are people who *are* victimized by events and circumstances beyond their control. The personalized response is an *overreaction* that is unnecessarily crippling—it is an exaggerated response to the normal stresses and strains of life:

AMPs That Promote Personalization
◆ "My life will always suck."
◆ "I was not meant to have any luck in this world."

(List continues on next page.)

- "Other people always seem to catch a break, but not me. My life was meant to be miserable."
- "God must be really pissed off at me to make my life this miserable."
- "Why do I always get stuck being involved with such morons?"
- "It doesn't matter how hard I work. I was meant to work until I die. I will never be able to take time off and relax, because if I do, something bad will happen to me."

Disputing AMPs That Create a Personalized View of the World

Bringing yourself out of a mindset that tries to convince you that you are the victim of an unusually cruel and awful life requires a lot of very difficult work. It is difficult because it requires that you give up the rather comfortable habit of self-pity. I know this sounds kind of harsh. After all, who am I to tell you that you have no good reason to be disappointed with the world? Getting off the pity pot is a decision *you* have to make, and this program is about you and your view of the world. I have nothing against self-pity. Everybody deserves the opportunity to look around and say, "Shit. Life is tough, sometimes I feel like I am beating my head against the wall." Interestingly, like beating your head against the wall, self-pity is one of those things that can feel a lot better after you stop doing it. As an initial response, self-pity is an acknowledgment that you have just gone through a difficult time and it feels painful. It's kind of like burning your hand and yanking it away from the fire. If you just kept on going as if nothing bad had happened, you would have a toasted hand. Acknowledging life's pain is a signal that you need to do something to try to make it less painful. That's what makes personalization such a self-imposed mind game—it actually does make life feel less painful because it gives you an excuse not to do any hard work to change it. It encourages you to live in a state of tolerable dissatisfaction and pessimism. I am not saying it is an easy task to change negative, pessimistic thinking into more hopeful, positive thinking, either. I also do not advocate adopting a foolishly optimistic point of view. Instead, I would suggest that the affirmations and self-talk you develop leave open the possibility that life can improve.

Also, reflecting on the important topics of empathy and forgiveness, you can move yourself past what any person is doing to you (or what you believe they are doing to you) and start considering what people who aggravate you are doing to themselves. When you realize that people who are annoying, rude, embarrassing, and inappropriate create their own horrible lives for themselves, it becomes less important to punish them in addition to how they do it.

The following examples are some affirmations to start you off. As always, putting them into language that is more consistent with your style and vocabulary will help make them more useful to you.

AMP-Fighting Affirmations

- "My life may be bad now, but bad is not necessarily horrible. People have lived through worse and life has changed for the better."

- "Ruminating over my bad luck will not make things any better. I have to try my best to look forward to easier times."

- "The world may seem as though it is set up to screw me, but that is just my reaction to feeling hurt. I can control a lot of what goes on around me, and I can influence it to be better."

- "I have felt sorry for myself enough. It is time to take some actions to improve my position."

- "Dealing with difficult people is always a pain in the ass, however, I am going to try my best to control the situation around the difficult people I must interact with, if for no other reason than to make my own life easier."

- "When people act negatively toward me, I am going to do my best not to take it personally. There were many people before me who got this treatment, and many people after me who will get it. The least I can do for myself is not let this person have the satisfaction of getting under my skin."

- "I refuse to let other people make me add to my own aggravation by remaining pissed off and bothered by someone who should simply not be this important to me."

Remember, these are not ideas that you can consider once or twice and proclaim yourself a new person. You have to practice affirmations and self-talk as though you are taking piano lessons, regularly and with dedication. The instrument you are learning to master is your head, which is substantially more complicated than a piano—at least I hope for your sake it is!

Step Five: Success Milestones

Focus and Direction

As you move forward through these critical paths, several things should be happening:

- You should be thinking a lot more about your behavior.
- You should be a lot less concerned about the behavior of others.
- You should be very focused on how your anger, impatience, and frustration influences your day-to-day interactions; and you should be convinced that much of how you perceive the world is influenced by your anger-maintaining presumptions.
- You should have had some success in making yourself less angry by disputing your AMPs with self-talk and affirmations.
- You should feel capable of exerting a lot more positive control over difficult situations.
- You should be a lot less critical of people in general, and much less critical of people you do not know, who you may have judged prematurely.

If you do not think that you have achieved success in these areas, don't worry. It's not a big deal. It would be a big deal if you have conned yourself into thinking you have made these changes and have not. Succeeding in managing yourself, even if it's only one in 10 times, is a step in the right direction. There is no need to move forward so that you can "finish." Trust me, you will never "finish." You will just continue to get less and less aggravated.

It's time to move ahead to the next critical path when you believe you have achieved all of the above, as well as the following:

Success Milestones: Overcoming Personalization

- You understand what the concept of personalization is.
- You are unwilling to live your life as a victim of a world that was constructed specifically to annoy you.
- You do not demand pity or retribution for your bad luck.
- You are willing to accept apologies without throwing them back into people's faces.
- You do not perceive other people's shortcomings as personal insults against you.
- You do not make yourself into a one-person police force to cure the world of "asshole behavior."
- You have achieved the very difficult skill of being able to see life through someone else's perspective.
- You can ask for and thank someone for forgiveness.
- You can control your use of extreme language and absolutism.
- You do not "un-apologize."
- You can listen to someone who is speaking to you in a rude or angry way, and listen for valid points they may be making about your behavior.
- You are successful at using affirmations and self-talk to short circuit angry behavior or lashing out at people who piss you off, even if it is for a good reason.
- You understand the relationship between anger and opportunity.

When you are comfortable in being able to say that you have mastered these skills, it is time to move on to the next critical path: "Controlling Predation."

Chapter 10

Controlling Predatory Anger, the Fifth Critical Path

Throughout this program I have been drawing a distinction between anger that is a result of chronic frustration (a more irritable and grumpy kind of anger that is an expression of failed expectations and disappointment in life) versus anger that is a result of predatory behavior (a more mean-spirited and territorial anger that is used to dominate and control people and situations). Technically, anger is always generated from *some* type of frustration. The distinction between chronically frustrated angry behavior and chronically predatory behavior is how the angry person perceives and reacts to frustration.

Controlling Predatory Behavior: Step One—Mastery Content

Frustration and Predatory Behavior

The kind of frustration that generates predatory anger is not the same as the disappointment and disillusionment of the chronically frustrated person. Instead, it comes from the angry predatory person's belief or perception that someone or something will stand in the way of his or her success at achieving specific goals.

Goals of the Predatory Person

1. The goal to compete to "win" (even if it is just for the sake of winning).
2. The goal to acquire (that is, money, power, status, fame, notoriety, advantage, and so on).
3. The goal to dominate or control other people in single relationships or groups.
4. The goal of achieving pleasure merely through the exercise of being able to exercise power or will. (For instance ,pleasure by killing, raping, or hurting another human being, that is achieved simply because it is a reinforcement of power and control).
5. The goal of eliminating any threat that stands in the way of attaining a goal.

To achieve these goals, predatory angry people will engage in a variety of behaviors, including:

Behavior of Predatory People

- Overly competitive behavior (competing to "destroy," not just win).
- Physical aggression.
- Bullying.

(List continues on following page.)

- Intimidation.
- Character assassination.
- Back-stabbing and gossiping.
- Purposely setting up someone to fail.
- Being deceitful to advance one's position.
- Manipulating people against one another to advance one's position.
- Participation in behavior that is illegal or immoral.
- Using the legal system in a deceitful way to get someone in trouble.
- Destroying personal property.
- Making someone look bad at work.
- Falsifying information to achieve one's goals.
- Risking the health or safety of innocent people to achieve your goals.
- Ignoring the emotional harm that may come to innocent people as a result of your behavior.

Is All Aggression Bad?

Aggression is a word we often use to describe the behavior required to compete hard, acquire success, or become a dominant figure in a relationship or group. When people compete hard in order to improve their position in life, it isn't always bad, sick, or unhealthy. The bad, unhealthy aggression is usually that which causes harm to someone else or is considered illegal or immoral. As a matter of fact, to possess the trait of being an aggressive "go-getter" is generally considered to be a positive attribute. Not surprisingly, the difference between the healthy form of the aggressive behavior versus the unhealthy and damaging form of behavior is very often seen by how people use or misuse the emotion of anger.

This critical path is about crossing the line that separates healthy competition from a desire to hurt others. For some people it is a rare occasion that they will hurt someone else purposely to attain something for themselves. For others, it is a way of life. I have been referring to people who exploit their anger and aggression as a way of succeeding in life as *chronically predatory*. This is not a path about how to "cure" chronically predatory behavior. It is a critical path about how to control and manage the instances when your anger is predatory. The true chronically predatory angry person would laugh at this critical path, and at the concept of anger management in general. As in the other critical paths, we will look at how to manage predatory anger in ourselves, as well as in others.

Want to or Have to? Can Be or Must Be? Who Is Chronically Predatory?

The desire to achieve certain goals for power, success, wealth, notoriety, and advancement in business can create an intense focus on carrying out whatever behavior is necessary to achieve those goals, even if it means hurting someone else, physically or emotionally. Although there are people who would disagree, you cannot hurt someone else without becoming angry first. Some people believe that the most horrible of psychopaths can hurt and destroy others without any feeling at all. They murder or hurt others and do not appear to have an angry face or demeanor. We see this portrayal in movies all the time—the "cold-blooded killer who destroys life without batting an eye." The presence or absence of anger cannot always be told by the look on someone's face or their demeanor. Just think of the last time you had an argument with someone who gave you "the silent treatment" when they were annoyed at you. They are plenty pissed off, yet they aren't saying a word. Some people are so skillful at it that the person they are angry at is the only person who is even aware that there is something "wrong." As with all other forms of anger, the person giving "the silent treatment" tries to hurt the person that they are angry at by treating them as if they do not exist. Just because the angry person is not foaming at the mouth with rage doesn't mean they are less angry than the person who is. What actively aggressive forms of anger have in common with more passive forms of aggression is the desire to hurt, and a lack of concern as to how the hurt will be felt by the person they are angry at.

Anger is an emotion with *many* components, only two of which are the look on someone's face or the tone of their voice. While these may be the more *noticeable* indications of anger I do not think they are the *important* ones. Instead, it is my opinion that the largest component of anger, the anger manifestation that is common to everyone that is angry whether you are yelling, punching, undermining at a business meeting, or not talking at all, is a disregard for the *consequence* of the anger and the desensitization to the physical and emotional things that happen to the recipient of your anger. In other words, what defines anger in general, and what makes predatory anger particularly scary, is the fact that anger suffocates empathy. Even when people are normally sensitive and kind, anger can short-circuit those tendencies and can be hurtful and damaging. This happens to most of us from time to time, especially when the general level of stress in our lives is high.

Loss of one's normal tendency for empathy as a result of stress is a pretty common occurrence between people who are in romantic partnerships. In cases where couples are bickering or arguing, they may both become so angry that, momentarily they do not care if they hurt the other person's feelings or damage their self-esteem. If the relationship is healthy, neither partner will let behavior such as this get too far out of hand before putting on the brakes and apologizing. For some people, however, hurtful remarks, insensitivity to a partner's feelings, or other angry behaviors are the rule, not the exception. Some people control their partner's behavior solely through anger. The "good times" in those relationships may be nothing more than the time between fights when nothing particularly terrible is going on, but there is little or no expression of genuine love and caring either. In other relationships, fights may be few and far between, but, when they occur, they are what I call a "history lesson," where one or both partners fight bitterly about whatever it is that made them angry, along with dozens of other things that have hurt their feelings in the past. In both of these cases, fights are characterized by people saying the meanest things they can think of to hurt the other person. This can create tremendous amounts of guilt later on, which can lead to promises of more sensitive behavior in the future, but the desire to hurt someone during a disagreement is a difficult habit

> ✔ **Check Point**
>
> *You can't always tell if someone is angry by the tone of their voice or the expression on their face. This is particularly true of people who are angry and predatory.*

to break. Even occasional fighting of this type can completely destroy a relationship.

In the case of chronically predatory people, they *never* care about what their anger does to others. As a matter of fact they *rely* on their anger to weaken or destroy others so that they may achieve some sort of gain as a result. In personal relationships, that gain might be control. It might also be a striking out or revenge for a hurt or disappointment that happened in the relationship. Even when the relationship is over, there is motivation to continue to hurt someone who has caused disappointment or who broke loose from the relationship. Here is an example of how the desire to hurt someone can continue long after the disappointing event:

He Started It; She Finished It

It had been a rough divorce for Mike. Not only was his wife going to take him to the cleaners for cheating on her, he knew that his 9- and 11-year-old daughters would never forgive him either. Their mother told them the whole story, and they haven't spoken to him in weeks. Mike's wife, Elaine, told him that after he was out of the house, she would make certain he would never see the kids again.

Mike desperately tried to explain to the children that he had made a mistake, and that he was sorry for what he did to the family. He told the girls many times that he would like them to try to forgive him, and that if their mother did not want to be married to him anymore, it did not mean that he would stop being their father. The girls were cold and told him several times they would rather be without a father. They had clearly sided with their mother, and Elaine was not making matters any easier by constantly badmouthing him to them.

One night, Mike came to kiss the kids good night as he had done every night since they were babies, and as he sat on the edge of his older daughter's bed, he became overwhelmed with emotion and started to cry. His daughter, feeling uncomfortable with his sad emotions said, "I hate you. Get away from me!" Within seconds, Elaine burst into the room and yelled at him, "What are you doing to my daughters, you pig!" She demanded he leave the room. She emerged about three minutes later and called 911. The police arrived and told him that his wife and daughter complained that he was making sexual advances toward the daughter in her room. He was arrested. He spent the night in jail. He had to hire an attorney. An investigation followed, first by the police sex crimes unit, and then by the state department of child welfare. Ultimately, he was found to be not guilty of any of the sex abuse charges. The judge who examined the case at trial concluded that the mother coerced the daughter into saying that she felt "uncomfortable" by the father's presence in the room. The daughter did not report any sexual abuse or behavior by the father, either in that instance or any instance in the past, but insisted she was frightened he would "do something."

Unfortunately, by the time the case was decided, the father was ordered out of the house with no visitation with his children until the charges were cleared. When the charges were cleared, the girls insisted they did not want to see their father. They had been told by the mother that "the judge made a mistake" by not putting the father in jail.

Three years later, after filing several lawsuits against the mother for interfering with visitation, the children could see their father one time a week in a counselor's office. After six months of counseling, the children still insisted that no one could make them see their father if they didn't want to.

Mike's story is not unusual, and there are plenty of others like it where the wife gets the short end of the stick. Even if we set aside the emotionally charged issue of sexual abuse, thousands of children are deciding they want to "divorce" one of their parents after the family breaks up. Often the children have no legitimate reason for not wanting to see or have a relationship with one of the parents. Their refusal to visit is in the service of helping the parent they have sided with express anger at the other parent. Many times, the children are coerced into saying they don't want to have a relationship with one of their parents because they feel that is what the parent they are closer to wants.

In the previous story, Elaine did a cruel thing to her husband and to her children, but if you ask her, he had it coming. Mike was a bad husband, therefore he was a bad person and a bad father. He hurt her. He set a bad example for the children. All of this led her to believe that she was protecting the children from the influence of a bad person. In her mind, if he cheated on her, who was to say he *wouldn't* sexually abuse the children? She knew that she was manipulating her children, but it had to be done in order to protect them. After they were grown up, they could make their own decisions about their loser father.

If you knew Elaine, you would probably consider her to be a vicious person. A nasty divorce or other stressful life circumstance can change that. Elaine was not what anyone would consider a "chronically angry person" before her divorce, but afterwards, in this instance and in many that followed, she became one. In her mind, she had to become this way because living life as a "wimp" and a "nice person," did not pay off for her. Her dissatisfaction with her relationship caused her to take up a different perspective on life, one where it was "eat or be eaten." She would teach her daughters not to make the same mistakes she did if it was the last thing she did.

All of us have the potential to permit anger and disappointment to turn us into cynical, hateful people. On this critical path, we examine whether we permit ourselves to edge up to the line by letting our predatory and aggressive tendencies get the better of us. For some of us, things have to get pretty bad before we activate the "dark side." For others, predatory, manipulative, and aggressive behavior is a way of life. It will become important for you to determine whether this sort of behavior is a *tendency* for you, or whether you are this *type* of person whether you have to be or not.

Do You Rely on Predatory Behavior?

Is there an angry predatory "type" of person, or does everyone show these traits every now and then? The answer to this question is most easily answered by trying to examine the extent to which people rely on predatory styles of behavior. In theory, given the right (or wrong) set of circumstances, everyone has the potential to behave in self-motivated and predatory ways. For instance, who would you be willing to throw to the dogs for a million dollars? Have you ever done anything that put someone else in a bad position for selfish or opportunistic reasons? Have you ever told a white lie to gain an advantageous position, especially when it involves someone else you don't particularly like?

The Person Who Is Truly Predatory Is Not Likely to Change

For most of us who seek to evolve into more compassionate, empathic human beings, gaining mastery over selfish and egocentric behavior is a matter of managing a *part* of us that *occasionally* gets out of control. Lack of feeling or empathy for others might be rare, but it happens. When it does, you want to correct it. For some people, an overly aggressive and predatory style *is* the problem. Anger is used as a "regular tool" for dealing with people and life in general.

Frankly, it is very difficult to convince people who use anger, control, manipulation, deception, and aggression as a regular or primary style of behavior that this kind of style is a problem. The chronically predatory angry person believes that the only "problems" that exist in the world are people or circumstances that prevent them from doing what they want to do. They are "in the way" and have to be "dealt with." This book is not likely to provide any help or insight to this type of person. As a matter of fact, at least with regard to predatory anger, this book is most helpful in teaching people how to spot and evaluate predatory anger so that you can avoid people such as this whenever possible.

> ✓ **Check Point**
>
> *For some people, angry acting out that is designed to hurt people is an occasional circumstance that happens under extreme conditions. But for the predatory person, the notion of physically and emotionally abusing people to attain what they want is an acceptable way of life.*

In business and work environments, it is impossible to avoid dealing with chronically predatory people sometimes. When that is the case, the goal of interacting with them is to keep as much of a low profile as possible and give them as little personal information about you as possible. Chronically predatory people rely on personal attacks, especially in business settings, to hurt and control others. (The coping step in this critical path provides more about this.) In love and social relationships, there is often the urge to approach the chronically predatory person as a sort of "science project," a person whose faults you believe you can cure simply by understanding and loving them because no one else has.

For the truly predatory person, there is far too much value in operating in a predatory way. No person is ever going to be important enough to the chronically predatory person for him or her to change that style.

Here are some of the reasons why chronically predatory people do not change their behavior:

> **Why Predatory People Do Not Change**
> 1. Chronically predatory people are seldom challenged (except by other very angry, predatory people) because most civilized people lack the motivation (and the skill) to fight or to be ruthless. Most people will go out of their way to avoid fighting, and chronically predatory people rely on that.
> 2. Chronically predatory people will always find people who admire them for their ability to intimidate and control. People will suck up to chronically predatory people merely to remain off their "shit list."
> 3. Chronically predatory people will not change to a less-aggressive style of behavior because they believe that less-aggressive styles indicate a personal weakness—it is exactly what they despise in everyone else.

The truly chronically angry person sees absolutely nothing to gain by changing their behavior. This is one of the reasons why I will always advise people who are in abusive relationships with chronically predatory people to get out of those relationships. No matter how patient, kind, supportive, loving, or tolerant you are, that person's behavior is not going to change. Your attempts will serve no other purpose than to make you a patient and supportive punching bag.

Aside from not being able to change the behavior of a chronically predatory person by being a good relationship partner, other unhelpful interventions for chronically predatory people are:

> **Things That Fail to Help the Chronically Predatory Person**
> 1. Hoping that dozens of failed relationships will teach the chronically predatory person to be better behaved.
> 2. Assuming that failure at work with bosses and coworkers will stimulate a desire to be more gentle and compassionate.

(List continued on following page.)

3. Figuring that physical injuries they have received at the hands of other angry people will motivate them to use less aggression in the future.
4. Believing that run-ins with the law or even jail time will persuade them to take a more civilized approach to life.

Ironically, the worst of these types of people, the monsters who rape, murder, torture, and disregard human life, often "learn" by getting killed during an angry interaction, or are otherwise prevented from harming anyone else when they make mistakes that cause the law to catch up with them. Even when chronically angry people are caught, punished, and incarcerated, their behavior does not change. Violent criminals have very high rates (between 50 and 70 percent) of recurring violent, criminal behavior when they are released from jail.

What about the lesser "monsters"? What about those who make other people miserable and unbearable because they are aggressive, but not aggressive enough to have to go to jail? What about those who are deceitful and opportunistic, but not criminally so? What about those who abuse power and authority, but hide it through careful manipulations and social savvy? I would not hold out any great hopes for these types of people to change significantly either. Again, if the gain that is derived from exercising angry and aggressive behavior is greater than the consequence, there is little motivation to change. Occasionally, a very disruptive life experience, a catastrophic event such as an illness or loss of something very important can motivate people to start a new life and correct chronically angry and/or aggressive behavior. Often, however, people can lead an entire life of taking advantage of others and gain so much that they are very willing to "write off" the occasional failure to achieve their goal.

Why Is Controlling Predatory Anger Considered a Critical Path?

If chronic predatory anger is so difficult to give up, is it worth devoting an entire critical path to? Most of us are not *chronically* predatory.

But as human beings, we all tend to use predatory styles *selectively* and *occasionally*, whether it be towards certain people, certain groups of people, or in certain situations or environments. Some people may use anger, intimidation, and overly aggressive or competitive behavior at work, but not at home. Others may be as gentle as lambs until the time community elections come around. Getting behind the wheel of a car stimulates others to maniacal proportions. Others may still focus on a single rival or a few rivals and let themselves fall into a bullying, angry, or intimidating style with them only. Sometimes, certain situations such as standing in line or shopping bring out unnecessarily predatory behavior.

While it is true that the sickest, most aggressive predatory people can probably never be helped out of their angry style by anything short of a miracle, this critical path is about when life brings out the worst in the rest of us in whichever circumstances we allow it to. Of course, as with any form of help, a true desire to change one's style is a step in the right direction. That is especially so with predatory anger, because the most predatory people would never admit to a shortcoming in their personality.

The fact that this critical path comes at such an advanced point in your dedication to living a more calm and less angry life is a reflection of how much work it takes to get to a point where you can concentrate on your *worst* moments. In some ways, everything you have learned or focused on up until this point has prepared you to take on your most ferocious demons. Addressing these issues earlier on, in my opinion, would not have been helpful because there would have been no foundation to relate it to. As a result of your success on the last critical path, you should be far less prone to personalizing the world as a place that was built merely to make your life miserable. Through your past efforts on this and other critical paths, anger should be far less a part of your life, and far less an important tool for you to have to rely on to cope with life's difficulties. That is precisely why, at this point in your mastery, you should focus on what might be the ugliest part of your anger, the part of your anger that is the most difficult to give up because, unlike the anger that is used in the service of expressing frustration, predatory anger can actually get you a good result, albeit for the wrong reasons. Here is an example of how intimidation and bullying can do just that:

Lewis and Clarke

"I hope you are not giving any serious thought to undermining my position on the Merriweather deal at the next meeting, Sanford," Mike Lewis told Sanford Clarke at lunch the other day. Clarke replied, "Well, I don't agree with it, nothing personal." Lewis shot back, "Nothing personal to you, because you didn't stake your career on pushing it through. I took some real chances for this deal. I made a lot of promises." Clarke was unimpressed. "Those were your decisions for your reasons. I can't abide by them." Lewis returned, "Look, don't make me have to play hardball with you, you smug, arrogant little piece of shit. My department will get this contract, and I will tell you why. I took the liberty of going through some of your numbers and they stink. I will have the opportunity to tear into your sorry ass at some point. And don't worry, when the time comes I will certainly point out a few things that a lot of people have obviously overlooked. Do what you want, but I can assure you there will be a price to pay if you cross me." Lewis was nose to nose with Clarke at this point. "Who said I was going to cross you, and why are you so touchy? Lay off on the caffeine, Old Bean. I never planned on making waves." Clarke did not think this was the best time to make his move against Lewis.

Competitive environments can bring out the worst in people, but they do not have to. Some people subscribe to the theory that it is a "dog-eat-dog world," and as long as you are not breaking any laws (or if you think you are not going to get caught breaking any laws), whatever it takes to advance your position is acceptable behavior. Office politics are a great example of this in more ways than for just business reasons. Office environments are social environments, as much as employers and managers of large organizations wish they weren't. Social environments within job environments are complicated networks of easily hurt feelings and jockeying for position within the group power structure. The "social politics" of the work environment comprise as much of the workday as the job tasks and responsibilities that people have. Social networks and office politics can destroy the bottom line. This is especially true in work environments where people do not earn a lot of money for the job they do. Social incentives become the main reason for coming to work, and social interaction can become more of a priority than work-related tasks. In the Lewis and Clarke vignette, intimidation and power plays formed the basis for the angry interaction between the main characters at the executive end of the business. The following vignette is a look at how predatory behavior can destroy a business at the most basic and fundamental level.

Hottech Electronics, Inc.

Hottech Electronics is a successful up-and-coming distributor of small components for computers and electronics. The warehouse crew ships and inventories tens of thousands of components an hour from their downtown warehouse run by Pensi Turbo, a 25-year-old dynamo, hired for his drive and energy by the founder of the company who was looking for people he could bring up through the ranks. Pensi had a bright smile and a persuasive banter. He was extremely protective of the girls in the back office, all of whom he personally hired, and all of whom were extremely attractive 19- to 22-year-olds. All of the girls were high school educated with no college experience, and very little life experience in general. They were all very efficient at taking and carrying out orders, and all of them were more than willing to burn the midnight oil so that parts could get packed and shipped for the next business day's delivery.

The secret to Pensi's motivational style was in a "side business" he was running on company time. The side business was an Internet pornography Website that featured the girls he hired in the shipping department posing naked. The entire setup was run from the warehouse with a digital camera, a computer (built with parts from Hottech's inventory), and an Internet connection. Pensi's approach was to hire young women who seemed eager to please and were good at taking orders. After a three-month "break in" period, he would take the newest girl to lunch in his late model Jag and ask her what she would think if he could show her a way to be able to own a brand-new luxury car in two months. He would then explain that he owned a "virtual modeling company" that sold "high-fashion photography" on the Internet. He explained that people would buy the pictures and then add the face or glamour shot into their own advertising. "The customers cut and paste the models right into their catalogs and we make money every time a picture is downloaded." After he saw signs of interest, he would offer the girls $500 just for a "test shoot." Five hundred dollars was more than two-weeks pay, and Pensi promised there would be "no nude shots and no monkey business." Pensi learned a long time ago that once he could get a "yes" to this, the rest was a piece of cake. Almost every girl he brought into the "business" had their clothes off for more explicit "erotic modeling" within the first two months of them agreeing to participate. The pay for "semi-nude" and "nude" photo shoots was triple what it was for "fashion photography," and by the time the girls were introduced to this kind of money, everyone at work was one, big, happy "family," so it wasn't even that embarrassing to the girls. To boot, everyone was making their regular salary for their day jobs at Hottech as well as their "bonus" pay for sticking around for two hours after work for a quick photo shoot.

No one's judgment is accurate 100 percent of the time, and when Pensi tried a little too hard to persuade a 20-year-old "fresh face" into coming into his side business, he got more than he bargained for—someone who threatened to expose the operation and get him in trouble. That was not cool. He wasn't going to let someone destroy his business just because he was giving her the opportunity to participate. What kind of person would do that to someone just for asking? Pensi quickly arranged for her to be "taught a lesson." Her car was keyed in the office parking lot. A week after than she came out to find three flat tires. Two days after that she quit. Newly relieved and thinking that dealing with this "temporary difficulty" was easier than he thought it would be, Pensi went to work on the next new recruit, who seemed eager to participate and "a low sell." Maybe the reason why she was so easy to sell was because she was already used to making money in a second job—she was a private investigator hired by Pensi's boss. Pensi and his "girls" were fired, but that didn't stop Pensi. Within three weeks he was up and running out of his own "warehouse" space—you can't get fired if you are the boss.

> ✓ **Check Point**
>
> *When people are understimulated in large work environments, they may seek to fill their day, jockeying for positions of power and control in the social networks that form when large groups of people work in the same space. Here is where a lot of workplace bullying and intimidation take place.*

Pensi's antics had a serious effect on Hottech's bottom line. In one week, the company had to fire more than one third of its shipping crew. The combination of the workplace becoming a social environment and a predatory mastermind who used the environment for his own selfish pursuits could have put an end to the business altogether.

In trying to use the "Hottech Electronics, Inc." story as an example of predatory anger, it is easy to see how people would find it hard to interpret Pensi's behavior as angry. It is opportunistic, manipulative, deceitful, and unethical, but is it *angry?*

In this critical path we learn that anger is not merely the teeth-gritting, screaming, punching, bar-room-brawling anger that is the obvious manifestation of rage. Pensi's anger is an anger that comes from feeling *entitled* to use the world to achieve whatever one believes they deserve. It is a generalized angry-at-the-world type of anger as opposed to an anger at one target or object. The anger that stems from feeling that the world "owes" you and you are "entitled" to get what you are owed forms the basis for a predatory orientation to the world. Pensi had to disregard the general health of the business he was working in, the wishes of his boss, the ethical implications of illegally using the business he was working in to conduct another clandestine business, and the feelings of the women he snookered and manipulated into his business. We all have selfish motives and wishes, and we all have thoughts and fantasies about quick paths to success. How many of us would rob a bank if we knew we could get away with it and no one would get hurt? Fantasies such as this are common to many people, but taking steps to carry out such a fantasy requires a predatory attitude. A large component of anger is being able to disable the empathy and sensitivity that would normally cause us to censor a plan such as that long before we were able to carry it out.

Pensi's "operation" required cunning, manipulation, and deceit that characterizes chronically predatory behavior. This critical path asks: "Does that type of behavior exist *anywhere* in your personality, and on *any* scale?"

Controlling Predatory Behavior: Step Two—
Coping Strategies

Success Without Destruction

The second step of each critical path examines coping strategies, which are specific exercises you can practice; a careful examination of your orientation to life; or, as in this critical path, taking stock of the way in which you structure your priorities and values.

For instance, if financial success is your highest priority in life, it would be great if all you have to do is work hard at your job and reap your rewards. Unfortunately, that's not the way it works. Financial success involves hard work, luck, opportunity, and probably a hundred other things that vary from situation to situation. The fact that hard work is only one element in the complex equation that brings financial success can be very frustrating for people. The culture we live in teaches that hard work "pays off," but it often doesn't. Instead, hard work without the payoff often produces disillusionment, frustration, and, of course, anger. This is especially true of people who work hard and feel underappreciated for their efforts. When this happens, it often stimulates a "me first" type of attitude, and the desire to "take" what might not have been given or offered. Stealing from one's boss or engaging in power plays with other coworkers are sometimes where frustrated and angry energies ultimately become directed.

Competitive behavior that occurs in an environment where frustration, failure, or disappointment are just as likely as success, often presents a basic conflict for people—in order to succeed you must weaken someone else's position. Consider the following dilemma: You and a friend are both interviewing for the same promotion at work. Advancing to the new position would greatly improve your financial and social position in life. As part of the job interview, the interviewer asks you to compare yourself to your friend in terms of your qualifications for the position. What do you do? Do you try to make yourself look good by emphasizing your friend's weaknesses? Do you approach the question diplomatically by side-stepping it, or giving a wishy-washy answer and risk that the interviewer will feel that your fear in answering the question in a more aggressive way will make a negative impression? Do you object to the question and hope to show strength by telling the interviewer you would rather not impress him by putting down a coworker? The answer to these questions will undoubtedly be driven by your values. There are some people who could devalue a friend's work performance to advance their own position and justify it by saying, "Sure he's a friend, and he's a great friend, but as a coworker he is not qualified for the position, but I am. The two have nothing to do with one another." There are others who would place the friendship at a higher priority than even a career. Still there are those who would lie and exaggerate to make someone else look bad, even if they were a "friend," because their own self-interests are *always* the priority.

Let's take the same sort of dilemma out of the work environment and into the social realm: You and a friend are both interested in dating the same person. Is it ever acceptable to do something that purposely makes your friend look bad in order to make yourself look better? For some people, "All is fair in love and war," for others, the behavior would be totally unacceptable.

The question we come back to repeatedly in this critical path is, "What does all of this have to do with anger?" This program considers anger as a complex emotion that includes all of the observable, volatile aspects of anger (yelling, hitting, intentional destruction of property), as well as the aspect of the emotion that short-circuits concern for the well-being of others in order to advance one's position. Using this aspect of the definition, behavior that is selfish, insensitive deceptive, manipulative, and which places another person's interests in jeopardy, is angry behavior. Competitive behavior is healthy. It is the *hypercompetive* behavior that is not. Cheating to win, hurting others to win, enjoying making someone feel like a loser more than appreciating the sense of satisfaction that comes from winning—these are some hallmarks of predatory behavior.

> ✓ **Check Point**
> *Most people will readily admit that it is important for them to live by a set of values; however, when it comes right down to it, very few people can put into words what values they believe are important.*

In the last critical path, we learned that empathy is a key component to releasing angry feelings. Manipulative, deceptive, hyper-competitive behavior, and outright physical aggression occur when people allow themselves to *suppress empathy*. When we become hyper-competitive, we lose interest in what happens to the people we are competing with. In its mildest forms, we may become unsympathetic, unsportsmanlike, or insensitive. In its extreme form, the hyper-competitive person enjoys hurting the adversary until it becomes the point of whatever competitive exercise or pursuit he or she is engaged in.

Adjusting Your Orientation to Success, Power, Approval, Winning, and Achievement

As a coping strategy, to suggest that people examine the values and priorities that relate to success, power, approval, and achievement seems like a very basic task that most people should do whether they are working on their anger or not. In fact, even though it is a basic task, it can be a very difficult one. To see how difficult it is, ask yourself these basic questions: "What personal code do you live by?" "What rules about dealing with people do you adhere to that you never break?" "What are the things your friends and loved ones can always count on you to do on their behalf?"

These questions are deceptively difficult to answer for most people because people will routinely respond with answers such as:

- "My friends can count on me to be 'nice.'"
- "My friends can 'call on' me when they are down."
- "People can expect that I will be 'good' to them if they are good to me."

The Importance of Commitments

When it comes down to it, all of these statements are either very vague or very basic, and they don't really say much about you as a person. Statements such as these probably mean that values are important, but not very well defined. That doesn't mean there isn't much to you as a person. It may simply mean that you are not in good touch with who you are as a person. It might also mean that you are not willing to make certain commitments regarding your behavior. Making commitments is an essential coping strategy for dealing with anger because the sacred promises we make to ourselves give less opportunity to make excuses for our behavior, and angry behavior (especially the predatory type) is what we most often make excuses for. For instance, can your best friend be certain that you will *never* talk about him or her behind their back? Can your partner or mate be sure that you will *never* make them look bad to others when they have done something to annoy you? Can your friends and loved ones be sure you will *never* hurt them to advance your own position in life? Can your coworkers feel comfortable working with you, making certain that you will *never* exaggerate their poor performance so you can gain status or power at work? Can the people who are close to you be secure that you will *never* "trade them in" when something that appears better comes along?

When relationships fail, it is often because people take advantage of one another, use each other selfishly and manipulate and deceive one another. Coming to terms with who you are when you are at your worst is a critical component of structuring your values and priorities. By the same token, striving to construct a set of rules that you can adhere to enhances a kind of dedication to values that will keep predatory behavior in check. The more important you make that set of rules, the more likely you are to reference those rules when you are confronted with a dilemma that places you in a position of choosing to make someone else's life more negative in order to make yours more positive.

Making yourself accountable to a personal code of values goes to the heart and soul of coping with the kinds of choices we make in our personal lives. It is a natural check against predatory behavior because predatory behavior is driven by an absence of personal values and a disregard for the feelings and well-being of others.

Everyone's Personal Code Is Different

While this critical path advises you to examine the areas in your life where you might permit your own self-interests to interfere with the quality of someone else's life, it would be far too presumptuous of me or anyone else to tell you how to go about living your life—that is up to you. The goal of your dedication to this critical path is to spend some time thinking about the kind of person you are, the kind of person you strive to be, and the principles and values that will keep you feeling comfortable about how you deal with people. Getting to a point in life where you can reflect on your behavior and determine whether it was right or wrong, and decide whether you need to do something to correct an error or insensitivity, is difficult enough for most people. This critical path takes you one step beyond that by asking you to predetermine the values and rules by which you will treat people. To construct your personal code or to reflect on your priorities and values, consider the following points in the box below:

Questions to Help Develop Your Own Personal Code

- "What selfish acts am I willing to do to gain attention, love, and affection?"
- "What selfish acts am I willing to do to gain financial success and achievement?"
- "What selfish acts am I willing to do to gain social approval among my friends?"
- "What selfish acts am I willing to do to gain power and influence?"
- "What selfish acts am I willing to do to protect myself when I am threatened?"

In the context of the question above, consider "What am I willing to do..." to mean "Who am I willing to hurt..." and "To what extent am I willing to hurt....", In addition, consider "hurt" to mean physical hurt, emotional hurt, or making someone look stupid, embarrassed, or incompetent.

Summing Up the Second Step

The further you go in your dedication to leading a less-angry life, the more choices and dilemmas you will encounter. Living a more calm and less-angry life is difficult, if for no other reason than the fact that being angry and acting angry is so *easy*. There is so much to complain about. There are so many bad drivers, inconsiderate people, incompetent people, slackers, idiots, and morons. Worse yet, many of these people seem to get more than their fair share of free rides, breaks, and "coupons." It almost doesn't seem possible to get anywhere in life without beating people at their own game. That's one way of looking at it. Another way is to ask yourself why you are spending so much time participating in that game, and why acquiring certain tokens of success has become more important to you than being a person you can feel comfortable with. Some would say that's fine, but you can't take good intentions to the bank. Of course, that is true. What good is being a person who is reliable, trustworthy, hardworking, honest, and respectful of others if all it brings you is aggravation? To see what "good" it is and how much it is worth is precisely the goal of this critical path. This critical path is about removing yourself (not necessarily physically, because it may be impossible) from situations where you rely on gossiping, back-stabbing, opportunism, revenge, hyper-competitive behavior, success at the expense of others, or worst of all, enjoying the feeling of arbitrarily controlling or hurting others just because *you can*.

For people who are already moderately successful, you will not believe how difficult this critical path is until you begin to try. As with many of the critical paths, you will have the hardest time owning up to the instances where you needlessly employ predatory strategies to gain success. If you are feeling brave enough, it might be helpful to seek the assistance of a "partner" or neutral party whose opinion you trust, to make you more aware of these behaviors.

When You are the Target of Predatory Behavior

As with every critical path, it is important to know and understand how to deal with anger in others as well as ourselves. Some common situations where people are victimized by predatory behavior are presented in the following box:

Situations Where People Become the Targets of Predatory Behavior

- Being the victim of a crime.
- Being the victim of a scam or con that causes you to lose a lot of money.
- Being the victim of rumors, gossip, or lies that hurt your reputation.
- Being "stuck" in a relationship with a boss or employer who is predatory either because he or she is a bully or a sexual predator.

(List continues on following page.)

- Being in a relationship with someone who uses your kindness as an opportunity to take advantage, berate, belittle, or abuse you.
- Being made to look bad at work by someone who has a personal problem with you.
- Being stalked, harassed, or followed by someone who wants to hurt you.

Whenever possible, it is important to get away from predatory types of people as fast and as far as you can. Physically removing people such as this from your life is sometimes a matter of life or death. Often people will stay in relationships where they are being victimized because they feel that it is better than being lonely. Sometimes people believe they are not entitled to a better or easier life. This is always a reflection of poor self-esteem. Not surprisingly, people who have low self-esteem are easy targets for predatory people because predatory people are control freaks, and people who have low self-esteem are very willing to be controlled and manipulated by others as a tradeoff for acceptance.

This is often a common dynamic in the lives and relationships of abused men and women.

Check Point

When people finally summon up the nerve to leave predatory and abusive relationship partners, life often gets worse before it gets better. Abused partners often suffer from loneliness, isolation, and fear over having to direct and control their own lives.

Sadly, after they finally get up the nerve to follow the advice their friends and family members have been telling them for years to ditch the abuser, they become angry and disenchanted because life is "harder" after the separation. Certainly that is often true, because people who leave abusive relationships have to work harder to make ends meet, may suffer loneliness just because there is no one else interacting with them, and have to make decisions on their own, which is generally something they dislike doing.

When You Can't Get Away

Sometimes you simply cannot "get away" from predatory people. This is especially so in business relationships where dealing with predatory people might be a necessary evil. If the predatory person in your life is your employer and you have to deal with him or her regularly, the advice is the same as if you are married to that person—get away. Of course that is much easier said than done. Most people rely on their jobs for survival. If you are being abused or taken advantage of by your boss, you must make the difficult choice of whether it is as impossible as you think it is to find someplace else to work. Sometimes the decision to "start looking" can be empowering enough to help you take the first step out of an abusive situation.

Bosses are not the only kind of predatory people you might find in your business or work environment. In highly competitive business environments, coworkers may treat you in manipulative and deceptive ways. Also, "office politics" can become a scene where power and control issues are part of the social environment of the office. There are ways to protect yourself from these types of situations in the office. Here are a few hints along those lines:

Establish Yourself as "Off Limits" in Office Politics

1. Learn to set limits in office relationships as soon as possible. Be wary of people who are overly seductive in business settings, who make offers that are too difficult to refuse, and who seem to want to "buddy up" without obvious reason. These people are often after control; influence; or at worst, a "fall guy" (someone who can be blamed for their screw ups later on). Watch your personal boundaries. Do not be so quick to do people any favors or form allegiances when you are new to a job.

2. Do not be quick to reveal personal information such as whether you are having a rough time in your marriage, or whether you are having a personal crisis to people you work with and do not know very well. Predatory types will use this information to capitalize on your vulnerability, or use it as fodder for the office or business gossip mill. If people "fish for information," say that you do not

---

(List continued on next page.)

mix business and personal relationships. There is almost always a side benefit to remaining "a person of mystery" at work. People will never know what or who you have up your sleeve. The less people know about you personally, the more power you will retain in a business setting. The more people know about you, the more they will lure you in to office cliques and groups (it is often worse than high school), demand loyalty, and seek to punish you with gossip when you do not defend the group leader. Be a "free agent." People are respected when they are seen as independent. You will be tested from time to time with gossip and speculation about "what you are all about." Not being part of any particular group and owing no loyalty makes it easier for you to slough it off because you will feel less like you owe anyone else at work any information.

Controlling Predatory Behavior: Step Three— Communications Skills

Revisiting the "Less Is More" Principle

We are a society that praises people for being "good communicators." We appreciate it in our presidents, mates, friends, doctors, teachers, bosses, and those who report to us. Good communicating isn't always about being a good talker. It's about knowing when to talk and when to shut up. Being a good communicator doesn't always imply a positive personality attribute either. Some of the most pernicious and dangerous people on earth were persuasive communicators. Hitler, for instance, was a masterful communicator, persuasive, commanding, and thoroughly evil and predatory.

Communication skills that advance people's interests in ways that are manipulative and deceptive are available to anyone who is intelligent and who has spent some time studying people. Con men (who make a living on predatory behavior) may not have extensive formal educations, but often have a keen sixth sense for persuasion, manipulation, and deception.

In this critical path, our attention is focused on predation. All forms of predatory behavior are *opportunistic,* designed to use a situation for as much personal advantage as it can offer. How many times have you been given the opportunity to comment on someone's behavior, performance, competence, physical appearance, or decision-making, where it would have made no difference if you said nothing, but instead, said something negative? It is a common observation that some people never have anything positive to say about anyone. From the perspective of those people who are angry, perhaps it is because people are less threatening when we can bring their negative behavior to light.

Boomerang Effect

I have pointed out in other sections of this book that life is a lot more complicated than angry people picking on people who aren't angry or who are easily intimidated. It has been my position all along that we live in an angry *world* where most of us could use some focus and direction about the role that anger plays in our lives. As a result of that, I have been saying, "anger begets anger." The same thing can be said about any manifestation of anger, such as, gossip, criticism, back-stabbing, and deception. In more practical terms, what makes you think that when you pass along negative information about someone else, the person who carries that message will not use it to make you look bad? The bottom line becomes, if that person is as opportunistic as you are, you might find yourself in precisely that position. How about what happens when you gossip behind someone's back to a third party, and the person you are gossiping to starts to feel as though you might also spread some gossip about *them*? In some circles it is so bad that *everyone* gossips about *everyone else.* In situations such as those, someone is always on "hot seat." The point of both of these descriptions is that giving someone "negative press" invites a kind of "boomerang effect." In the end, it may not bring you as much positive advantage, as it causes you to be placed on the defensive yourself.

This critical path encourages people to talk less and listen more. This applies to situations where you might be tempted to go overboard with self-promotion, as well as situations where you might be tempted to attack someone to make yourself look better, or simply because the opportunity is there and you can't resist it.

Here are some communication pointers to help tame predatory tendencies:

Communication Strategies for This Critical Path

1. When you have earned success, let other people notice it; don't gloat.

2. Be kind and gracious to the people you have surpassed—you may see them again on the way down from your ivory tower.

3. Remember what your mother told you about not having anything nice to say about someone. (What she said or *should have said* is, "If you don't have anything nice to say about someone, don't say anything at all.")

4. Resist the opportunity to join the group when the topic of discussion is bashing someone who is not there to defend themselves.

5. Examine your style or approach to people. If you exert power over them by bullying, intimidating, name-calling, threatening, or embarrassing them, think about how that experience will affect them in the long run. You might forget about what you said or did, but they might remember it long enough to catch you off guard sometime when it is very inconvenient for you to have another enemy.

6. Spend more time observing the people you feel are threatening to you. Don't be so quick to engage them in a war. Oftentimes, the people who are most threatening at first can become your biggest allies when you start by showing a little kindness and tolerance. Your first effort with any new person, venture, or encounter should be *cooperation*. It takes less work, gets you further faster, and often produces no aggravation. As opposed to competition, cooperation requires little strategy or damage control.

(List continues on next page.)

7. Keep your friends close and your enemies closer. Be gracious and cordial even to people who know are bashing you behind your back. This is especially true in work environments, where alliances can be made and broken very quickly. Positioning yourself openly as an adversary merely identifies that you are in a power struggle with someone. Remaining civilized and "friendly" will make the conflict appear one-sided. In doing so, you are also controlling the situation by preventing escalation.

Controlling Predatory Behavior: Step Four—Affirmations

Affirmations: Being Mindful of the Damage We Cause Others

This is a very difficult critical path because, as we have seen, the chronically predatory person does not seek or accept the need for change, and the occasional predatory act can be easily excused or justified. One of the most essential tasks of this critical path is to make and keep the promises you make in your personal code of conduct. It is important for people to create limitations on their own behavior because these limitations guide decision-making as well as determine the extent to which you can accept success and achievement at someone else's expense. The limits and boundaries we set for ourselves are also extremely important ways of controlling angry impulses. As with every critical path, the fourth step combines examining your AMPs with practicing the type of self-talk and affirmations that help you retrain your attitudes and beliefs. Here are some of the more common AMPs that excuse and justify predatory behavior:

AMPs That Excuse Predatory Behavior

- "I know he got hurt, but business is business."
- "If he wasn't prepared to lose, maybe he shouldn't have played the game."
- "All's fair in love and war."
- "She would have done the same thing to me if I didn't do it first."
- "Maybe hurting him this much is good for him in the long run. It will educate him that this is not the best way to be spending his time."
- "I got so caught up in the heat of the competition that I didn't realize what the outcome would be."
- "I didn't say anything about him (or her) that hasn't been said by someone else."
- "I had to do what was best for me."

A common theme of these AMPs is a lack of responsibility-taking for the outcome of what happens when behavior is opportunistic. It *is* possible to go into adversarial circumstances with an eye toward controlling damage to your adversary. When you can't you are operating purely on ego. Here are some affirmations that offer a balanced view of competitive situations:

Affirmations to Use in Competitive Environments

- "I can win and still be fair to my opponents. I do not have to destroy my adversaries to get out of this ahead of the game."
- "It is a good idea to protect the feelings of people I don't particularly care for because that reduces their motivation to hold grudges that might come back at me at an inconvenient time."
- "Gloating might make me feel good in the short run, but always makes a negative impression on others."

(List continued on following page.)

> - "Am I really considering what my drive for success might be doing to others?"
> - "I am going to keep promises I have made about my character and values."

Finally, here are the affirmations you can practice to help you deal with people who are engaging you in a predatory way:

> **Affirmations to Help Deal With Predatory Behavior From Others**
> - "I am going to give this person as little information about me as possible."
> - "I will not give this person the enjoyment and strength he gets from pushing my buttons."
> - "If I cannot control and manage the behavior of this person, I will get away from them."
> - "By playing with 'finesse' and 'stealth' I will retain my advantage and give this predatory person very little to attack me with."

Controlling Predatory Behavior: Step Five—

Success Milestones

Owning up to Predatory Behavior

Success milestones in this critical path are few, but difficult to master. They require a lot of "owning up" to behavior that is not so desirable, and they require letting go of excuses you have made in the past for taking advantage of others.

That's it! However, as they say, "walking the walk" is a lot harder than merely "talking the talk." When you are confident that you have mastered these milestones, it is time to put the icing on the cake. The last critical path is called "Cool Under Pressure," and it is about mastering those circumstances when life puts your back up against the wall. Good luck!

Success Milestones for "Controlling Predatory Behavior"

1. Be able to acknowledge that you have caused other people to suffer needlessly so you could gain success, popularity, financial reward, or social power. (Don't be so quick to say, "I've never done any of those things." If you have ever gossiped or spoken behind someone's back, you have gained social power by putting someone else down.)

2. Create a personal code of values that places limits on what you are willing to do in order to achieve personal gain.

3. Be able to control your desire to strike out at people who try to make you look bad by their own predatory behavior.

4. Understand the value of downplaying, ignoring, and becoming "invisible" to personal attacks.

5. Refuse to "telegraph" the strategies you will use to oppose people who are trying to make you look bad.

Chapter 11

Cool Under Pressure, the Sixth Critical Path

This last critical path is about life's toughest times, when keeping cool under pressure can make the difference between making life significantly better or significantly worse, all within a relatively short space of time. When stress is high, frustration can build quickly and emotions can spiral out of control. The steps in this path prepare you for dealing with these situations.

Step One: Mastery Content

Examples of Life's Toughest Times

Poor anger management will often bring negative consequences. However, the times when consequences are the greatest are the times when your back is up against a wall, the stakes are high, and you lose control of yourself. These are examples of some of those times:

- You are engaged in a hostile legal conflict and have to deal with adversarial circumstances that are unusual to your style of dealing with people. For instance, you are being sued by someone, or you are being investigated by the government or other important organization.
- Your productivity and/or performance is being evaluated harshly or wrongfully criticized in a business setting or at work.
- You are in the public eye as a result of an achievement, honor, or bid for a political position.
- You are caught in the middle of a stressful circumstance or emergency, where keeping your wits about you, managing others, and/or managing your emotions is essential to your survival. This includes being part of a disaster, or being the target or victim of a crime.
- You are immediately forced into a situation of major life change (For example, divorce, death of a family member, or economic hardship).
- Any circumstance in which you are wrongfully blamed for doing something that you were never a part of or had no association with.
- Any circumstance where you or your work is being judged (For example, a competition where you are judged on your personal presentation as well as your work.)
- You are the subject of investigation by an important organization or agency.

Going to Court

If there were ever a life experience that everyone could do without, it is having to go to court for *any* reason whatsoever. Having to go to court for anything is a good example of a major life stressor that places you in a position of having to reorient yourself and your priorities to deal with a circumstance of extreme frustration. Dealing with court and legal difficulties requires that you learn to be "cool under pressure," which is what this critical path is about. Whether you are suing someone or being sued, accusing someone or being accused, fighting for something or against something, the experience of being involved with the legal system is never what we imagine it will be.

Part of the reason court is not what we expect boils down to a very basic contradiction, which is that we expect everyone to see "fairness" the way *we* see it, from our own point of view. In reality, what fairness *really* reflects is a balanced consideration of *two* points of view. Ultimately, even if we get half of what we want in court, it is not getting the other half, which can often make us upset. Add to this the fact that going to court is usually expensive (if not in terms of what it costs in dollars, then certainly in terms of what it costs in time and emotional stress). It also involves having to deal with lawyers, some of whom are outstandingly talented human beings, some of whom are merely mediocre, and some of whom are the scum of the earth and the reason for all the bad-lawyer jokes out there. Going to court takes you out of your natural environment and places you in a position of helplessness and lack of control. This is true, even if you work in a legal environment. It is a whole different ball game when you are one of the people personally involved in the legal action as opposed to one of the people involved in "putting on the show."

Check Point

Going to court is always a stressful and frustrating experience, because very rarely does anyone perceive "fairness" exactly the same way as the people involved in the law suit.

The next vignette is a good example of how, regardless of your profession or life experience, having to be a litigant (person who brings on a legal action or is the subject of one) is different than operating in a professional role.

Mike and Michelle Judge

When Michael Judge became a judge, everyone made the obvious jokes. He was a good judge and, like all good judges, he was an excellent political campaigner. When election time came around, he was out there shaking hands, and passing out flyers. Right there next to him was his wife, Michelle, a tireless workhorse and Judge Judge's biggest supporter.

As with many positions of power and influence, when things get out of hand, they get out of hand in a big way, and when the Judges marriage began to break apart, it broke apart in a million pieces. Worse yet, The Judge's had two children under the age of 16, and apart from financial issues surrounding the breakup, Mike was threatening to sue Michelle for custody of the kids. During one particularly difficult night, the police were called to the house because of the racket they were making, "discussing" family issues.

It was Mike's allegation that Michelle was drinking too much. It was Michelle's allegation that some of the late nights Mike was keeping were not related to his political obligations, but were social and with members of the opposite sex. These complaints formed the basis of what was becoming a more and more bitter breakup by the minute. It was all complicated by the fact that the local courthouse gossip mill was making minced meat out of both of them as stories, some real, some extremely exaggerated, and some completely fabricated went circulating through the always gossip-hungry local community of lawyers.

The prevailing perception was that Mike was an eager go-getter, but that Michelle was the backbone of the family. No one, except Mike and the children, saw that Michelle's over-consumption of alcohol was a huge problem. They could, however, easily observe Mike flirting and at times going out to dinner with younger female attorneys. The real problem was that little was being done to address both problems, and each was interested in garnering sympathy from the community in which they operated.

Eventually, Mike did sue for custody, requesting that the case be handled in another jurisdiction where they were not as well known. This would protect Mike as well as Michelle. Unfortunately, because he was a judge, Mike was used to having his words accepted without dispute. Not so, in his own case, especially when he was put on the witness stand and had to testify to the thousands of hours of work his wife did on his behalf, and to the number of nights out he spent each week. After all, his wife was good enough to raise the children while he was "campaigning," but was now too sick and too much of a drinker to be trusted with them alone. "I know where this is going," Mike thought to himself. "I've seen it a hundred times...." Seeing it a hundred times did not stop him from acting the way he had seen many people in that position act—defensive, nasty, sarcastic, and critical.

Michelle had no history of alcohol abuse, no DWI convictions, and Mike couldn't produce a single witness to testify that they had ever seen her drunk at a political event. Michelle, on the other hand, did produce a witness who testified that Mike was very drunk on the night he was elected to his position and had to ask Michelle to drive him home. The reality was that Michelle had developed a serious drinking problem over the last six months. Like many people who abuse alcohol, she did not do it in public or in front of anyone except her family. The children loved both of their parents. They would never do anything to hurt either parent, so they would not testify to witnessing their mother drunk almost every night for the past six months.

At the end of the portion of the trial that had to do with the children, the lawyers for Mike and Michelle spoke, and they finally settled on custody to Michelle with liberal visitation to Mike, thus sparing both parties the stress of a legal decision. Mike knew that the outbursts he had on the witness stand did not make a favorable impression on the judge presiding over the case. Wisely, he decided to cut his losses and avoid the stories that would circulate around his courthouse if he went to trial on custody and lost.

Unfortunately, political strategizing and a hundred other factors took precedence over the needs of the children. Within three months after The Judges ended their marriage, Michelle's alcohol use worsened and required an inpatient hospitalization and rehabilitation, which ultimately was the best thing for her. It would have been much healthier for the children to have seen her get help without crashing and burning. In the end, everyone suffered from the loss of opportunity. Mike lost the opportunity to assist his children by assisting their mother (regardless of whether he wanted to remain married to her or not). Michelle lost the opportunity to become sober at a much earlier part of her alcoholism.

The children lost the opportunity to see their parents part as friends and co-supporters, a role they had enjoyed seeing them in for their whole lives. If Mike had a better handle on his anger in a tough situation, both before he decided to sue for custody and once he was in the situation, the outcome might have been very different.

There are a number of lessons to be learned from this story, but especially the lesson that no one is immune to circumstances that can become difficult, uncontrollable, and pressure-filled. I have tried to explain in the other critical paths that frustration is to anger like gasoline is to fire. Staying in touch with how fast stress can rise, and counteracting that stress using the coping strategies in the steps of this critical path, will help keep you "Cool Under Pressure."

High-Pressure Environments and Situations

High-pressure environments—those that place your health, safety, career, family, or reputation on the line—produce a unique type of stress. Anger is related to the "fight" or "flight" system that is designed into the human nervous system. Fight-or-flight reactions are those emergency or high-pressure situations that we react to by either running away to save ourselves (flight) or reacting aggressively to ward off the threatening stressor (fight). The kinds of situations I have been discussing in this chapter are those that activate this emergency response system. Pressure-filled situations do not permit us as much time to think through the solution to a problem, and instead we rely on the emotional equivalent of "autopilot" to get past the dangerous or threatening situation. Frustration, feelings of being threatened, anxiety, and worrying about the outcome of a tough situation can make people impatient and angry. This critical path is about those situations where anger comes to a "quick boil," as opposed to a "slow burn." It is, by far, the most difficult type of angry emotional reaction to have to handle. For most of us, encountering these situations is, thankfully, rare.

Some personal and occupational roles place people in these situations all the time. For those people, it is vitally important to physical and emotional health to develop a set of tools to handle large amounts of daily stress.

Avoiding Superman Syndrome

One of the ways that highly stressful situations damage us physically and mentally is when we assume that we can take on more and more of life's most demanding situations, ignore the effects they have on our emotional and physical health, and not suffer as a result of it. Here's an example:

Dr. Karen Corazon

Another completed day of work in the coronary care facility of a large hospital saw Dr. Karen Corazon weaving through rush-hour traffic to pick up her 3-year-old bundle of joy from aftercare. There was relaxing music on the radio for once, and tonight was not a cooking night. Dinner was already prepared and required only heating up. Another small favor life was throwing Dr. Corazon's way was that the kitchen was clean, and no clothes had to be washed. It was a night where all she had to do was kick off her shoes and enjoy the company of her daughter and husband.

Work had been very stressful. After becoming the chief resident of cardiac surgery at her hospital, her responsibilities changed. Truth is, she chose a rough profession, operating on the organ that pumps the life into each and every one of us. She had operated on the very young and the very old, and on everyone in between. A good day of work meant that someone's family would experience the joy of a loved one's presence for more time than anyone had previously bargained for. A bad day of work, well, that needs no explanation. For now, however, her sights were focused on seeing her daughter's smiling face. One more block to go, and one more traffic light to make. It was the "long light" on Northern Boulevard. Seven minutes of waiting, waiting, waiting if you were unfortunate enough to miss the left-turn signal—and it looked like that was going to happen. If she could get into the left-turning lane she would make it. The problem was that there were four cars ahead of her and, in order to get into the lane, she would have to drive outside the "safety zone" for about three seconds. She went for it, and wouldn't you know it, the last car before she could jump into the turning lane was a squad car. The police officer, a woman, raised her head as Karen was passing by and immediately jumped on the accelerator, lights flashing. "Shit! Why is this happening to me?" Normally, Karen would have been very apologetic to any police officer stopping her for any reason, but not today. A woman cop should have a little sympathy for another woman in rush-hour traffic (at least this was her reasoning).

Karen pulled over to the other side of the intersection and waited for the police officer to approach. Instead of waiting for the police officer to speak, she barked at her, "Are you really going to give me a ticket for short-circuiting that turn signal by 30 feet?" The officer replied, "One foot, 30 feet, 100 feet, you can't enter the turn lane until you pass the striped marks." Karen shot back, "That is such a *crock*. I endangered no one. I want to pick up my daughter at daycare. She has been waiting all day to see me. I put in 10 hours of surgery today, and I am wiped. You should know how it is to maintain a career and a family." The police officer replied, "Yes, I do, as a matter of fact, I am performing the responsibilities of my career as we speak, and that is to enforce the law which you have just broken." Karen was getting angrier. "Oh, really, so now harassing innocent citizens is part of your job. This is so stupid. It's beyond stupid. If you are going to write me a ticket, go back to your cruiser and write it so that you can get your quota or whatever and go bother someone else." Karen herself could not believe how she was acting, or the words that were coming out of her mouth, but she could not control herself.

Although it would have been a perfect opportunity for the police officer to lose her cool, she did not, but the officer could not resist the final word. "You know, Ma'am, I had absolutely no intention of writing you a summons when I stopped you. I simply wanted to make you aware of what you were doing and give you a warning. Now, after listening to your nasty attitude, I do not think a simple talking to will change the way you drive in the future, so you are getting a ticket. Wait here."

Karen just sat there dumbfounded.

This story is important because it shows the uncharacteristically angry way Karen dealt with the situation, because she had let herself become unaware of the level of stress she had been experiencing. She thought she could handle it *all*. The consequences of not being able to manage her stress could have been a lot worse if she lost control of her frustration while a patient was on the operating table. People in high-stress situations must stop to decompress. It is possible to become overly focused and absorbed on job tasks or any responsibility in life, to such an extent that it can cripple you when an unexpected source of stress or unexpected problem enters your life.

Avoiding the Anger Ambush

Anger can get the better of you when life brings unpleasant "surprises" that demand immediately switching gears and changing priorities. A tax notice, an unexpected expense, illness, sudden loss of your job, becoming aware that you are the subject of an inquiry or investigation, are all events that can ambush you. Impulsive and panicky reactions to these events can quickly turn to anger and frustration, most of which begins with the question, "Why *me*?" Part of staying "cool under pressure" requires that you go back to the critical path of avoiding personalization by realizing that, even if you knew "why," it would most likely not remove the source of the stress. Nonetheless, "Why me?" is a typical first reaction to large-scale unexpected stress. The key to overcoming feelings of being ambushed by life's unexpected stressors is to switch from "why" to "how" and "what," as in "Now that I am in this mess, *how* can I solve the problem or control the damage" and "*What* can I do first?"

Avoid Fast-Forwarding

"Fast-forwarding" is a way of describing what happens when we are confronted with something that makes us nervous and worried, and by imagining what *could* happen when we start to believe it *is* happening. Most of what we think of when we imagine what could happen is bad (for instance, "I could lose my job," "My reputation could be destroyed," "I will be humiliated," or "I will become poor and homeless"). As a result, we assume that there will be unfairness and injustice done to us. Naturally, when we *imagine* all of those horrible outcomes, we begin to feel as though unfairness and injustice is inevitable. When we reach this point, it is easy to fall into the habit of relying on AMPs that twist our thinking to conclude that we are the victims of unfairness, and that can lead us to act in angry ways. Here is an example of how AMPs progress to the point of prematurely convincing us that we are victimized and treated unfairly:

> **AMP's That Make Bad Situations Worse**
> - "I always knew this would happen to me someday."
> - "This is awful and horrible, and it will never go away."
> - "This is going to destroy my life."
> - "I will never be able to recover from this."
> - "I can't wait to get back at the people who are doing this to me."
> - "If they are going to play dirty, I am going to play dirty."
> - "I must have done something to deserve this."
> - "I am the only one who has to deal with shit like this."
> - "These people must really hate me in order to pursue this type of action against me."
> - "I would rather run away from everything than have to deal with this."

Taking the focus off "why," resisting the temptation to allow your fears to force you too far into the future, and disputing the AMPs that prevent you from thinking logically and clearly are the points of emphasis that form the coping strategies in the next stop on this critical path.

Step Two: Coping Strategies

First Aid for Tough Times

Tough times are inevitable and, although instinctively we know this, they can take us off guard and create a sense of panic, lack of control, and angry responding. Tough times create psychological injury, almost like a broken leg from a bad fall. Here are some tough times that may require some mental mending:

Tough Times That Require Mental Mending

- A letter in the mail informs you of an IRS audit.

- A process server hands you documents that say you are being sued for more money than you have made in the last five years.

- There has been a theft from your company involving several hundreds of thousands of dollars. The questions that internal security are asking you lead you to believe that they suspect you did it.

- News of a mistake you made more than 20 years ago is resurfacing at an inconvenient time. People who are your adversaries are trying to use the information to discredit you from achieving a major step forward in your career.

- Your performance is being reviewed by a panel of people who will decide whether to advance you to the next level on you career path or keep you where you are. The panel is developing tough questions for you to answer based on your history and performance, and you will be defending your career.

- You are with a group of people, some of whom have become injured by a terrorist attack. A threat to your health and safety may still be present. Several of the people in the group have fashioned themselves as "leaders" and are directing you and other members of the group to do things that you do not think are safe.

There are a host of very difficult situations people can suddenly encounter in life that require a kind of mental "first aid," or emergency actions and reactions. These situations have all or some of the following ingredients:

Common Characteristics of Tough Times

- They come on strong (and sometimes suddenly).
- They involve a threat to your health, social status, safety, or well-being.

(List continued on next page.)

- ◆ They require cool thinking and strategizing.
- ◆ They can get much worse if you lose your temper.
- ◆ They often involve some antagonistic person or situation.

These moments can create some of the most significant turning points in your life, but they do not have catastrophic endings. Even those situations that seem to start badly, when handled properly, can build confidence, character, and ultimately success.

Preparing Is Key

The difference between thinking about "worst-case scenarios" and letting your worries and fears "fast-forward" your feeling as though the worst has already happened is that "worst-case" thinking focuses you on controlling the damage as the end result of the exercise, and worrying about the worst-possible outcome merely focuses you on the negative end result.

Training your mind and decision-making before things get tough makes the kind of "automatic" thinking and behaving that is required in tough situations easier and more efficient. Going over various scenarios and techniques reduces the level of anxiety and stress you feel when you encounter tough situations. Sometimes this is referred to as "stress inoculation." Training your behavior and decision-making will take away some of the sting and feelings of ambush and surprise that come with taking on difficult situations.

Training your emotions away from angry outbursts and temper tantrums during tough times is essential in situations where your behavior is being judged by others. Although it is rational and logical to conclude that any human being under considerable stress may lose his or her temper from time to time, this kind of leeway is almost never afforded to people who are under accusation, scrutiny, or investigation. Instead, people who lose their tempers in these situations are often assumed to be guilty of whatever it is they are being scrutinized for. People who lose their tempers in difficult situations are judged more harshly, punished more severely, and alienate themselves from the people who support them.

Emotions can run especially hot in situations where your honesty and reputation are questioned. It is very important to practice imagining how you will behave if you are challenged in these areas. It is equally important to practice fighting off or censoring behaviors that might make you appear hotheaded, out of control, or enraged.

"This Can't Be Happening to Me"

When life is going along relatively smoothly, we do not feel any large measure of threat. When something terrible happens, we are usually more than willing to let the "people who take care of it," take care of it. A lifetime of living in a culture with the presumption that "on most days everything will be all right" can leave us in bad shape for handling ourselves when we do encounter a seemingly impossible-to-handle situation. (September 11 is a good example.) It is only natural, then, that when people encounter any severe crisis, their first reaction is *denial*. The denial is supported by thoughts such as "This must be some kind of mistake" or "I can't believe this is happening to me." As a momentary reaction, this is natural. But as a working strategy, waiting for someone else to handle a problem that directly involves you is not a good coping plan.

Whether it is a terrorist attack, a lawsuit, an accusation for an activity you had no part in, or some other threatening event, it is important to start gathering information about what is happening *and start dealing with it*. Eventually, when you realize that something bad *is* happening to you and that it is *not* a mistake, without a plan, you will become fearful if not terrified. Feeling afraid and terrified intensifies feelings of helplessness and loss of control. Intensified feelings of helplessness and loss of control produce frustration. And as you know by now, frustration produces anger.

Why Me?

Initial shock and anger are the predictable results of feeling ambushed by circumstances that make you feel helpless or have threatened your reputation, family, survival, or freedom. The previous critical paths emphasize that anger is supported by anger-maintaining presumptions. By way of review, your initial "first aid" treatments when encountering tough situations in life require two actions. The first is to attack your disbelief and acknowledge that you are in a tough situation. The second is to short-circuit all of the angry AMPs that keep you away from solving the real problem, averting the crisis, or presenting information that will make accusations for things you are innocent of go away. That means you must catch yourself in the act of repeating those messages that interfere with productive problem-solving.

Your previous efforts from completing the first few critical paths should immediately tell you that obsessing over the "why me's" is an unproductive type of *personalization*. Often life's toughest situations are attributable to chance, bad luck, bad timing, being in the wrong place at the wrong time, and so on. Leave it at that. When the bad time is over with, you can go back to pondering the mystery of your place in the universe. Right now, it's time to take care of business.

After the Shock and Sting

Your coping plan for tough times should take into account that, after your initial impulsive or momentarily angry reactions to accusations or bad news, you will want to keep screaming to anyone who will listen, and to a few people who might not want to. Try to confine excessive and repeated reactions to people whom you know and love, and in the privacy and solitude of a place where no one else can see you. I am not advising this because I am opposed to emotional displays. Expressing one's feelings is an important part of communicating—it's the *intensity* of how you express those feelings that can get you into trouble. Remember, people tend to judge angry, intense, emotional reactions in a negative way, whether they are justified or not. Your best demeanor is always to appear interested in what is going on, and your best way to move forward is by being active in your participation in solving the problem.

While angry, defensive reactions to tough situations are not in your best interests, giving the appearance of avoiding the situation or being disinterested will make you seem uncooperative and appear as though you are "hiding something." The impression to shoot for is *concerned but not hysterical*. Think about what it is like to be stung by a bee. The initial reaction is usually, "Shit! That hurts!" most people will understand that for the moment. However, if you spend the next six weeks of your life maintaining that level of emotional intensity, people will think there is something wrong with you. Similarly, if you let the sting swell up to the point where you have to have a body part amputated, they will also think there is something wrong with you. The reasonable response is that you are going to get it looked at, help yourself as much as you can, and act as though your life is going on as usual, albeit with a little extra inconvenience from where the sore spot is. Likewise, if you have fallen under scrutiny or some of your dirty laundry is being aired in a malicious attempt to discredit you, show that you are handling it, and move through the regular motions you take through life. Make it so that people will wonder whether those who are either challenging you or threatening are concerned for no good reason.

What to Do With Your Energy

Encountering life's most difficult situations, especially those that affect your career, reputation, social life, and emotional health usually create intense feelings of anxiety, fear, and discomfort. Often it will feel as though you are "jumping out of your skin." The worst thing you can do with all of the energy is play a mental tape of all the horrible things that will happen to you if "no one gets it." The natural and normal fear of anyone who is being needlessly scrutinized, investigated, or blamed is, "What will happen to me if, by some chance, people do not or cannot see that I have done nothing to warrant this?" Those of us who are creative can spend days writing unhappy and catastrophic ends to the drama that surrounds us. All this does is create pessimism, and worry on top of worry. Instead, use your energy to *gather information* and *get help*. Whatever your problem is, it is probably not a new one. Use your library, your computer, the telephone book, and your network of friends to research help that's available. You must actively fight the impulse or tendency to believe that problems of this type will go away on their own, or that someone will appear out of nowhere to rescue you. If you do engage in this type of thinking, you will become depressed, avoid working on solutions to your problem, and you will procrastinate. What you will find, and this is vitally important, is that after the initial shock of knowing that you are being sued, investigated, scrutinized, evaluated, or reviewed, things may calm down for a while. Many of these kinds of events stem from within large organizations, and the internal mechanisms of large organizations turn slowly. *Use this to your advantage.* Do not take a vacation from doing something about it, especially if the potential consequences are far-reaching. On some days, you may want to concentrate on it less than others. Or you might want to schedule in advance some time off, after which you immediately get back on track.

Check Point
Having to deal with a situation that creates tremendous stress and nervousness will often leave you with a lot of excess energy. Put that energy to good use by gathering information and talking to people who might help you. Taking action and gathering information can go along way to convince you that there are things you can do to make the situation better.

However, if you get into the habit of putting off dealing with the process of solving the problem, before you know it you will be smack up against deadlines, court dates, and other pressure points—and you will hate it.

Do not be shy about asking for help, begging for help, or calling organizations that deal with your particular problem. Now is not the time to yield to tendencies to be shy or embarrassed. Instead of being shy or embarrassed, promise yourself to be properly thankful or give a volunteer effort to others after your difficult time has passed.

Some Important "Don'ts"

Keeping "cool under pressure" is as much about not making certain mistakes and assumptions as it is about gathering the right help and information. Here are some important guidelines about what "not" to do.

Don'ts for Controlling Anger During Tough Situations

1. Do not develop "instant hatred" for people who are investigating you, lawyering against you, or reviewing you, especially if they are strangers to you and it is part of their job. Chances are if you make it personal, they will too. Why would you want to make anyone *more* motivated to give you a hard time? I have seen countless examples of investigators who are not passionate about what they have to investigate or review and are simply looking for a reason to refuse to go forward, or go forward without passion. Similarly, I have seen lawyers who are more sympathetic to their adversary's case than they are to

(List continued on next pages.)

their own client. People whose job it is to review and even prosecute others often look for reasons to back off. On the other hand, if you get up in someone's face and imply that they are stupid or incompetent, all you are doing is giving them motivation to find something, *anything* to make you look bad.

2. Do not grant your adversaries "superhuman powers." Just because someone is scrutinizing you doesn't mean they are an expert who can make anyone look bad, even if there is nothing bad there. If you give them that power, you will have more reason to feel threatened, more reason to behave defensively, and less of an ability to communicate.

3. Do not give your adversaries the impression that you think they are morons. This is true even if they *are*. Chances are, if your adversaries are idiots and incompetent, that is good for you. Always be polite to your adversaries, even when they are nasty to you. It makes a better impression on everyone and will almost always take some of the wind out of their sails. Do not let your adversaries know which buttons they can push, because they will wear those buttons out at every opportunity. Finally, an adversary can be a moron in every other aspect with the exception of the issue he or she is dealing with you about. Anyone who does something a hundred times a day is going to have an advantage over someone who is doing it for the first time.

4. Do not criticize the process you are involved in. As you will see in the next step, there are ways of expressing your disapproval, but it has to be done very carefully. You may think a legal proceeding is "bullshit," but if you express it, or even act in a manner that is consistent with it, you are making your hill higher and steeper.

5. Do not expect that after you present yourself, people will act convinced of your truthfulness, sincerity, or righteousness. Not everyone will "look" as thrilled to endorse

your side of the story as you will be thrilled to learn that your hard time has come to an end. Many people who investigate or analyze facts for a living do it with a kind of coldness and poker face that cannot be easily read. Do not make assumptions based on the look on someone's face, their body language, or their eye contact. Misreading these signals will make you frustrated, upset, and angry, and you could easily turn a positive outcome into a negative one if you presuppose what someone else is thinking or how they are feeling.

6. Do not expect that anyone evaluating your behavior will think you are a "nice person," even if that is the reputation you have enjoyed your whole life. People who evaluate others for a living have been fooled a hundred times by people who seem nice, but who turn out to be not so nice. Again, do not get angry or frustrated if anyone evaluating you cannot immediately see how wonderful you are. In the end it doesn't matter, as long as you influence things as positively as you can.

7. Do not expect that everyone else will understand your indignation even if it is well deserved. It is normal and natural to become furious over being blamed for something unjustly or being called out onto the carpet for no good reason. Do not turn the situation into an exercise in correcting whatever system has brought you into the center of it. Work on that problem later when all of this is over with. Do not suggest that when your ordeal is over, "heads will roll." Bullying your way out of a situation where you are on the defensive is not a good strategy.

8. Do not lie. Credibility is a crucial issue in impression formation in all types of difficult situations. In the vast majority of circumstances, lying will cause more trouble than it will ward off.

9. Do not permit yourself to be totally consumed by your difficult situation. Do not isolate yourself or become a "cavedweller." Day-to-day survival is still a necessary aspect of life. Whenever possible:

- Go to work.
- Go shopping for necessities.
- Feed yourself.
- Do not overdo your use of substances such as caffeine or alcohol.
- Exercise.
- Read for enjoyment.
- Enjoy your family.
- Maintain your friendships.

Some Important "Do's"

Here is a list of things you can and should practice prior to having to answer questions, testifying, or making a presentation about a topic that may involve pointed or tough questioning:

Do's For Controlling Anger During Tough Situations

1. Learn how to listen and pause before responding to allegations. Never talk or write about the first thing that comes to your mind. Respond in your head first, and then review what you would like to say. At the very least, your pause will make you seem less "jumpy," antagonistic, or "snappy."

2. Quiet your body. Practice sitting still. Relax the muscles in your face when someone is talking to you. You can moderate your body's transmission of signals that make you anxious by breathing in and repeating the sentence (to yourself), "I can count to three," and then exhaling while repeating the sentence, "I can count to three and four."

3. Limit your range of emotional expression in both directions. Do not explode in laughter or in anger. Smile when you are pleased. Try to remain neutral when you are displeased.

(List continued on following page.)

4. When you can accept responsibility for something, do so, especially if the accusation that is being made against you is complicated and involves some transgression of your behavior. Admitting to some mistakes is often seen as a positive. Blaming everyone and everything and being critical is almost always seen as a negative.

5. Always, always, always remain polite and respectful. All people who judge and scrutinize others take either formal or informal notice of the demeanor of the person they are dealing with. Be pleasant. Give the impression that the process going on around you is uncomfortable for you but that you understand the necessity and importance of it. That is what most reasonable people expect— cooperation amidst discomfort. Any behavior that is outside that perception, if you are either too comfortable or too angry, may be assessed negatively.

6. Often the best impression you can make is no impression. You want people to think: "This is a 'regular person' out there trying to make a living doing his job, and trying hard to be helpful and cooperative to those around him." The power of many kinds of accusations (not all kinds, but many) lies in an attempt to make a person appear larger than life and, therefore, capable of doing things that most people would not do. Keeping a low profile, speaking when you are spoken to, and addressing people in authority with the proper terminology will assist in showing that you are not larger than life, not above politeness and civilized behavior.

Lawyers, Lawyers Everywhere…

As a forensic psychologist, I have spent a good deal of my professional life interacting with lawyers, judges, and people in authority. Some lawyers complicate the process of finding out the truth and make their money by steering people away from finding the truth, and that disturbs me. That being said, some of my best friends are lawyers, and boy, when you need them, they certainly can perform a valuable service.

Having to deal with lawyers as an expert witness can be difficult. My opinion and my reputation are always on the line and under attack. Most good lawyers make me work hard for a living. However, it doesn't compare to the stress of having to deal with lawyers when you are on either end of a lawsuit. If you are suing someone, you will always have a lawyer on the other side trying to make you look unfair and unreasonable for bringing the lawsuit. If you are being sued, you will always have a lawyer trying to attack you for whatever it is you are being sued for.

The best lawyers are often the biggest pains because they have a natural ability to ask questions that make you feel uncomfortable, foolish, and as though you are lying even when you are telling the truth. The good news is that judges know this because they are lawyers, too. The bad news is that it is hard to trust that judges will know this, because even judges appear to be swayed by lawyering that is less representative of the truth and more representative of showmanship.

To end this section, I am going to give you some tips on how to handle lawyers, based on almost two decades of having to interact with them.

How to Handle Lawyers

1. If you are not getting along with your lawyer, try as hard as you can to get a new one. Wittingly or unwittingly, a lawyer who you are not getting along with can seriously damage your case by complaining about you in public or ,worse yet, to a judge. Whenever I hire a lawyer I always ask him to promise me, point blank, that they will never say anything negative or derogatory about me to an adversary or to a judge, even in casual conversation. If nothing else, I believe this will serve as a cue and an extra measure of censorship if the impulse arises.

2. Be polite and courteous, but never speak to an adversarial lawyer, even socially, without your lawyer present. Information you speak even in a "casual conversation" can and often will be used against you.

(List continues on next page.)

3. Never think you can outsmart a lawyer at his own game. You don't get extra points for making a lawyer look stupid. If you fail, the lawyer gets extra points for making you look stupid. It is as easy as that.

4. Never harass a lawyer. As I mentioned before, why would you want to increase anyone's motivation to make your life miserable?

5. Take your time when answering any questions posed to you by a lawyer. And unless it is an answer you have rehearsed with your own lawyer, answer with as few words as possible.

6. Resist the opportunity to make speeches. Answer questions directly and honestly.

7. Be polite and respectful to everyone you encounter in a courtroom. Judges and attorneys are often very familiar with court staff, clerks, court officers, and other personnel. A "bad report" from any one of these people can have a negative impact on a case (even though it shouldn't, it does, so be careful).

8. Controlling your emotions is essential, but particularly so with judges. If a judge corrects your behavior, say, "I'm sorry, Your Honor," and don't do it again.

9. If a lawyer is questioning you and really getting under your skin, ask for a break, a recess, or an opportunity to go to the bathroom. Even if the judge denies your request (unlikely unless you are doing it every five minutes) the request itself and the time it takes to consider it may break the lawyer's momentum. Always take your time answering. Judges sometimes become very impatient with attorneys with long lines of questions about the same topic. The longer you take to answer, the more time will be spent. Eventually a judge may tell the attorney who is hammering you to move on.

10. When things become very tense and anxious, soothe yourself with the thought that the process has a beginning and an end, even if it is an end for "just today." Though it often feels like it, you will not be spending the rest of your life on the witness stand.

Step Three: Communication Skills

Wearing Your "Game Face"

Wearing your "game face" is an expression I use with my clients to describe the "mask" we need to wear in order to accomplish what is necessary in difficult situations. Imagine that you have to go into your boss's office an hour after he screamed at you for something totally unrelated to anything you did. You can scowl at him and communicate with your face, comments, and gestures how much of an ass you think he is, or you can get through the meeting as if nothing had transpired. What's that you say? You don't need to lick anyone's boots to make a living? Fine, if that's what you consider bootlicking, call him an ass and, if necessary, find another job. However, sometimes there is more to it than that. You may have more opportunities at that job than you can have somewhere else. You may think enough of yourself to know that having to deal with a stupid boss on an occasional basis is worth some of the other benefits. You might perceive that one day you will be in his position and he will be out on his rear end. It all depends on your situation, but there is something to be said for being able to act in your own best interests by keeping some of your feelings to yourself and putting on a happy show, just to get you through a tough time.

Please don't confuse this with being a "fake" or a "phony." Instead, look at it as an exercise in social judgment or part of the cost of doing business. In the end, if it benefits you and it decreases needless conflict, that is what should count more than anything else. Let's say you have to appear before a judge who, at a prior time, made it clear he didn't like you and gave you a very bad decision. Or you have to give a presentation to a client you know does not like or respect you. Does it make any sense at all to reinforce negative perceptions and make life more difficult for you? Or does it make more sense to put your best foot forward and try and prove them wrong? I guess that depends on whether you feel it is more important to try to control the damage that can be done to you by those who don't like you; or give yourself the satisfaction, if there is any, to let someone who doesn't like you know that you're smart enough to know they don't like you, but not classy enough to keep it to yourself.

Standing on Ceremony

We are a "free country" and we should be allowed to say what we think, right? Wrong. The belief that people should accept your feelings regardless of what they are just because we live in a free country and we are guaranteed freedom of speech is a fantasy and an AMP. Sure we can say (almost) anything we want without being thrown in jail for the words, but there is no guarantee that we won't suffer in other ways. It is not against the law to tell your boss to go screw himself. Your boss can't get you arrested, but he can fire you. This very sobering fact of life presses on the most stubborn nerve of almost everyone who has a problem with anger. They will always say, "it shouldn't matter what I say, how I say it, or who I say it to. As long as I am right, I should be treated fairly." Sure, that would be a great philosophy if only the world operated solely on the basis of "right" and "wrong" and there was a 100 percent accurate measurement of both. Unfortunately, this is where the logic breaks down. This critical path is about what happens when people stumble into a situation where they are accused, mishandled, victimized unfairly, scrutinized, evaluated by others, and judged. Everyone who is in this position, wants to be judged on the basis of what is truly "right," especially if the scrutiny or investigation that they are the subject of is undeserved. The problem is that the people who are doing the judging don't have enough information to know that it is undeserved and are mostly just doing their jobs. They have to evaluate you, understand you, poke at you, and observe you before they know it is undeserved. Your angry behavior might not be the correct criteria for them to focus on. In fact, it might be the worst, but it is the one that is often used to formulate judgments about what you might or might not have done.

It is insulting to be evaluated and judged. It impinges on privacy and freedom, and places a great amount of wear and tear on your nerves. however, if you stand on ceremony and tell the world in an angry way and with angry types of communications that you should not be judged on your angry behavior, but instead on the facts of whatever it is people are examining, you are speaking into deaf ears. It doesn't happen. It doesn't happen when you are stopped by a police officer who says you are speeding when you are not and you tell him to get his equipment checked and his eyes examined. It doesn't happen when you speak in a sarcastic, irritable, or nasty tone to judges, review boards, and almost anyone in any role where your behavior is being examined or criticized. Your demeanor, your "game face" is what people judge you on, whether you like it or not; whether it is fair or not.

Putting Together Your "Game Face"

Hopefully, the times will be few and far between when you will have to appear before a person or a group of people who will judge your behavior or decide whether your life will become better or worse after they get through with you. When it does happen, angry emotions can easily get the better of you. You can become nasty, condescending, sarcastic, rude, disrespectful, or oppositional. These are all ways of showing that you resent having to go through the process, and, often, the process is seemingly unfair, unnecessary, and inconvenient.

Check Point

A "game face" is the mask we wear when it is not in our best interests to make our true feeling (mostly angry) show. It is not a comfortable role to have to play, but is always best chalked up as part of the "cost of doing business."

The point of putting on your best set of manners for appearances sake is that it operates in your best interests and stops you from making a bad situation worse. When you are confronted with a difficult situation, the first priority should always be to get through it in the shortest possible amount of time. Some essential communication skills are as follows. A lot are merely the kind of common sense rules of polite conversation your mother should have taught you before you were 6 years old. Remember, common sense will get you through most situations in life, but teaching people common sense is rarely the hard part. It's motivating people to use it that's tough.

Finishing Touches

Communicating in a difficult situation is an exercise in "impression formation." The words we use, the way we dress, posture, cleanliness, and the looks on our faces all communicate something whether we like it or not. I can't tell you how many times I have heard judges, law enforcement officials, or other people who are in a position of authority and should know better, describe a man wearing a goatee or dressing in a certain way, by saying, "I didn't like that guy. He looks evil." Should a person be judged by whether or not he has facial hair or dresses in leather pants and a T-shirt? Of course not. Do you think that sorty of thing does not happen? If 20 years of experience watching people being judged means anything, I can tell you it does. I can tell you that people are judged if they wear dirty clothes to court, if they dress provocatively, if they have tattoos in obvious places or if they are loaded down with gaudy jewelry. If flavors were the best way to describe the best impression one could make in court, at a tribunal, or in a situation where you are being accused of something, "vanilla" would be the flavor I would choose. Plain Jane and Plain John have the best chance of being judged on the facts and not misjudged on their looks.

Here are some communication strategies for dealing with tough times:

Commonsense Communication Strategies for Tough Situations

1. Speak when you are spoken to and do not be a smart ass to anyone who is in a position of authority. If you are in a position where you have to respond to people in authority, use "Ma'am" and "Sir," "Mr." or "Ms.," or whatever professional or legal title they go by when you address them.

2. Do not imply that anyone in authority doesn't know what they are talking about or does not have the requisite amount of life experience to judge you.

3. If you are not certain about whether it is appropriate for you to speak or respond, ask politely, "May I respond to that?" or "Would it be all right if I spoke to that issue?" If this is not the way you usually speak, make it that way. It will be a pleasant surprise for the person you are speaking with to discover you took the time to learn.

4. Watch your body language, the sounds you make under your breath, and your side comments.

(List continues on the next page.)

5. If you are in a situation where you have hired an attorney to speak for you, let the attorney speak for you and do your best to be quiet.

6. If and when you do have to speak, speak loud enough so that others can hear you.

7. If you have to disagree, do it apologetically and by acknowledging what the opposing person said. For example: "I have listened carefully to what you have said, and I'm sorry I cannot agree." Avoid emotional reactions such as "That's a crock of shit" or "That's a lie!"

8. Do not interrupt someone when they are speaking. If someone interrupts you, say as politely as possible, "I listened very carefully while you were speaking. May I finish?" This does not apply when you are speaking to a person in authority.

9. Intelligent people are often very sarcastic. Sarcastic comments and a condescending attitude toward authority are dumb strategies. What is the point of trying to prove that the people who are judging you are stupid, if they were at least smart enough to put themselves in a position in life where they will have the last word?

10. Use polite forms of speech where they are appropriate including "Good morning" (or whatever time of day it is), and always say "Please" and "Thank you."

11. Try to avoid expressions such as, "To be perfectly honest..." and "I swear...to God...on my life...on my mother's grave...on my children's lives, and so on." These may be statements of emphasis and sincerity from your point of view, but they are almost always seen as "oversell" by people you are talking to.

Step Four: Affirmations

Fighting the Feeling of Being Singled Out, Victimized, and Scrutinized

If you are ever caught in the middle of a difficult situation, try to stay connected to the present. Force yourself to respond to what is happening *right now*. If you are pessimistic and prone to creating doom and gloom fantasies for yourself, you will become frustrated and act as though you have *already* been wrongfully judged, and that will make you angry. Your anger will become your biggest problem, because it will prevent others from seeing the truth.

AMPs can play a major role in reinforcing fantasies of being wrongfully judged or punished; as a result, they complicate your reactions to difficult situations. Here are some of the AMPs you should jump on top of and dispute right away:

Jumping to Conclusions With AMPs

- "Why is this happening to me?"
- "I don't deserve this."
- "How dare this happen to me."
- "I know that no one is interested in the *real* truth of all this."
- "I should not be subjected to this type of treatment."
- "Why are they picking on me?"

AMPs such as these tend to stimulate nonproductive and self-destructive thinking that interferes with your finding effective solutions to your problems. Here are some of the unhealthy thoughts and ideas that these AMPs will promote:

Other Nonproductive Thoughts That AMPs Promote

1. What is happening to you is punishment that was earned from something else and catching up with you.
2. Thoughts of revenge against those who are bothering you.

(List continued on next page.)

> 3. Feeling alone and isolated as a result of the difficult time.
> 4. Need to escape because the pressure is too great.
> 5. Feeling that this is the worst thing that will ever happen to you and it will ruin your life.

Letting yourself play and replay AMPs and the ensuing guilty, panicky, and sometimes foolish thoughts that follow them is a form of self-punishment you can learn to do without. Always emphasize *solving the problem*, and doing it in the best possible frame of mind.

Being Your Own Best Friend

In developing my anger management program and counseling people with anger problems, I have met hundreds of people who are "their own worst enemies." Many are victims of a combination of bad luck, stress, and a kind of intense stubbornness about insisting that they should be judged on what is fair, not by how they act and react. Here are some affirmations that will start you off on a perspective for managing tough times that is self-promoting as opposed to self-destructive. Remember, you need to practice them in order for them to be helpful.

> **Affirmations for Tough Times**
> - "I will not permit tough times to damage the rest of my life."
> - "I will seek information wherever I can to help me out of this difficult situation."
> - "I will practice being cool under pressure and imagine myself standing strong in front of those who question my integrity."
> - "I will not give people who oppose me the satisfaction of pushing my buttons."
> - "I will remain polite and cordial, because I know that is in my best interests."

(List continued on next page.)

- ◆ "I will not permit myself to lose control of my emotions in public, where it will create a negative impression of me."
- ◆ "I will try to concentrate on the fact that this terrible event will someday have an end to it."
- ◆ "I will rely on people I trust for help, and take their advice when I am too emotional to think on my own behalf."
- ◆ "I will resist the urge to run away or avoid dealing with difficult times."
- ◆ "I will dedicate the proper time and energy to solving my problems but I will not let difficult time rules my life or my emotions."
- ◆ "I know other people have gone through this and successfully weathered the storm."
- ◆ "This difficult time will not kill me, and anything that does not kill me ultimately will make me a stronger person (first expressed by the German philosopher Neitsche)."
- ◆ "I will not waste my time seeking revenge against my accusers. Living through these tough times without letting my adversaries think they can hold me down is the best revenge."

Step Five: Success Milestones

You Have Come a Long Way

Succeeding at the milestones in this critical path means a lot more than just completing a critical path. It means that by completing all of the critical paths, you have taken a thorough and comprehensive look at the role that anger plays in your personality, your approach to life, and your relationships.

Hopefully, you will not have to rely on being "cool under pressure," because your lifestyle and your life experiences won't require it. If you choose a profession or avocation that requires remaining calm and collected against the odds and in stressful situations, perhaps this critical path will help center and focus you. If you come into an occasional circumstance where you are in "hot seat," I hope that reflecting on the topics in this critical path, reviewing the coping skills, and practicing the affirmations will bring you through the tough time with a minimum of discomfort and aggravation.

Success Milestones for the Sixth Critical Path

1. You can look at difficult times with confidence that you will be able to ultimately succeed despite the stress you will be experiencing.

2. You can get through difficult times without making things worse for yourself before you can make them better.

3. You can confront tough times without being afraid to ask for help from people who have experience with solving problems, or being hesitant to lean on the people who love you for support.

4. You are able to control your emotions when people are confronting you.

5. You refuse to make your enemies and adversaries "larger than life."

6. You avoid the trap of antagonizing people who may be scrutinizing you, denying them more motivation to make your life difficult.

7. You have successfully developed a "game face," an attitude and style you use to cope and deal with difficult times and difficult people. You have also developed a set of behaviors that will get you through a situation as quickly as possible, with the least possible aggravation.

8. You can avoid the urge to "prove a point" at the wrong place and time.

9. You have eliminated sarcasm, facial expressions, and behaviors that make you appear uncooperative, disinterested, or oppositional when you must deal with authority or scrutiny.

10. You have eliminated AMPs that reinforce unproductive and self-destructive thinking when you are unfairly accused, observed, evaluated, or scrutinized.

Conclusion

See You Again Sometime

Please don't take it personally, but regardless of how hard you have worked, you are not finished yet. Learning the skills and techniques of successfully managing anger is a lot like learning a new language. You can never learn "whole language," because you can spend the rest of your life learning nuances, local phrases, and new vocabulary. Anger is an emotion that is exceedingly complex. You may find that you will encounter new annoyances at new phases of life—new pet peeves or new habits about people that drive you nuts. You will lose your patience in new and creative ways. All of that is normal and predictable. After going through this program, the advantage you gain is that fewer things will make you angry and those that do should strike you in a different way. Hopefully, you will not feel the need to hold on to, nourish, and invest in angry ways of interacting with people. I would be delighted to learn that after going through this program, your conclusion is that investing in anger is just not worth the trouble. What is worth the trouble is keeping your anger in check so that you can spend some time making the world a slightly better place.

Peace,
Peter Favaro

Index

About the Author

Peter Favaro, Ph.D., is a practicing clinical and forensic psychologist with offices in Port Washington, New York; Houston, Texas; and West Palm Beach, Florida. Over the last 14 years, Dr. Favaro has worked with over 4,000 high-conflict divorced and divorcing families, helping find solutions to protect the best interests of the children caught between their parent's struggles.

Dr. Favaro is the author of numerous text and consumer books in the areas of parenting, child development, education, and electronic learning. He has lectured throughout the country on parenting, psychology, and the law, as well as on conflict resolution strategies. He is also a regular expert on the psychology of crime and domestic violence for *The Montel Williams Show*. Readers can visit the Anger Management Website at *www.angermanagementcourse.com,* where they can have access to more anger management materials, lectures, videos, and support bulletin boards.